HAIRDRESSING MADE EASY

FLEMING DUNBAR BEd (Hons), Cert Ed, M C Dip, LCG.

PUBLISHED BY ACORN TRAINING CONSULTANTS, BELLANALECK, COUNTY FERMANAGH, N. I.

Acknowledgements

The author wishes to express his gratitude to all the members of the hairdressing staff at Fermanagh College for their enthusiastic support, their cooperation and their help in evaluating the material.
Cartoons and some of the diagrams by Barry Slevin

Copyright © Fleming Dunbar 1993

All rights reserved, this work is copyright. For copying prior permission must be obtained from the publishers and a fee may be payable. No part of this publication may be reproduced, stored in a retrieval system, or transmitted in any form or by any means, electronic, mechanical, photocopying or otherwise, without prior written permission of the publishers.

Published 1993 by Acorn Salon Training Consultants

ISBN 0 - 9516933 - 1 - X

Printed in Great Britain by The Bath Press, Avon

Hairdressing Made Easy

Fleming Dunbar BEd (Hons), Cert Ed, MCDip, LCG, lectures in Fermanagh college where he has been in charge of hairdressing for eighteen years. He started his hairdressing career in Glasgow and on completion of his apprenticeship there, moved to USA where he gained valuable experience. On returning to Scotland he set up and ran his own successful business for many years. Fleming's teaching career began when he accepted the post of lecturer in hairdressing at Fermanagh college in 1974. He rapidly built up an excellent reputation for quality training recognised throughout Northern Ireland and the border counties of Eire. After completing his teacher training he went on to gain a 1st class honours degree in Educational Management. For many years Fleming was an assessor for City and Guilds throughout Ireland.

CONTENTS

Introduction vi

Reception 1
Personal hygiene. Clothing. Hair. Skin care and makeup. Feet. Teeth. Interpersonal skills. Verbal communications. Non-verbal communications. Duties performed by a salon receptionist. Reception area. Receiving visitors. Making appointments. A typical appointment book. Service times. Appointment cards. Filing records and documents. Dealing with complaints. Receiving and delivering messages. Making and receiving telephone calls. Preparing clients for hairdressing services. Handling Banking. Security and safety. Receiving delivery of stock.
Practical Section
Receiving clients. Receiving visitors. Preparing clients for a hairdressing service. Processing a credit card purchase. First aid in the salon.

Consultation and Diagnostics 19
Hair structure. Structure of skin. Types of hair. Growth cycle of hair. Hair and scalp disorders. Infectious disorders of the hair and scalp. Factors which affect the condition of growing hair Porosity and elasticity. Choosing a style, pattern of hair growth, natural hair movement, hair texture and density. Face shapes. Facial features. Client's lifestyle. Choosing a colour. Precautionary tests. Health and hygiene in the salon. Salon hygiene. Poor salon hygiene.
Practical Section
Precautionary tests. Consultation and diagnostic procedure.

Conditioning Hair and Scalp 44
Conditioners. pH what is it? Effects of heat and cold on the hair. Porosity and elasticity. Types of conditioners. Massage techniques.
Practical Section
Conditioning the hair and scalp.

Shampooing the Hair 53
Shampoo and water. Action of shampoo. The detergent molecule. pH and shampoo. Tips on shampooing. Shampoo chart.
Practical Section
Procedure for shampooing.

Haircutting 59
Tools used to cut hair. Cutting techniques. Club cutting with scissors. Tapering with scissors. Tapering with a razor. Thinning hair. Angles. Establishing basic guideline. Sectioning. Bobbed cuts. Graduated cuts. Layered cuts. Choosing a style. Hair texture. Natural growth pattern of hair. Hair condition.
Practical Section
Cutting the hair. Bob cut. Graduated cut. Layered cut.

CONTENTS

Blowdrying and Setting 74
Cohesive setting. Setting lotions. Styling aids for both blow drying and setting. Tools used to blow dry. Blow drying techniques. Styling dry hair.
Practical section for blowdrying
Applying styling aids. Practical hints on blow drying. Blow drying classic and graduated bobs, wedge style, layered style. Finger Drying. Scrunch Drying. Stying dry hair with curling tongs or a hot brush. Crimping.
Setting the hair
Rollers. Pincurls. Placement of rollers and pincurls. Finger waving. Drying to set the hair. Dressing out a hairstyle. Plaiting the hair
Practical procedure for setting
Hints on roller setting. Roller setting. Setting and dressing out pincurls. Procedures for reverse pincurling. Forming finger waves. Backbrushing and combing. Plaiting procedures. Styling tools chart.

Perming and Neutralising 99
Theory of perming the hair. Perm lotions. Rod size. General guide. Winding. Winding techniques. Application of perming lotion. Processing time. Neutralising. Common problems and causes.
Practical procedure
Perming the hair. Preparing hair for perming. Winding. Application of perm lotion. Assessing curl formation. Removing the perm lotion. Neutraling and condition. When the perm has been completed.

Colouring the Hair 115
Colour formation. Basic principles of colour. The colour star. Hair composition. Hair structure. Permanent colours. Types of colourants. Application circle. Ancillary product range. Hints and tips. Colour problems resolved. Condition of hair. Permanent colours. Semi-permanent colours. Temporary colours. Lightening the hair by bleaching. Decolourants.
Practical procedure
Selecting a permanent colour. Strand test. Applying a permanent colour or bleach. Colouring a retouch.. Applying a semi-permant colour. Applying a temporary colour.

Selling 147
The right image. The right atmosphere. The right attitude. A positive attitude. Conveying sincerity. Avoiding high pressure selling. The right time to sell. Know your job. Be prepared.

introduction..........

Welcome to *Hairdressing Made Easy*, the new practical guide for every potential hairdresser - from the complete beginner to the salon apprentice and college student. Its easy to read format and lighthearted cartoons are designed to make learning interesting and fun. Even the experienced hairdresser will find it a useful and stimulating reference book.

Hairdressing Made Easy is both comprehensive and concise. It contains all the information and 'know-how' needed to successfully complete recognised training courses, such as the City and Guilds / Hairdressing Board's NVQ level 2, but presents it in such a way that even the individual with no experience whatever will find it simple to follow. This is because the author comes to the point quickly and logically without adding trivial details, complex explanations and elaborate descriptions-all of which make learning a time consuming chore.

The book is divided into 11 units, each covering specific areas of hairdressing. With the exception of 'Selling', each unit finishes with practical step-by-step instruction in how to carry out the procedures discussed in the text.

1 RECEPTION

The receptionist

Never underestimate the importance of giving clients a good reception. First impressions are lasting impressions, so the receptionist should reflect the salon's standards in her appearance, her attitude and her communication skills. Most large salons employ someone to carry out reception duties, but in small salons they are usually undertaken by the hairdressing staff. It is not easy to do both jobs at once, so it is vital that staff in small salons work out an efficient system for dealing with this.

Let's start by looking at some of the personal factors associated with reception work.

No matter how fashionably dressed and pleasant a receptionist may be, if she has dirty nails, an unpleasant body odour or stained clothing, potential clients will not be impressed. They will naturally assume that the salon itself is not too clean.

Some salons require the receptionist to wear a uniform; otherwise wear an outfit which is in harmony with the image the salon wants to present. Very trendy salons, for example, will expect their staff to wear the latest fashions. At the same time it is important that you feel good in what you are wearing, so choose styles which suit your figure, colouring and personality. Needless to say your clothes should always be clean and fresh.

Your hair should be a good advertisement for the salon. Keep it clean, attractively styled and in good condition.

Wear comfortable, well fitting shoes. Aching feet do nothing to encourage a pleasant manner! Keep your shoes clean and scuff free. If your feet tend to sweat wash them frequently and use a foot deodorant. Treat infections such as Athlete's Foot immediately.

Receptionists spend a lot of time talking to people so clean teeth and fresh breath are a must. Halitosis (bad breath) can be caused by poor dental hygiene, gum disease, smoking and eating highly spiced foods. Clean your teeth and gums thoroughly after eating. Breath fresheners should be used when required. These vary from mouth washes to sprays and tablets.

Interpersonal Skills

The way a receptionist relates to clients depends very much on her attitude to her work. If you are interested in promoting the salon's business, you will be enthusiastic, efficient and pleasant to clients. A good receptionist will realise the importance of interpersonal skills and develop these to the best of her ability.
These skills can be divided into two categories, namely verbal and non-verbal communication.

Verbal Communication

This refers to the spoken word, what we say and how we say it. All clients appreciate a courteous, cheerful and accurate response to a query or request, not an off-hand or abrupt reply. They should be made to feel important and never treated as nuisances.

Answer the telephone politely in a clear voice. Record any messages accurately. Be a good listener, and do not interrupt without good reason. Not only is it rude, but it makes the other person feel you are not interested in what she has to say.

Never ignore a client even if you are busy at another task. It only takes a few seconds to acknowledge their presence and indicate that you will attend to them as soon as possible.

It is a good idea for the receptionist to wear a badge with her name on it so that clients know how to address her.

Non-Verbal Communication

Non-verbal communication or 'body language' is the means by which we convey a message to someone without having to say a word. We use body language when we approach someone with a smile to make them welcome or turn our backs to give them the 'cold shoulder.' It can be a very effective means of communication. A nod and a wink can speak volumes!

Most body language is extremely subtle and open to misinterpretation. Avoiding eye contact, for instance, can make the recipient feel you are not interested in them, or that you are not telling the truth, when in fact you might just be very shy. A good receptionist will use appropriate eye contact to assure the client that she is listening to her and interested in what she is saying. 'Appropriate' does not mean staring. Too much eye contact will embarrass the client.

Learn to be aware of the messages you are conveying through body language. Studying other people will help you to do this. It is fascinating to discover how efficiently a yawn can indicate boredom, or a quick glance at a watch convey impatience.

What does a salon receptionist do ?

You may not be required to carry out all these duties. It will depend on the policy of the salon in which you are working.

* Keeps reception area clean and attractive
* Receives clients and visitors
* Makes appointments
* Files records and documents
* Deals with any complaints
* Receives and delivers messages
* Makes and receives telephone calls
* Prepares clients for hairdressing services
* Handles money
* Keeps a record of financial transactions
* Banks money
* Receives delivery of stock
   * First aid
      * Reception Area

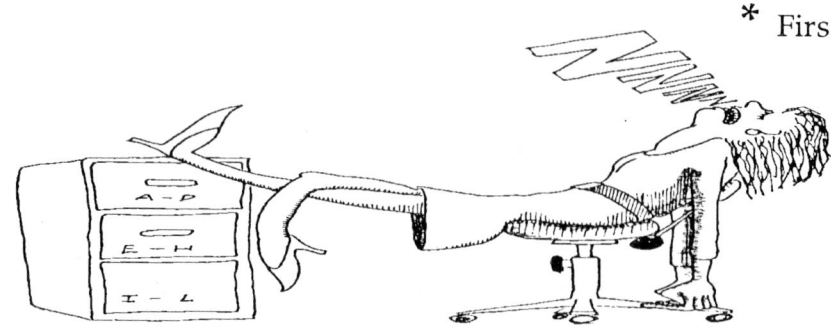

Reception Area

If the reception area is dull, untidy or in poor decorative order it doesn't matter how well a receptionist carries out her responsibilities and presents the right image, the client's impression of the salon will be adversley affected.

There is no need for the reception area to look like a Hollywood film set to make it attractive. This can be done with minimum outlay. Comfort, cleanliness and attention to the details below are the main ingredients.

All reception areas should be welcoming. Sometimes ultra-modern, sophisticated salons can be quite off-putting to clients, so it is important to balance this image with a relaxing atmosphere. Warmth, soft lighting and comfortable seating can all help to achieve this.

The reception area, like the salon itself, should be spotlessly clean and tidy without looking clinical. A cluttered desk, for instance, looks messy and gives an impression of inefficiency. Wallcoverings and paintwork should be kept fresh and clean.

Retail products should be attractively displayed where clients can see them easily, not placed haphazardly in a corner out of reach.

Artistically arranged floral displays can bring a plain background to life and give a sophisticated image. These can be quite expensive as they have to be renewed frequently. An attractive alternative is a group of well chosen pot plants which will last indefinitely if properly tended. Avoid using artificial flowers as they are not easy to keep clean, tend to be stiff and difficult to arrange and are rarely as attractive as real ones.

A variety of up-to-date magazines should be left in accessible spots.

A cup of tea or coffee will be welcomed by most clients, especially those who have to fit in an appointment during lunch breaks or in the middle of a busy schedule. It will also help the client to relax and enjoy her visit. Facilities for purchasing refreshments are also a good idea.

Receiving clients and visitors

"AN APPOINTMENT!!?"

All clients and visitors should be received with friendly courtesy. Visitors, such as company representatives or tradesmen, should be asked to remain in the reception area until the person they wish to deal with has been consulted.

The receptionist is responsible for issuing the client's record card to the appropriate stylist and, in some salons, you may also be required to keep the record up to date. All information given by or about clients should be treated as confidential.

Receptionists must have a thorough knowledge of the cost of all services offered by the salon and which manufacturers' products the salon uses.

Treat every member of staff with respect, from the junior to the manager.

You should know every staff member's range of expertise and responsibilities. Some stylists, for example, may be better at cutting than others, or may dislike working with long hair. You should therefore be in a position to team up clients and stylists appropriately as required.

From time to time the receptionist will have to deal with awkward situations. You must be able to do this with courtesy and diplomacy. If the salon has set policies for dealing with particular situations make yourself familiar with these. Clients or visitors likely to cause 'a scene' should be attended to promptly or they may become increasingly difficult. They should always be treated fairly and tactfully. If you feel unable to deal with a situation, explain the problem to the manager or other capable member of staff and she will advise you how to proceed, or she will deal with it herself.

* The procedure for receiving clients and visitors is given in the practical section at the end of the unit.

Making appointments

It is essential that the salon's appointment system is run efficiently. Mistakes in appointment times lead to confusion and frustration. Overbooking results in staff having to work longer hours than necessary, missing tea or lunch breaks, and clients having to wait a long time. This in turn leads to irritability, dissatisfaction and inferior workmanship which are bad for staff, clients and business alike. All entries in the appointment book should be written clearly and neatly in ink to avoid being accidentally erased. A page from a typical appointment book is reproduced at the end of this unit.

The receptionist should be able with experience to estimate fairly accurately how long a particular service should take and make appointments accordingly. If you are not sure about a particular client or service consult the stylist before making the appointment.

Below is a guide to the average time taken for the services listed.

SERVICE	Time
Shampoo & blow / Scrunch dry	45 minutes - 1 hour
Shampoo & set (short hair)	40 minutes - 1 hour
Shampoo & set (long hair)	1 hour
Styled haircut add	30 minutes
Plaits	15 - 30 minutes
Conditioning treatment	15 minutes
The following treatments include styling	
Permanent wave (regular)	2 - 3 hours
Spiral perm	3 hours
Straighteners	2 - 3 hours
Permanent colour (full head)	2 hours
Permanent colour (retouch)	2 - 3 hours
Semi- permanent colour	1 hour 30 minutes
Hair Lightener (full head)	2 hours
Hair lightener (retouch)	2 - 3 hours
Highlights / Frosting	2 hours
Lowlights	2 hours

Appointment cards

Most salons use cards to remind the client of her appointment time. The card should record the date, time, service required and the stylist. These cards are inexpensive to print and help to cut down mistakes in appointment dates being made. They also help to advertise the salon.

Filing Records and Documents

You will need an efficient system for storing and retrieving records. Filed documents can be classified in several ways.

* **Alphabetically**
* **Numerically**
* **Chronologically**

Salons normally file client's records alphabetically on a card system, but computers are becoming increasingly popular for keeping all kinds of records.

Dealing with complaints

Clients, or indeed other members of the public, may be dissatisfied with some aspect of the salon or its services. It depends on salon policy who deals with complaints.  Very often a client will approach the member of staff she knows best, or the person whose work she wishes to complain about. Most complaints will eventually be referred to the salon manager but sometimes the receptionist will be required to deal with them herself, at least initially.

Treat the person making the complaint courteously, but do not discuss the problem in front of other clients. Instead, move to a quiet area where you can talk to her without interruption. It is better to refer the matter to an appropriate member of staff if you think it will take more than a few minutes to resolve the problem so that the reception desk is not left unattended

If the complaint is justified deal with the matter according to salon policy. If there is no salon policy about that particular matter, and it is too serious for you to deal with yourself, you must refer it to a senior member of staff. Take whatever steps you can to regain the person's confidence in the salon.

If you feel the complaint is unjustified, how you proceed will depend on how serious the matter is. If it is a comparatively trivial matter it is sometimes better to give the person making the complaint the benefit of the doubt, especially if she is a valued client. However, more serious matters must be referred to a senior staff member.

Receiving and delivering messages

Telephone callers often ask the receptionist to pass on a message to another member of staff. A telephone message pad should be kept beside the telephone for this purpose. The message should be recorded accurately at the time the call is made and given to the person for whom it is intended as quickly as possible Some salons have answering machines to record messages from callers telephoning after closing time. These messages should be replayed and answered as soon as possible.
If a call comes in for another member of staff ask who is calling and inform the staff member of this before she accepts the call.

Points to remember when taking messages

*   Listen carefully to what the caller says.

*   Record the message immediately or important details may be forgotten.

*   Note the time and date the message was received.

* Write your name with the message so that the recipient can refer back to you.

* If the message is urgent, make sure it gets to the person for whom it is intended right away.

Making and receiving telephone calls

The telephone is a vital link between the salon, its clients and its business contacts. The receptionist has to acquire good communication skills so that she can 'sell' the salon and its services to callers.
Below is a list of some do's and dont's which will help to achieve this.

Do
*   Answer calls with a pleasant greeting and introduction such as "Good morning, this is .... salon. Can I help you?

* Use the caller's surname. First names should be reserved for personal friends and those clients who have specifically requested their use.

* Be polite and helpful.

* Memorise services and tariffs so that you do not waste the client's time and money while you search for information. For the same reason always keep the appointment book open near the telephone. If a client requires information that is not immediately accessible, explain this to her and ask if she would like to hold on while you find it. If you think it might take some time offer to ring her back. (Make sure you get her phone number!)

Don't

* Answer with 'Hello, who's calling?' as the client wants to know who she is speaking to first.

* Let the telephone ring for a long time before answering.

* Have a radio or other source of noise near the telephone. Background noise above an acceptable level is distracting to both parties and can lead to information being picked up wrongly.

Types of calls

The receptionist should also know the cost of making calls. Up-to-date information about services and costs is available from British Telecom free of charge.

There are three call rates
Peak rate.............. 9am to1pm. Monday to Friday.
Standard rate......... 8am to 9am and 1pm to 6pm. Monday to Friday.
Cheap rate .... 6pm to 8am Monday to Friday and all day Saturday, and Sunday.

Depending on the distance of your call, the amount of time you get for each unit will vary.

The charging rates are;
'L' rate - Local area rate
'A' rate - Up to 56km (35 miles)
'B' rate - Over 56km
'B1' rate - Some 'low cost' routes over 56km
'M' rate - Dialled calls to mobile telephones

Keeping telephone charges to a minimum

It is not the number of calls that determines the cost but the number of units recorded on the meter at British Telecom exchanges. A unit is measured according to the time of day, the day of the week, the distance between callers and the length of the call.

* Keep calls as short as possible.

* List all the relevant information you wish to receive or pass on before you make a call.

* Be sure of the number you wish you call and avoid being charged for a wrong number.

* Replace the receiver promptly and firmly at the end of the call.

* Using the operator to connect you increases the cost, so dial the number yourself whenever possible. This is called Subscriber Trunk Dialling (STD).

Telephone numbers are pre-fixed with a code number if dialled from outside the immediate exchange area. There are local codes, national codes and international codes.

To make calls to:

* the same exchange area as your own, dial the number only.

* a local area, dial the local code and then the number.

* outside you local area, dial the national code and then the number.

* other countries, consult your telephone book as some countries cannot be dialled directly and you may require assistance from the operator.

Telephone Services Available through the Operator

* Alarm calls.

The telephone operator will ring you at any time of day or night. There is a charge for this service.

* Person to person calls.

No charge is made until the caller begins speaking to the person he is calling. This avoids paying for time wasted trying to locate someone although there is a charge for the service itself. It is therefore only economical when making high rate calls.

* Transfer charge calls.

Reversing the charge so that the other party pays for the call is useful for representatives wishing to contact their company from a salon without running up the salon's bill. There is a charge made for this service over and above the cost of the call.

Dial 100 to contact the operator about the above services.

* Emergency Calls

Dial 999 and tell the operator which emergency service you require - Fire, Police or Ambulance.

* Information Services

Information about the weather, motoring, tourist facilities, correct time etcetera is available by dialling the appropriate numbers listed in the telephone book. The service is charged at normal rates.

* Directory Enquiries

Dial 192 The operator deals with UK and Republic of Ireland directory.

* Freephone

This facility allows you to call numbers beginning with 0800 with the cost of the call being automatically paid by the company concerned.

*Telephone faults

Dial 151 This wll put you through to the telephone engineer

Useful numbers to keep available for emergency use

* Local doctor

* Local hospital

* Local police station

* Gas Board

(The Gas Board provides a 24 hour emergency service. Contact them immediately if you smell a gas leak.)

* Electricity Board

(The Electricity Board also provides a 24 hour emergency service.)

* Local electrician

* Local plumber

* Water Board

Other useful numbers to note

* Local transport services including train, bus and taxies

* Wholesalers

  * Company representatives

    * Credit card companies

Preparing clients for hairdressing services

Some salons require the receptionist to prepare the client for the stylist after checking her in.

Release forms

If the salon uses release forms the first thing you should do is ask the client to sign one.

Release forms, or disclaimers as they are sometimes called, are designed to give the salon or training establishment some degree of exemption from responsibility for accidental injury or damage to clients or their belongings. Commercial salons are usually reluctant to use release forms in case clients infer that something is likely to go wrong. However, most training agencies such as colleges of further education and private schools do use such disclaimers.

* Clients signing these forms retain the right to sue a stylist, trainee or agency who causes her injury or damage by not following health and safety practices correctly.

Protecting the client"s clothing

The client's clothes must be well protected from the harmful effects of chemicals used in hairdressing processes. Colourants, for example, will cause permanent staining and perm lotion will bleach. A variety of gowns, capes and wraps are availableto prevent this, including disposable plastic ones.

For most salon procedures, the client wears a plastic cape over a towel and gown.

Dark gowns and towels are usually used with colourants. Lighter ones can be kept for shampooing and cutting.

Neck strip tissues help to prevent cut hair getting into clothing, and on to the skin causing irritation.

* **The procedure for preparing clients for a service is given in the practical section at the end of the unit.**

Handling money

The receptionist is responsible for accepting payment from clients, and perhaps dealing with other financial transactions.

Value Added Tax

Many salons charge VAT. Most salons who charge this tax include it in the cost of the service but others add it afterwards. At the time of publishing, this tax is 17.5% of the total bill.

Receiving Payments

Normally the client's bill is itemised on a salon sales slip which is then removed from the pad and given to the receptionist for totalling. Cash should be kept separate from other forms of payment in the cash register.

Different methods of payment

* Cash
* Cheque
* Credit Cards
* Vouchers

Cash

Most clients pay for their hairdressing services in cash. To avoid delay in giving change, it is advisable to have an adequate 'float' in the cash register at all times.

It is important to check the denomination of bank notes carefully before putting in the till, or giving to a client in change, as it is quite easy to confuse notes from different banks. When notes of a large denomination have to be changed, it is advisable to invite another member of staff to witness the transaction. Customers should always be given a receipt preferably detailing the cost of each service given.

Cheques

A cheque is a written order to a bank or building society authorising it to pay the amount of money it specifies from the cheque writer's account to the individual, or company, named on the cheque. Although cheques are legal documents, they are not legal tender, therefore no one is obliged to accept a cheque as payment instead of cash. Many companies refuse to accept cheques unless they are satisfied that the customer is reliable and that the bank will honour his/her cheque. Banks often charge their customers a small fee for each cheque cashed, although this varies from bank to bank.

Every cheque account customer is issued with a cheque card by his bank or building society. This gives the customer's number, the card's expiry date, a specimen of the customer's signature and guarantees that the bank will pay up to **the amount indicated on the clients cheque card** if it has been completed according to the conditions laid down by the bank. Anyone who has a current account with a bank can be issued with a cheque book, regardless of age, as long as they are able to understand the procedure. Some building societies also offer this facility.

The account holder must fill in the following information and sign her name on the cheque

* Date of issue
* Name of recipient, which can be an individual or a company
* Amount to be paid out both in figures and writing

She may also wish to 'cross' the cheque by drawing two parallel lines across it. Some cheques come already printed with crossed lines. 'Crossed' cheques are not transferable. That means they can only be paid into the account of the individual or company to whom they have been made out, and not cashed by any other source. Some cheques may have 'Not negotiable' or 'A/C Payee Only' written between the crossed lines to emphasise that they are not transferable.

Reasons why a bank might refuse to honour a cheque.

* The account holder does not have sufficient money in her account to make the payment.
* The signature does not match the specimen signature of the account holder.
* Alterations on the cheque have not been initialled by the account holder.
* The cheque is dated in advance of the date that cheque is presented to bank.
* Written amount payable does not match figures.
* Cheque was issued over six months before being presented at the bank, and is no longer valid.
* Cheque has been cancelled by account holder before it was presented at the bank.

Advantages of paying by check.

* It avoids the need to carry cash which can be bulky.

* If a cheque book is lost or stolen the owner can cancel the remaining cheques by informing his bank immediately.

* If, after paying by cheque, a customer is dissatisfied with some aspect of the purchase she can ask the bank to withhold payment of the money. This does not apply to cheques with a value less than £50 which has the check card number recorded on it.

* It is an ideal method of transferring money by post.

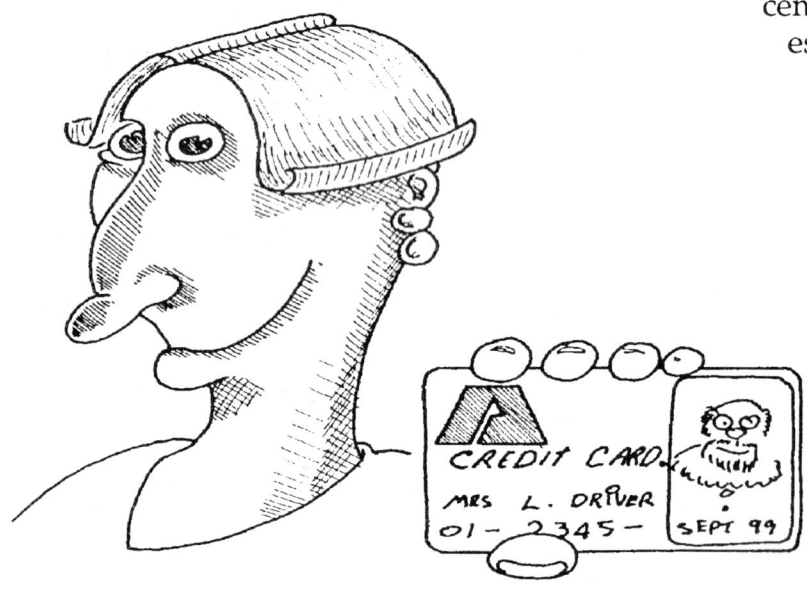

Credit cards

Credit cards are a convenient method of paying for goods or services, and safer than either cash or cheques. The card, with a specimen signature on the back, is presented to the seller who makes an imprint of the card on a voucher and asks the customer to sign it . If the signature matches the specimen signature the transaction is completed and the customer is given a copy of the voucher as a receipt. Some businesses telephone the credit card company before accepting a card to ensure the card is valid and the customer has not borrowed over the limit allowed by the company.

The most popular credit card companies in this country are Access, Visa and Barclaycard. Users are sent a monthly statement of what they owe. They are required to pay a specified amount and interest is charged on the remainder. If however the customer pays for the goods within a month of purchase no interest is charged.

Advantages of using a credit card

* Avoids having to carry cash.

* Most chain stores, and many salons, accept credit cards.

* They are accepted abroad.

* Credit card holders are allowed to borrow relatively large amounts so expensive goods can be purchased easily and paid for whenever the customer desires, although a small percentage must be paid monthly and interest rates are high.

* Can be used for 'armchair' shopping. Purchases can be made from mail order companies by ordering by telephone and quoting the credit card number.

Procedure for processing a credit card purchase is given in the practical section at the end of the unit.

Charge Cards.

Some large department stores operate their own in-house charge cards. These cards are given to customers who have opened an account with the store. Many of these companies have their own salons where customers may charge the service to their personal account using such cards. Larger companies offer charge cards which can be used in a large number of places. Two large charge card companies which operate this way are American Express and Diners Club.

Charge cards differ from credit cards in that the the amount charged must be paid off at the the end of the period allowed and no facilities for extended credit are offered. The receptionist completes the transaction in exactly the same way as a credit card.

Gift Voucher

Some salons offer gift vouchers that can be purchased at any time of the year and redeemed to pay for a salon service or product. They are popular during the festive seasons when clients often purchase a voucher as a gift for a friend.

Discount Vouchers

These are aimed at promoting a particular service or product on special offer in the salon. The amount allowed is simply deducted from the total bill.

Product Vouchers

There is an increasing trend for manufacturers to promote their products directly in the salon or in magazines and newspapers. The client gets money off the product and the salon can claim back the face value of the vouchers from the manufacturing company.

Keeping a record of financial transactions

The amount of takings during the day in a busy salon can be quite considerable, so for security reasons and good accounting principles, all transactions involving cash and cheques should be recorded with supporting documentation. The documentation and payments should always be available for inspection by management. Accurate records allow the proprietor to obtain an accurate day to day picture of the salon's performance and to analyse its strengths and weaknesses. It is also important that a salon keeps accurate payment records for taxation purposes at the end of the financial year. The salon owner may also want to know which staff are building up the business and which are not. Many salons operate a commission system so staff and management alike have a vested interest in accurate record keeping.

Reasons for keeping accurate records of daily takings

* To compare takings with those of other years.
* To identify areas of wastage.
* To show to prospective buyers.
* To detect changes in demand for services and retail sales.
* To identify individual payments made for retail products and treatments in case of dispute and as a safeguard against fraud.
* To maintain a record of stock used.
* For tax purposes.

The receptionist may not have access to receipts for the larger salon expenses such as from product manufacturers, in which case you will only be responsible for recording small daily outgoings such as postage, coffee, cleaning products etcetera.

Operating a payment recording system

After a hair service or buying retail products the client is given a sales docket by the stylist which serves as the bill. This is given to the receptionist who totals the amount, adds VAT if necessary, and retains the docket. The client is then given a receipt of payment.

Purpose of sales dockets

* To check at the end of the day if the takings total is correct by comparing it with that of the sales tickets.
* To calculate the commission due to individual stylists.
* To assess each stylist's contribution to the profitability of the salon.

Banking

You may be required to pay money and cheques into the salon's bank account and will use pay in slips for this purpose. Most pay-in slips are labelled 'Bank Giro Credit'.

To complete the pay-in slip you will need to know the salon's bank account number, the sorting code and the name under which the account is held.

You may have to sort the monies into different denominations and enter the amount in the appropriate columns. Cheques are listed on the back of the pay-in slip.

During bank opening hours the money is usually deposited via the bank cashier. This may take some time if the bank is particularly busy. Some banks recognise that businesses cannot afford to have staff wasting time queuing and have introduced express lodgements. This new service enables you to make lodgements and bank Giro credit transfers without any delay at cash points. A depository is installed where you can drop in the lodgements without queuing. Specially designed vouchers are accompanied by envelopes for express lodgements. These may be used to lodge money at any branch into the salon's account. The maximum that can be lodged is £300.

* The procedure to follow for express lodgements is in the practical section at the end of the unit.

Night safe

This is a facility offered by banks for those depositors who wish to place money in the bank after banking hours. The money is put into a special wallet or box issued by the bank. You will be able to unlock the night safe with keys issued by the bank.

Security and Safety

Never discuss the salon's banking routine with anyone other than authorised personnel. If possible vary your route to the bank. Do not make it obvious that you are carrying money. Make it a routine that on busy days you make more than one visit to the bank. Do not have large amounts of money in the till or on the premises. If you are ever threatened by a thief give him the money and do not put your personal safety at risk.

Receiving delivery of stock

The receptionist may be required to accept and check deliveries of stock, as well as attend to any mail or parcels which arrive in the post. Normally salons have laid down procedures for dealing with these items.

All packages containing stock will be accompanied by a delivery or consignment note which lists the number of packets, their contents, reference number and supplier's name. Packages should be checked very carefully.

Only sign for receipt of a delivery if the following conditions have been met.

* **The goods were ordered.**
* **The packages contain the goods listed.**
* **The quantity delivered is correct.**
* **The goods are undamaged.**

If there is no delivery note, check with the appropriate member of staff that the goods were actually ordered. If it is not possible to check the contents because the delivery men do not have time to wait, then the delivery note should be signed 'received but contents not checked'. Personal letters and parcels should be kept in a safe place until they are delivered to the appropriate member of staff.

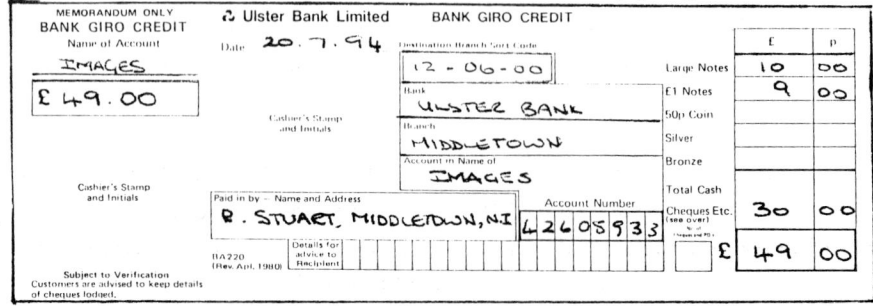

PRACTICAL SECTION

Receiving clients

Procedure

1 Welcome the client or visitor by name if known, giving a pleasant greeting and smile.

2 Establish why she is there. If she wants to make an appointment ask what services she requires and whether she wants a particular stylist. Record her name etcetera in the appointments book. Mix-ups over appointments or stylists should not occur if the client is correctly informed and the appointment recorded accurately.

3 Make the client comfortable if she has to wait and offer her a choice of magazines to read and a cup of tea or coffee if available. When a client finds her visit relaxing and friendly, she is much more likely to return. If a client wishes to chat, keep a pleasant conversation going without asking personal questions and avoiding any gossip.

4 If a client is late for an appointment, do not show that you are annoyed or ask for an explanation. Reassure her and try to re-schedule the appointment for as soon as possible without delaying clients who are on time. If it is not possible to fit the client into her own particular stylist's schedule, offer her an appointment at a later date or, if another stylist is available offer her services.

Receiving visitors

Procedure

1 Visitors should be treated initially in the same way as clients. When you have established the reason for the caller's visit she should deal with the situation courteously and according to salon policy. Visitors should never be left to wander round the premises on their own, both for the visitor's sake and for security reasons.

2 Company representatives often call and each salon has its own policy in dealing with such people. Some salons insist that representatives only call by prior arrangement and refuse to see them without an appointment. In others it is the receptionist's duty to deal with them and, as most representatives would rather deal with the manager directly, you must make this clear from the start. If the representative insists on seeing the manager, you should relay this information to him through another member of staff and await his decision. Managers who deal with representatives themselves should be informed of the caller's arrival, his name and company before being called to see him.

3 Tradesmen and other official personnel such as telephone engineers and health officials who arrive unexpectedly should be asked politely for some form of identification. If you are not satisfied you should telephone their place of business to verify their identify.

Preparing clients for a hairdressing service

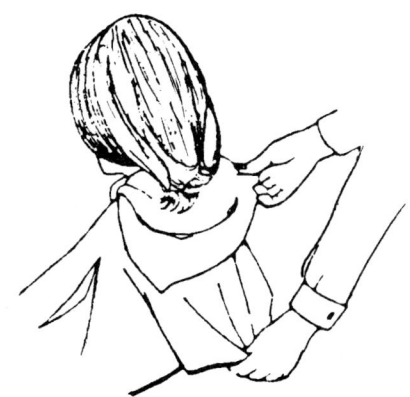

Procedure
1 Put a clean gown on the client.

2 If client is having her hair cut, place a neck strip and fresh towel round her.

3 Tuck in collar if above gown level. Do not tuck towels into client's neckwear as this allows liquids to soak into the garment.

4 Place a plastic cape over the gown and towel covering both.

5 Check record card and release form, if used, before service is carried out.

Processing a credit card purchase

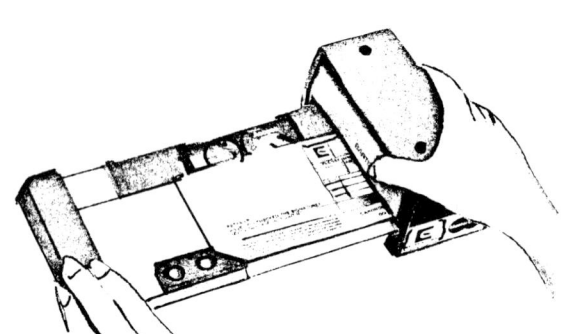

Procedure
1 Check the card is acceptable.

2 Imprint the sales voucher with the card.

3 Complete the sales voucher.

4 Ask the customer to sign the sales voucher and card match.

5 Check that the signature on the voucher and card match.

6 Complete sales procedure by checking that the details are clear on all the copies.

7 Hand the top copy to the customer with the card.

8 Place your own carbonised copies of the sales voucher in the till.

Making express bank lodgements

Procedure
1 Complete lodgement voucher.

2 Retain your copy.

3 Place cheque, cash and completed voucher in the envelope and seal.

4 Drop envelope in special depository which is prominently displayed in the bank.

First Aid in the Salon

When someone is injured or suddenly falls ill, every second counts. Most first aid is practical common sense and can be learned from a textbook, but some, such as artificial respiration combined with chest compression, should be learned from a qualified instructor.

Before finding yourself called upon to treat a casualty study the following pages as the information could save vital moments in a emergency.

The Health and Safety Regulations (1982) require that all salons, no matter how small, should have a first aid kit readily available in case of accidents.

First aid kit

* Waterproof plasters
* Absorbent gauze
* Triangular bandages / slings
* Camomile lotion
* Antiseptic wipes
* Eye pad
* Open weave bandage
* Round ended tweezers
* Safety pins
* Antiseptic cream

Bleeding due to minor cut

Sometimes even small injuries bleed profusely, which can be alarming. Bleeding normally stops of its own accord and can usually be quickly controlled by holding the cut closed with the fingers. Because of the risk of **AIDS or hepatitis,** wear disposable gloves when in direct contact with blood. Alternatively, ask the client to apply pressure herself using a sterile piece of cotton wool over the cut area. Keep the cut clean. Do not use 'stiptic pencils' to stop bleeding as these can spread infection. Blood stained cotton wool etc should be put in a sealed container and disposed of safely.

* Clients suffering from haemophilia, a condition in which the blood does not clot, require urgent medical attention for even a relatively slight injury.

Nose bleeds

Ask the client to sit with her head forward and pinch her nose for several minutes until the bleeding stops. Warn the client not to blow her nose for some hours, as this may dislodge the clot. If the bleeding is profuse, and does not stop within a reasonable time medical attention may be necessary.

Severe bleeding

Apply firm pressure with a clean gauze or any absorbent material on the area from which the blood is coming. Protective gloves should be worn. Phone for an ambulance immediately.

Blood spillage

Contaminated towels and gowns should be placed in a sealed container prior to sterilising. Any blood on the floor or surrounding area should be cleaned immediately using neat bleach. Allow the bleach to remain for one minute before removing with hot water and detergent.

* The same procedure should be used for the spillage of any body fluid.

Superficial burns and scalds

First aid treatment is the same for burns caused by dry heat, electricity, chemicals or boiling liquids. Cool the affected area by holding it in cold water for at least ten minutes. Cover injured area with a sterile bandage.

Electrical accidents

Electricity can kill or produce a wide range of injuries, including severe burns and asphyxiation. Never touch the victim of an electrical accident until the source of power has been removed. If the electricity cannot be turned off and the casualty is in direct contact with the power source, lever her away from it with a brush hande or similar object made of insulating material. Get immediate medical attention for the casualty.

Fainting

Fainting occurs when the blood supply to the brain is suddenly and temporarily reduced.

Warning signs

* The person's face becomes pale.
* Her skin may become cold and clammy.
* Beads of sweat may appear on her face.

If the client has passed out but is breathing normally, lie her on her back and raise her legs above the level of her head. Loosen her clothing at the neck and let fresh air into the salon. Reassure client when she gains consciousness, and allow her to remain lying down for a few minutes before gradually raising her into the sitting position. Give sips of water if required.

Fits

Do not use force to restrain the client's movements. Rough handling may bring on another fit. Remove any furniture or other objects against which the victim may hit herself. When she regains consciousness reassure her and seek medical advice if necessary.

Eye Injuries
Any chemical which enters the eye is extremely dangerous. If it is a strong alkali or acid act quickly. Tilt the client's head over a sink and flood the eye with gently running lukewarm water, or splash water into the eye with your hand. When the injured eye is thoroughly flushed out put a clean eye pad dressing on it and get the client to hospital immediately.

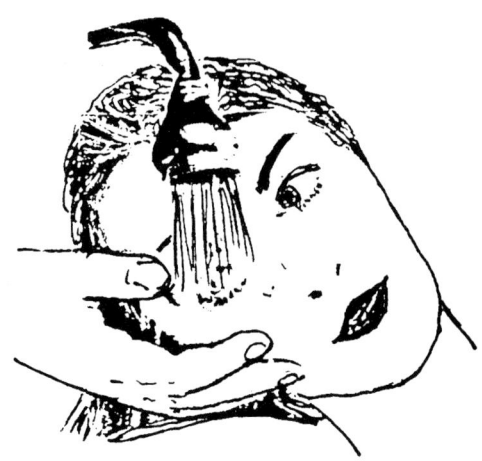

Heart Attack
Symptoms
* Severe and constricting pain in the chest, sometimes radiating down the left arm and left side of the neck.
* Shortness of breath.
* Weak or irregular pulse.
* The casualty may collapse and lapse into unconsciousness.

Phone for a doctor or ambulance immediately. Check breathing and pulse. If they have stopped give artificial respiration and chest compression if you are competent to do this until medical assistance arrives.

Typical Appointment Page

DATE: TUESDAY 10th FEB.

	Gail	Laura	Emma	Kerry	Daniel	Jamie	Stuart
8.30	↓	K. Mohan French Plait	↑	Mrs Bell Tint	↓	↓	
9am	N. Stuart B/Dry	D. Spence Restyle		E. Ford Frosting		P. White Restyle	
9.30		↓ Mrs Jacob	↓	M. Noble S/Set	↓	↓ B. White	↓
10am	D. Brown S/Set	Perm ↓	↓ 0	N. Dawson Perm	Ms Wood Frosting	Perm ↓	C. Mitchel Perm
10.30	P. Ards Perm	M. Thatcher Scrunch		↓	C. Quinn Colour	N. Kinnock Colour	
11am	↓	B. Dunn L/Lights	↓ ↑	K. Moss Straighteners	Full Head ↓	Semi-Perm B. Reid	V. Elliot Restyle
11.30	S. Creamer B/Dry		↓ ↓	↓	D. Bell B/Dry	French Plait A. Taylor	L. Johnstone B/Dry
noon	Lunch ↓	Martin Cut	↓	Ms Shaw B/Dry	Lunch	Frosting ↓	Lunch
12.30	↓	L. Nixon Restyle	↓	E. Dixon Conditioner	↓	Ms Robb B/Dry	↓
1pm	M. Cassidy Spiral	↓	B. Walsh Colour	↑	J. Robb Perm /	Lunch	A. Gunn Colour
1.30	Perm ↓	Lunch	Retouch D. Ford		Restyle ↓	↓	Semi Perm J. Orr
2pm	D. Turbitt Highlights	↓	S/Set Ms West		Ms Cox Highlighter	Mrs Hart Perm	Lowlights ↓
2.30	Mrs Wilson S/Set	Ms Orr Semi Col	Restyle ↓	↓	↓ K. Baker	↓	B. Donaldson Colour
3pm		A. Hall Perm	Mrs Smythe Scrunch	↓ 0	French Plait	M. Smith S/Set	Full Head C. Nash
3.30	Mrs Green Perm	↓ Ms Gunn	A. Woods Tint	↑ ?	↓ J. Major		S/Set
4pm	↓ D. Smith	Spiral Perm	Retouch Ms Ward	0 0	S/Set D. King	W. Ray Spiral	M. Adams B/Dry
4.30	B/Dry P. Miller	↓ C. Gunn	Perm ↓	? ↓	B/Dry ↓	Perm	
5pm	S/Set ↑	S/Set ↑	G. Barr Semi Colour	↓	A. Brown B/Dry	↑	C. Murdoch Perm
5.30					J. Wilson Cut		↓
6pm			S. Black S/Set	↓	Blow Dry ↓	↓	E. Dunbar Trim

NOTES: IF ANY CANCELLATIONS FOR DANIEL TODAY RING MRS WOODS - BLOW-DRY - Tel 327 8541.

Note see how more time is allowed for longer processes

2 CONSULTATION

KNOW YOUR CLIENT

Every human being is unique, and so are their hair and skin. These vary from one individual to another in colour, texture, condition and rate of growth. This variation is of primary importance to the hairdresser and is the reason why every client must be consulted, and an analysis made of her hair and scalp before any service is carried out. A client, whether she actually says so or not, is consulting you, the expert, about her hair.

Consultation is the discussion which takes place between you and your client about the client's hair. The client will tell you what services she would like, any problems she has with her hair or skin and how she wants the finished result to look. Your part is to advise, make suggestions, tell the client what is or what is not possible, and come to an agreement about which service should be carried out and the cost of these services.

KNOW THE BASICS

Before it is possible for you to offer advice and suggestions to the client you must make a *diagnosis* about the condition of the client's hair and scalp. To do this you need to know about the structure of the hair and skin, what they are made of, how they are affected by chemicals used in the salon and be able to recognise the various disorders to which they are susceptible.

You are not in a position to give advice about styling until you understand how texture and natural growth patterns affect cutting and styling techniques, and how basic hair designs will accentuate or camouflage the individual's facial features, bone structure, height etcetera.

Consultation skills also include the ability to give advice on styles which are appropriate to the client's age and lifestyle.

Let's look first at hair itself.

Hair is made from a special protein called *keratin*, as are skin and nails. Unlike other proteins keratin contains *sulphur* and it is the presence of sulphur which enables hair to be permed.

The keratin in skin is soft, but in the hair the keratin becomes hard by a process called *'keratinisation'*. It is composed of millions of *amino acids* which are the *'building blocks'* of protein. Healthy hair contains eighteen or more different kind of amino acids.

Each hair grows from a long narrow canal called a *follicle* which stretches down from the surface of the skin into the dermis for about one tenth of an inch.

At the bottom of the follicle is a small dermal *papilla* which contains microscopic blood vessels known as *capillaries*.

The capillaries transport oxygen and nutrients to the group of cells surrounding the papilla. This group of cells grows out into the follicle to form the *hair bulb* which is the anchorage and living part of the hair.

The cells of the hair bulb increase and push outwards in a column of keratinised cells which become the *hair shaft*. These cells are no longer living having been cut off from the blood supply. In other words the hair we see on our scalp is dead.

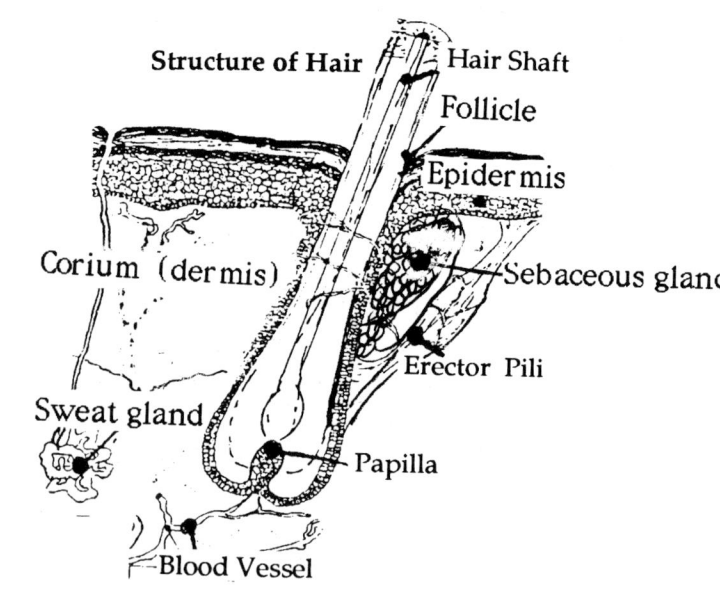

Hair Composition	
50%	Carbon
25%	Oxygen
15%	Nitrogen
5%	Hydrogen
5%	Sulphur

Cells produced from the top of the papilla form the centre core or *medulla* of the hair. Because these cells are loosely packed the medulla is soft and spongy. Cells from the side of the papilla form the next layer, known as the *cortex*. The cells of the cortex become elongated and spindle shaped and form the bulk of the hair shaft. The cortex is surrounded by an outer layer, called the *cuticle*.

Let's look more closely at these three layers.

Cuticle

The cuticle is the *outer layer* of the hair and is made up of overlapping scales, rather like the tiles on a roof only several layers deep. Its purpose is to protect the cortex which is much more delicate and can be easily damaged, weakened or even destroyed. The cuticle, in conjunction with an oily substance called sebum, keeps the cortex fairly water-proof, only allowing the right amount of moisture to be absorbed.

When the cuticle is in good condition the acid in the sebum keeps the scales tightly closed and they lie smoothly along the surface of the hair. This smoothness allows light to be reflected giving the attractive shine usually associated with healthy hair.

Damage to the cuticle results in the scales being raised or broken off. When this happens, not only does the hair become dull because the light is not reflected but, if the lower layers are affected, the cortex which they were designed to protect is left exposed.

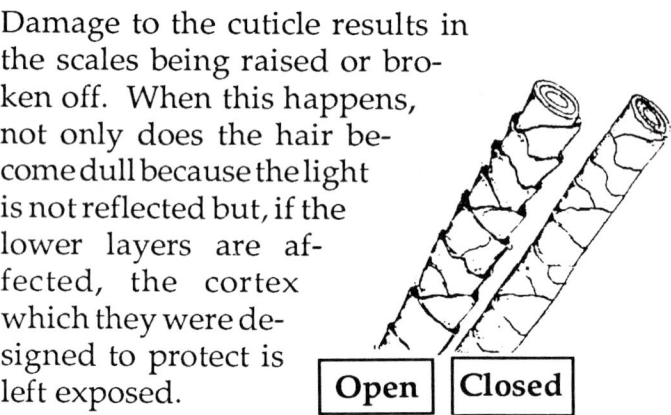

Unfortunately, it is very easy to damage the cuticle scales by both harsh physical treatment and chemical abuse. Very often the ends of the hair are in a worse condition than the roots because they have suffered longer abuse.

Physical damage to the cuticle can be caused by a number of factors.

* Over-exposure to sun and wind
* Excessive heat - often from tongs and hair dryers
* Backcombing
* Harsh brushing

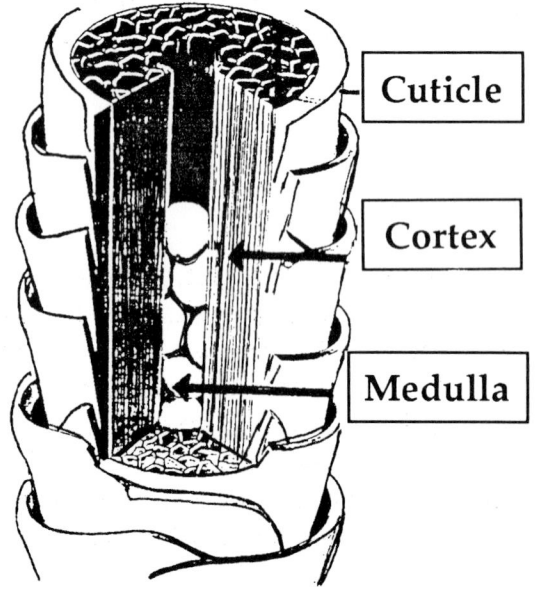

Chemical damage to the cuticles is usually caused by *alkaline* **hair products.**

Alkalies cause the cuticle scales to open up so are used in hairdressing treatments to raise them enough to allow the active ingredients in perm lotions, lighteners and colouring agents to penetrate into the cortex. If not used extremely carefully or left on too long these alkalies can cause permanent damage. Even alkaline shampoos, although they clean the hair thoroughly, can cause cuticle damage.

NOTE It is important to remember the *opposing* actions of *acids* and *alkalies* on the cuticle. Acids shrink and tighten the cuticle scales. Alkalies make them swell and open up. *Heat* and *cold* have similar effects because cold makes the scales contract while heat makes them expand. These two laws of chemistry and physics are made use of in many hairdressing processes.

Cortex

This is the main body of the hair, being anything between **75** and **90** percent of its bulk. It is the cortex which determines the following properties of hair.

* Tensile strength
* Elasticity
* Porosity
* Texture

The cortex is made up of millions of parallel keratin fibres, known as *polypeptide* chains, which are twisted around one another like a rope. Each chain is made up of molecules of *amino acids* joined together by very strong vertical links called *peptide bonds*. These bonds are the strongest in the hair and can only be broken by strong alkalies or excessive stretching.

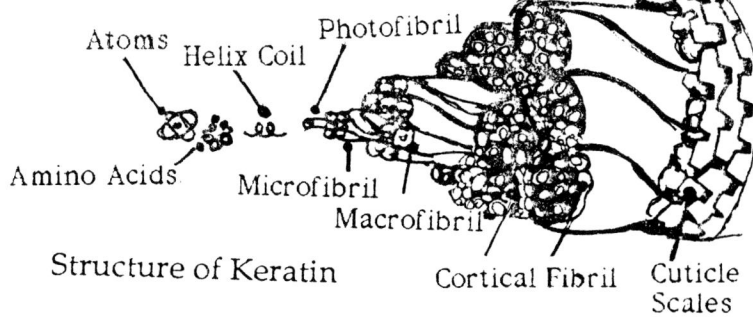

Structure of Keratin

Several different types of horizontal *cross-bonds* hold the polypeptide chains together. It is important for the hairdresser to understand something about *two* kinds of cross-bonds, because it is the breaking and reforming of these which allow you to style the hair.

Some cross-bonds are strong and not easily broken. The strongest of these contain *sulphur* and are called *sulphur bonds, S-bonds* or *disulphide bonds*. They attatch themselves to a special amino acid in the polypeptide chain called *cystine*. Sulphur bonds are only broken by boiling water and certain chemicals.

Hydrogen bonds, on the other hand, are weak and easily broken by the application of heat, or by the physical action of water, making wet hair very elastic. Hydrogen bonds help to give hair *'body'* and assist the sulphur bonds to keep the chains of keratin together.

Re-arranging the cross-bonds in hairdressing treatments will cause minimum damage to the hair if carried out carefully, although no matter how particular you are chemical treatments will always leave the hair slightly more porous than normal. You will appreciate therefore just how *important* it is to follow the manufacturer's instructions when carrying out these processes.

If either vertical peptide bonds or sulphur cross-bonds are destroyed, the hair will lose its *elasticity* and may break off. Note also that if the cuticle has been damaged by chemicals it is inevitable that the cortex, being more fragile, will also be damaged.

The natural colour of hair is due to the presence of a pigment found in the cortex called *melanin* which is formed in the *epidermis*.

Medulla

The medulla is the soft, spongy centre of the hair and is really just an air space although it may contain a little melanin. Some hairs have a medulla throughout their length, others only in part and in some the medulla is absent altogether. As it does not play a significant role in any hairdressing processes we do not need to give it any further consideration.

Structure of skin

The next thing we want to look at is the skin. With a few exceptions the skin covering our bodies contains hair follicles and functions in the same way as scalp skin, so although hairdressers are primarily concerned with the scalp there is no need to discuss different areas of the body separately.

Skin is our bodies' *protective* outer coat. It is the largest organ of the body, and weighs about six pounds.

As the diagram indicates, skin is extremely complex. It contains numerous nerve endings which give us our sense of touch and make us aware of our environment.

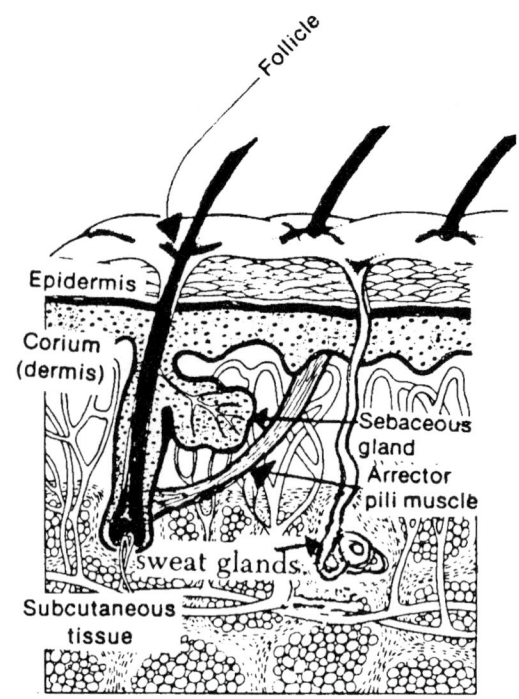

It also contains *sebaceous glands,* which secrete an oily substance called *sebum* to lubricate the skin and hair, and sweat glands to help regulate the body's temperature.

Sebum and sweat are *acidic* and together cover the surface of the skin, including the scalp, with an *acid mantle.* This acts as an antiseptic because bacteria do not grow readily in acid conditions.

Hair follicles are found in nearly all skin, the main exceptions being the soles of the feet, the palms of the hands and the lips. A muscle called the *arrector pili* is attatched to each follicle and causes the hair to stand on end when activated by fear or cold.

The skin we see on the surface of our bodies is dead, just like hair. Underneath this layer of dead tissue are several layers of living cells and together they make up the *epidermis.*

The bottom layer of the epidermis is known as the *germinating* layer because the cells here multiply by a process of cell division called *mitosis.*

The new cells formed push upwards and, after becoming full of keratin they die. These dead cells form a protective waterproof layer with the assistance of sebum. This helps to prevent moisture loss from the body, saving it from becoming dehydrated.

Melanin, the dark pigment which colours the hair and gives the skin a tanned appearance when exposed to the sun's rays, is manufactured in the germinating layer. It protects the skin from the ultra violet rays of the sun.

The *dermis* or true skin, as it is sometimes known, lies below the epidermis and contains the tiny blood vessels which feed the living cells of the epidermis. It also contains the nerve endings which, although they do not penetrate the epidermis, are so sensitive that they react to changes in temperature and even the slightest pressure on the skin's surface.

Although the outer layers of both hair and skin are composed of keratin, hair keratin is hard and skin keratin is soft. The latter is much more delicate and sensitive to chemicals. Hair products are designed to have the desired effect on the hard keratin of the hair without damaging the soft scalp keratin. Incorrect use of chemicals can cause severe irritation of the scalp.

Now that you have been introduced to the basic structure of the hair and skin we will look at the different types of hair found on the body and the growth cycle of scalp hair.

Types of hair

There are three basic types of hair.

Terminal hair

Terminal is the name given to the hair produced by the scalp, and of course is the type we are interested in. It is coarser, denser and more pigmented than any other type of hair.

Terminal hair itself can be sub-divided into three types according to race.

* European hair which has less than seven layers in the cuticle
* Oriental hair whas between seven and ten layers in the cuticle
* African hair which may have as many as fifteen layers in the cuticle

Vellus hair

Vellus hair is the fine hair found on most parts of the body.

Lanugo Hair

This is the fine, downy hair which covers the body before birth and is shed around the eighth month of pregnancy. Premature babies are often born with lanugo hair still on them.

Growth cycle of hair

Hair does not keep growing indefinitely. Each hair has its own growth cycle.

It grows actively for anything from one to seven years, which is known as the ANAGEN stage.

When the hair has stopped growing it becomes detached from the base of the follicle and dies over a period of two weeks. This is called the CATAGEN stage. After a hair has died it is easily removed by brushing and shampooing. Fortunately only about fourteen percent of scalp hairs die at any one time, so we do not usually notice any hair loss.

The follicle then goes through a resting phase known as the TELOGEN stage for about four months after which a new hair begins to grow.

The three stages of hair growth

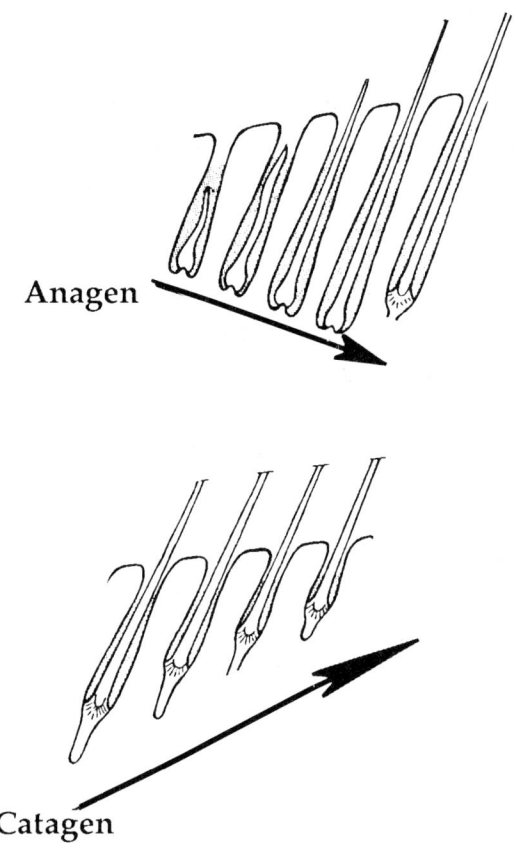

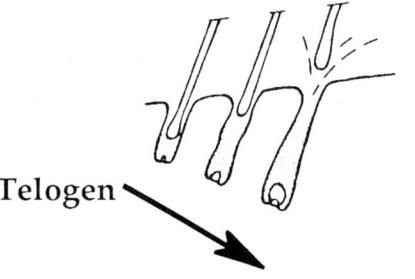

The average human scalp produces in the region of 100,000 hairs which grow about twelve milimetres, or half an inch, a month. The maximum length a hair can grow depends how long the *anagen* stage lasts.

Both the quantity and the rate of growth decrease gradually with age. However, hair growth can be stimulated by certain hormones such as those produced during pregnancy.

Physical stimulation of the scalp by brushing or massage increases the blood supply to the papillae and it has been claimed that this promotes faster growth.

The growth rate of hair is also affected by the climate and increases with the temperature. You may have noticed that your hair grows more quickly in summer.

Hair and scalp disorders

The first step in any consultation and diagnostics procedure, after sitting the client comfortably and covering her shoulders with a protective gown, is to examine the hair and scalp for any signs or symptoms of disease or abnormality.

To do this you must have some knowledge of the most common disorders of the scalp and hair. It is particularly important that you should be able to distinguish between infectious and non-infectious conditions.

You should NEVER carry out a salon service on a client with an infectious condition, or make any attempt to treat the syptoms, because you will put not only yourself but other staff and clients at risk.

It is sometimes very difficult for even a medical practitioner to diagnose a disorder which does not present the more obvious symptoms and occasionally infectious conditions are confused with non-infectious in the salon. This results in either an unnecessary loss of business or putting others at risk of contamination. Study the disorders listed below carefully, and learn the various signs and symptoms of each so that you will know what to look for.

Infectious conditions are passed on either by direct contact with the source of infection, or indirectly by coming into contact with infected tools, towels, gowns, etcetera.

An infection passed on by direct contact is said to be *contagious*. Infections are caused by bacteria, viruses, fungi or parasites.

Non-infectious conditions cannot passed on to another person. However, many of these disor-

ders are distressing to clients because of the discomfort they cause and their unsightly appearance. It is important that they are diagnosed correctly and treated where possible.

A few non-infectious conditions can benefit from salon treatment but most require some form of medication and no attempt should be made to offer medical advice.

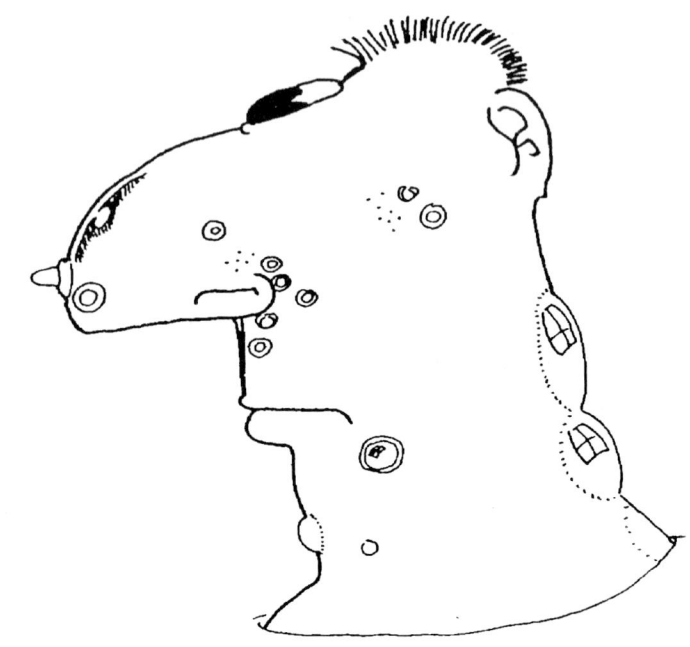

Infectious disorders of the hair and scalp

Tinea Capitas (ringworm)

Cause
Ringworm is a highly contagious fungal infection spread by direct contact with infected people, animals and soil. It is very common in children. Despite its name no worm is involved.

Signs and symptoms
There may be no symptom other than mild irritation. Usually it starts with an inflamed patch which enlarges for a few weeks then stops growing. Another patch then starts up somewhere else. The centre of the patch returns to normal looking skin, leaving the characteristic ringed effect. There may be some scaliness, and the hairs break off at the site of infection giving the hair a moth-eaten appearance.

itch Mite

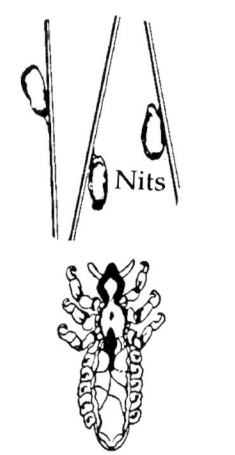
Nits

Pediculosis Capitis

Treatment
Recommend that client seeks medical advice as antibiotic treatment will be necessary over a period of one or two months.

Scabies

Scabies can occur anywhere on the body and is highly contagious.

Cause
Infestation with the parasite Sarcoptes scabiei. The female **mite** burrows into the skin and lays its eggs. These hatch and mature in the skin and then emerge on to the surface again. Symptoms are caused by an allergic reaction to the mite and its eggs.

Symptoms
Very itchy pimples. Sores develop where these are scratched and tiny ridges can be seen where the mite has burrowed in.

Treatment
Medical treatment is required.

Pediculosis Capitas (head lice)

Cause
Insect parasites which feed by sucking blood. They lay eggs, commonly known as nits and cement them on to the hair shaft so, unlike dandruff, they do not come off easily. Although very small, nits are clearly visible through a magnifying glass.

Signs and symptoms
Intense itchiness often occurs at the site of infestation and both nits and lice may be seen on the head. They are generally located in the nape area and around the back of the ears.

Treatment
Shampoos containing malathion or carbaryl are used to destroy head lice. Sterilise all contact areas.

Impetigo

Cause
Bacteria, usually streptococcus or staphylococcus, get into breaks in the skin, often as the result of scratching another irritating skin condition. **Impetigo is highly contagious.**

Signs and symptoms
Impetigo starts with a red spot. This becomes a blister which bursts and discharges, forming a yellow crust. The crust spreads and more spots errupt near the site of infection.

Treatment
Can be treated at home by bathing and applying an antibacterial paint such as gentian violet, but this is unsightly and therefore embarrassing. It is better to seek medical advice.

Plane Warts

Cause
There are several different types of warts, all caused by viruses and slightly contagious. The plane wart is the one which normally affects the face and scalp area.

Signs and symptoms
Plane warts are smooth, solid growths on the surface of the skin. They are either skin coloured or light brown. They generally grow in clusters often along the site of a scratch.

Treatment
Warts sometimes disappear without treatment, but more usually persist or spread. Although proprietary treatments are widely available, medical advice should be sought to confirm the diagnosis and because warts have a tendency to become infected.

Non-Infectious disorders of the hair and scalp

Monilethrix (beaded hair)

Cause
Unknown. It is thought to be an inherited condition.

Symptom
Swellings and constrictions alternate along the hair shaft due to uneven cell division in the hair follicle. The hair is usually coarse, dry and dull. It breaks easily at the constricted areas leaving stubble on the scalp.

Treatment
None. Treat hair very carefully to avoid breakage.

Trichorrhexis nodosa

Cause
Physical or chemical damage to the cuticle of the hair causing the cortex to swell outwards. Occasionally it is caused by a metebolic disorder.

Signs and symptoms
Nodular swellings are apparent along the hair shaft. The hair is dry and very easily broken.

Treatment
Damage cannot be repaired. If condition is very bad salon services should be avoided. Otherwise treat very carefully.

Fragilitas Crinium (split ends)

Cause
Physical or chemical damage

Signs and symptom
Dry brittle hair that has split from the ends along the hair shaft.

Treatment
No treatment will cure this condition. The ends should be removed by cutting.

Alopecia

Alopecia is the medical name for baldness. There are different types of alopecia with different causes.

Androgenic Alopecia

This is the name given to the common type of baldness in men.

Cause
Associated with male hormones.

Signs and symptoms
The hairline begins to recede gradually and there is a thinning at the crown.

Treatment
None.

Diffuse Alopecia

Cause
Hormone disorders and other illnesses seem to bring on this form of alopecia.

Signs and symptom
Gradual thinning of the hair commonly seen in women.

Treatment
Refer to a medical practitioner.

Traction Alopecia

Cause
Constant tension on the hair roots, usually brought on by the hair being pulled tightly back into a pony tail or similar style.

Signs and symptoms
Usually the hair loss is more noticeable at the front hairline, unless it has been pulled out in a rage!

Treatment
Remove source of pressure.

Alopecia Areata

Cause
Sufferers may have an inherited tendency towards this type of alopecia. It seems to be brought on by stress or shock.

Signs and symptom
Small circular patches appear and gradually enlarge.

Treatment
Usually the hair begins to grow in again after a few months without treatment, but it is as well to get professional advice.

Cicatrical Alopecia

Cause
External damage to skin either by chemicals, heat or a cut.

Signs and symptoms
Bald patch where the hair follicles have been permanently damaged.

Treatment
None.

Pityriasis (dandruff) There are two types of dandruff. *Pityriasis simplex* is the common dry variety, and *pityriasis steatoides* is a greasy form.

Cause
The disorder is thought to be linked to the presence of too high a level of pitysporum ovale, a micro organism present on normal scalps. The greasier the skin, the worse the dandruff.

Signs and symptoms
Instead of cells of dead skin being shed individually, they stick together to form large visible flakes which can be seen in the hair and on clothing. In pityriasis steatoides the dead scales are greasy and stick to the scalp. They tend to clog the pores, and cause severe irritation.

Treatment
Regular washing with medicated shampoos containing selenium sulphate, zinc pyrithione (ZPT) or hexachlorophene will control, if not cure, this disorder. Medical advice is required if the condition does not clear, or becomes infected.

Seborrhoea

Cause
Occurs after puberty and seems to be associated with the sex hormones

Signs and symptoms
Excessively greasy scalp and skin following puberty.

Treatment
Can be controlled using cetrimide based shampoos regularly. The greasiness can often be reduced by keeping to a diet free of dairy products and sweet stuff, especially chocolate.

Sebaceous cysts (pilar cysts)

There are two types of sebaceous cysts, but the ones found on the scalp are known as *pilar cysts*.

Cause
Unknown, but tend to run in families.

Signs and symptoms
Little painless lumps appear and enlarge to form dome-shaped swellings.

Treatment
Surgical removal. Normal hairdressing services can be given.

Psoriasis

Cause
Unknown, but can be inherited and usually starts between the ages of 5 and 25. It is often precipitated or aggravated by stress, streptococcal infections and some drugs.

Signs and symptoms
Recurring scaly eruptions on the skin or scalp Patches are deep red and covered with silvery scaling which can be scraped off. The centre of the patch may revert to normal skin. Sometimes there is pitting and destruction of the nails.

Treatment
Medical treatment is required. Sometimes psoriasis is mistaken for an infectious condition because of the inflammation involved. It is not infectious and normal salon services can be carried on if the scalp is affected although the use of chemicals is not recommended.

Eczema

There are five different types of eczema, all with different causes ranging from heredity to allergic reactions to various substances. The two types most likely to affect the scalp of adults are contact eczema and seborrhoeic eczema.

Cause
Contact eczema is an allergic reaction to certain substances. Seborrhoeic eczema develops in areas of the skin where the sebaceous glands are numerous, but the cause is unknown.

Signs and symptoms
The different forms of eczema are characterised by different symptoms. With contact eczema there may be itching, small blisters and redness. When the blisters burst weeping occurs, followed by flaking as the skin dries.

Hairdressers often develop contact eczema on their hands as a result of not wearing protective gloves when carrying out services involving the use of chemicals. Seborroeic eczema is characterised by red scaly areas with cracks frequently appearing in the creases around the ears. This type does not produce the same degree of irritation as others.

Treatment
Contact eczema will clear up when the irritant is removed. Further outbreaks can be prevented by wearing protective clothing if contact with the offending substance is likely. If there is a discharge of pus, tenderness or boils associated with eczema immediate medical attention is required. Seborroeic eczema cannot be avoided but early medical treatment will clear it quickly.

Factors which affect the condition of growing hair

When we were discussing the structure of the hair we noted that hair in good condition can be recognised by its shine and smoothness, whereas hair in poor condition looks dry and dull.

The condition of the hair is extremely important to the hairdresser because, no matter what service is carried out, if at the finish the hair is lifeless and dull it will not look attractive.

We have already seen that hair can be damaged after it has grown, but it can also be damaged during the growth period itself.

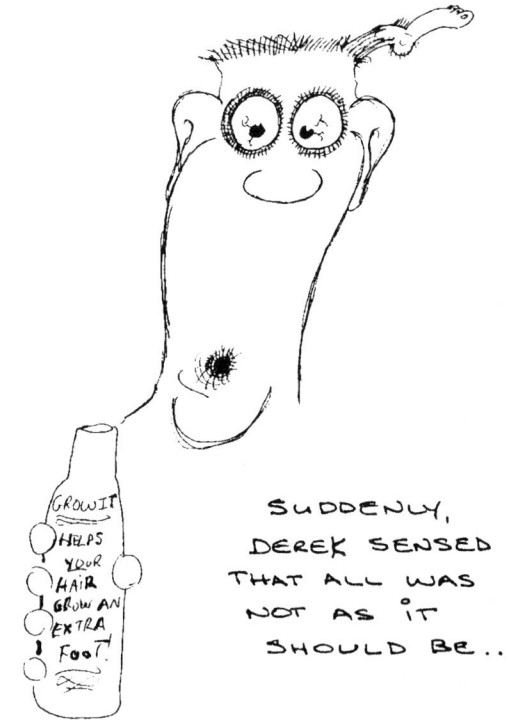

Suddenly, Derek sensed that all was not as it should be..

The hair we see growing above the scalp is dead and, although we can temporarily alter its appearance and the way it feels to the touch if it has been damaged, we cannot make it 'healthy'.

When hair is being produced all the essential nutrients are carried directly to the papilla by tiny blood vessels. If for some reason vital ingredients are in short supply, or missing altogether, the cells will not form properly and the resulting hair, if it grows at all, will be deformed in some way and not in the condition it should be.

With the exception of genetic defects in the hair's structure, it is the quality of the blood which determines the quality of the hair as it emerges from the scalp, and therefore healthy people usually produce healthy hair.

Porosity and elasticity

The hair's condition can be assessed by examining its porosity and elasticity. <u>These are extremely important concepts for the hairdresser to grasp.</u>

Porosity

Porosity refers to the amount of *moisture* hair will absorb. The cortex can hold several times its own weight of water.

When the cuticle is lying flat and tight against the cortex only the amount of moisture required to keep the cortex healthy will be absorbed.

The following can have a detrimental effect on hair while it is growing.

* Illness
* Mineral deficiencies such as anaemia
* Stress
* Hormone deficiencies or over-production
* Drugs
* Contraceptive pills
* Menopause
* Radiotherapy

Problems arise when the cuticle has been damaged because the cortex is then able to absorb too much moisture and is said to be over-porous.

Several chemical treatments, such as perming, colouring and lightening, require the cuticle scales to be slightly raised temporarily to allow sufficient numbers of the relatively large molecules of the active ingredients to get into the cortex. Heat and alkalies both cause the scales to swell and lift up and are used for this purpose.

If the scales have been damaged previously and therefore already raised, the over-porous cortex will absorb too much of the chemical too quickly. This leads to over-processing and damage to the bonds holding the polypeptide chains together, as well as further damage to the cuticle. Also, because cuticle damage is not evenly distributed the result of the treatment will be patchy.

If the hairdresser knows in advance that the hair is over-porous she can take steps to minimise further damage by using either weaker chemicals or *'buffers'* which prevent over-penetration of the cortex. You will learn more about these in the appropriate units.

Hair in very poor condition should not be subjected to any further chemical treatment.

Elasticity

Keratin resembles a spring in structure which allows it to be stretched and to return to its original state when the tension is released. This property is called elasticity.

Dry hair in good condition can be stretched about a third of its length without breaking and still return to its original length.

Wetting hair increases its elasticity because water enables the numerous hydrogen bonds to stretch further.

Porous hair which allows too much water into the cortex is very easily over-stretched and broken. It loses its elasticity and will not return to to its original length or shape.

Elasticity is measured by the amount of pressure required to stretch a hair to breaking point. This measurement is known as the *tensile strength* of the hair.

Porosity and elasticity are inversely proportional to one another. As the porosity of hair increases its elasticity decreases. The ability to assess the porosity and elasticity of hair develops with experience and is of major importance in the consultation and diagnostics procedure. Simple tests for assessing porosity and elasticity are given in the practical section at the end of this unit.

Choosing a style

We will now go on to look at properties of the hair which are particularly relevant when choosing a suitable style for a specific client. These include the different patterns hair tends to grow in, the hair's natural movement, its texture and its strength.

Patterns of hair growth

The direction which the hair takes when it emerges from the scalp depends on the angle at which the follicle is lying to the head. Although each client has a unique growth pattern certain formations occur frequently in particular areas of the scalp.

Patterns

* Widow's peak - caused by hair at the centre of the front hairline coming forward into a peak.

* Cowlick - occurs at the front hairline and is caused by hair lifting up and curling forward.

* Crown - circular pattern at the back or on top of the head.

* Double crown - as the name indicates there are two crowns present.

* Natural parting - the hair lies at opposite directions on either side of a line from the front hairline to the crown.

* Nape hairline - sometimes hair at the nape grows towards the centre of the neck.

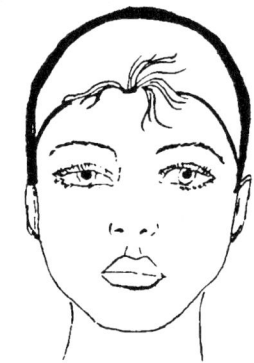

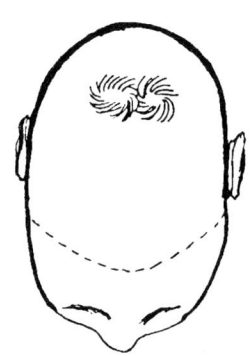

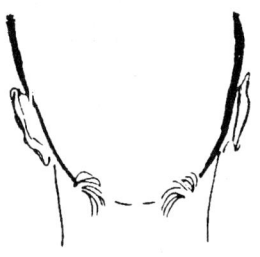

Important

All growth patterns must be analysed and taken into consideration when designing a style. A straight fringe, for example, will not lie properly if the client has a cowlick. If you try to force the hair to lie against its natural growth pattern it will always tend to spring back, making the style difficult for the client to keep. Also, you must be careful when cutting the hair short over certain growth patterns as the hair will tend to stick up.

The natural growth pattern is best recognised when the hair is wet and not disguised by previous styling.

Natural movement of hair

The natural movement of hair, that is, whether it is straight, curly or wavy, depends on whether cell division in the papilla is even or not.

If the cells divide evenly throughout the hair will be straight.

If they divide more rapidly at one point than another the hair will curl or wave. Sometimes this uneven division stops, either permanently or for a period of time, which explains why a curly haired child can grow up with straight hair and why hair can become straight after an illness.

Again it is important to take the hair's natural movement into consideration when styling, although it can be chemically altered by perming or relaxing.

Hair density and texture

The *density* of the hair is simply the quantity of hair on the head. Hair is 'thick' because there is plenty of it, and 'thin' because it is sparse.

Density is determined by both the number of hairs and their *texture.*

Texture refers to the degree of fineness or coarseness of the hair. It is associated with the number of cuticle layers and assessed according to the diameter of the hair - the more layers, the wider the diameter and the coarser the hair. Texture varies with racial type.

The diameter of the hair also depends to some extent on whether the hair has a medulla or not.

The tensile strength of hair tends to vary according to its texture.

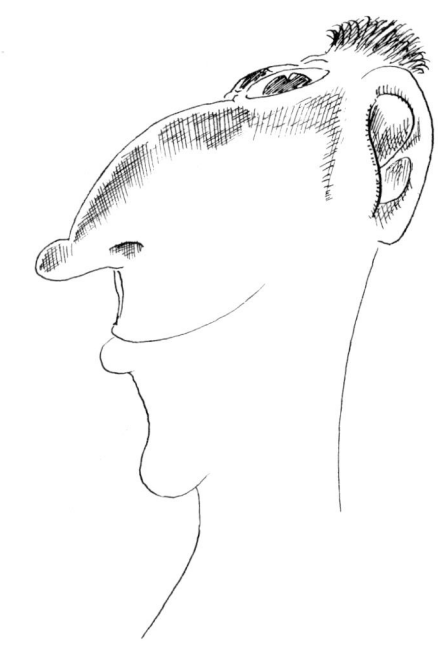

Fine hair

Fine hair does not usually have a medulla and is inclined to be limp with less tensile strength than other hair. Styles requiring plenty of volume and movement are more difficult to achieve with fine hair, and do not last long. Long fine hair tends to look 'stringy' and shapeless.

Coarse hair

Coarse hair usually has a medulla and has more cuticle layers than fine hair. It is typically strong and wiry. It will not readily follow the contours of the head smoothly, but tends to be bushy and difficult to control. Coarse hair in good condition is very elastic and therefore resistant to having its natural movement altered. If cut very short it will tend to stick out.

Medium hair

Hair which is neither fine nor coarse may or may not have a medulla. It is the most easily managed type of hair because it is strong without being wiry and difficult to control. Most styles can be adapted to suit a client with this type of hair.

Other important factors to take into consideration when creating a style are the client's face shape, her facial features, her size and her lifestyle.

Face shape

Oval shaped faces have traditionally been considered ideal and are the standard against which other shapes are judged. Stylists usually try to balance, or camouflage, features of other shapes to give an oval appearance. This is, of course, a matter of personal taste and it is fashion which usually dictates which shape is considered desirable at any given time. However, as a general rule the chosen style should compliment the client's face shape rather than exaggerate it.

Oval face

Oval faces suit nearly any style, so it is basically a matter of designing a style which appeals to the client and emphasises her most attractive facial features

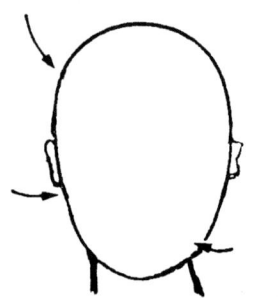

Forehead in proportion to jawline

Round face

If the hair is long a soft style which frames the face will make a round face appear longer and thinner. A full fringe tends to accentuate the roundness of the face. Short casual styles brushed gently onto the cheeks make the face look thinner.

Heart shaped face

Heart shaped faces suit most styles. If the head is very broad across the temple area heavy or fluffy fringes and fullness below the ears will help to camouflage this.

Pear shaped face

Pear shaped faces have a broad jaw line and narrow towards the forehead. Fullness at the temples and softness over the jaw help to even out the different widths.

Long face

Fullness at the sides adds width to the long face giving it a more rounded appearance. Long or upswept styles emphasise face length and are best avoided. Shortish styles with a heavy full fringe help to reduce the length of the face.

Square shape

Squareness can be softened with a soft half fringe and hair brushed over the jaw line. Straight lines emphasise the angular lines of a square face so keep the outlines rounded.

Diamond shape

Diamond shaped faces are wide across the cheekbones and narrow across both jaw and forehead.
Fullness around the temples and jaw will give width where it is lacking. Brushing the hair on to the cheeks helps to narrow the face in this area.

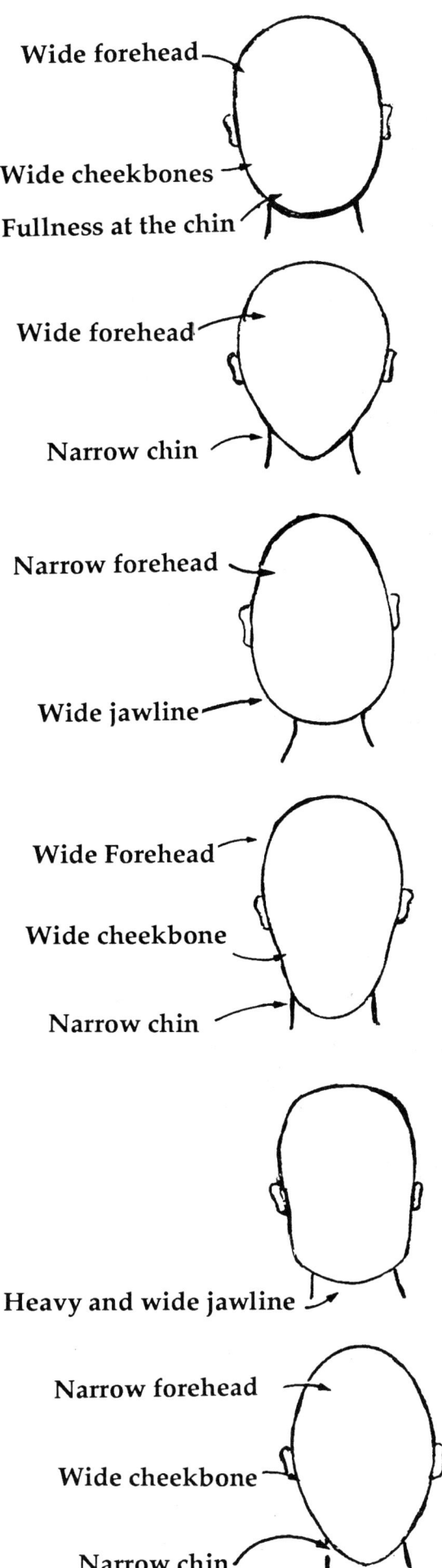

Facial features

Clients want a hairstyle which emphasises their most attractive features and draws attention away from less pleasing ones. Examine the client's profile as well as the front of her face.

Remember 'beauty is in the eye of the beholder' and you might have quite different ideas from the client, so do not automatically assume that she will agree about which features are attractive and which not. If, for example, a client with large ears asks to have her hair swept back from her face you can either very tactfully suggest she might suit her hair forward better, or assume she does not mind having big ears and comply with her wishes.

Hairdressers need a lot of tact and diplomacy! Never make a client feel embarrassed or insulted by showing amusement at her suggestions. It is important to respect her wishes and approach her sympathetically.

There are no hard and fast rules to follow when designing a style to suit facial features.

Certain styles emphasise the eyes more than others. For example, the eyes will look larger if the hair is brushed up and away from the forehead but full at the temples. A style with the hair brushed on to the face around the eyes makes close set eyes appear further apart.

Cropped hair, or long hair worn up, will make a short neck look longer. Other styles tend to emphasise the jawline, or the cheekbones.

You will learn with practice to recognise the effects of different styles.

Body type

Height and general size may not seem relevant to the choice of a style but you will discover that a style which looks perfect when the client is sitting down may be far from it when she stands up.

The finished style should be in proportion to the body. For instance, if a client has a large head and relatively thin body, giving her a style with lots of volume will make her look top-heavy.

A very tall person may not want the extra inches added by a bouffant hairstyle, whereas a small person might be pleased with an extra inch to her height.

Client's lifestyle

Most people lead busy lives and do not want fussy hairstyles which will keep them at the mirror for an hour each day. Neither do elderly people with stiff joints or weak muscles.

If a client appears with a photograph of an intricate creation she would like without having considered the work involved in maintaining it, you should discuss this with her. Usually such styles are reserved for special occasions and the client does not expect to keep it for any more than a day or two. However, even some apparently casual styles can be very time consuming to maintain and this should be pointed out.

Choosing a colour

Before selecting a shade for a client who wants her hair coloured, the natural colour of her hair, her skin tone and her eye colour must be taken into account. This is particularly important if a 'permanent' tint is being used. Again, you will learn by experience which hair colours complement the client's natural colouring. Study the product manufacturer's shade charts with the client to see what suitable colours are available.

Precautionary tests

Before chemical treatments are carried out in the salon it is often necessary to carry out certain tests on the hair or skin. You may want to determine the effects of previous treatments which might cause problems. Perhaps you need to find out if the client is sensitive to a particular product, or to determine whether the hair will take the particular treatment.

We will discuss these tests now and you will learn how to carry them out in the practical section at the end of the unit.

Allergy test

Permanent and some semi-permanent colours contain either para-phenylene-diamine or para-toluene-diamine, known as 'para dyes'. These substances can severely irritate sensitive skin and you are legally bound to carry out a skin test before using them for a full treatment.

The skin test is done on a small patch of skin 24 to 48 hours before you plan to do the colouring. If a positive reaction occurs the product must not be used. This test is also known as a skin test, patch test, hyper-sensitivity test or predisposition test.

Incompatibility test

Some hair colouring agents, particularly those intended for home use, contain metallic dyes. The metallic salts remain in the hair and if it is then treated with chemicals containing hydrogen peroxide a reaction will occur which will damage the hair. These salts cannot be removed, other than by cutting the affected hair off, and no chemical treatments which make use of hydrogen peroxide should be carried out on hair which is shown to have traces of metallic salts left in it. This includes most perms and permanent colours, and also some semi-permanents.

Always ask the client if she has used any colour on her hair in the past eight months. The client may have forgotten, or not want to admit to having used any, so do not accept her response without reservations.

Metallic dyes tend to leave the hair with a greenish tinge, so look for this and if you have any doubts at all carry out an incompatibility test.

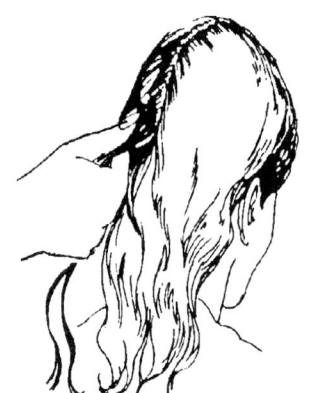

Pre-perm test for residual curl.

Although a client may not have had a perm for several months there may still be some curl left near the ends of the hair, or indeed most of the hair if it is long. This may not be immediately obvious if the hair has been blow dried or set, so the hair must be wet before you can see if there is any permanent curl in it.

Do not re-perm hair which has any permanent curl left as it could damage the hair. If the curl is only at the ends suggest to the client that it could be cut out.

Pre-perm test curl

If you have any doubts about whether a particular client's hair will perm successfully it is better to test a small section of hair first than run the risk of damaging the whole head.

Test curls are done using different perm lotions on small sections of hair so that you can ascertain which lotion, if any, will give the best result.

The test will also indicate which size of rod to use and how long the processing stage will take.

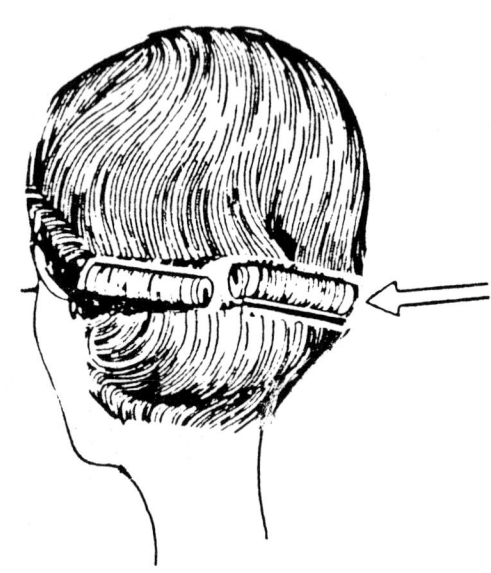

Test cutting for colour

Test cuttings are used to assess the effects of colourants or lighteners on the hair before applying them to the whole head. Strands of hair are removed and coloured as directed by the manufacturer. When processed the results are assessed.

Effects of henna treatment

Henna was frequently used in the past to give the hair a red colour and may still be used occasionally. Unfortunately it combines with the sulphur bonds in the cortex and interferes with the perming process. If a client has a reddish tinge to her hair it is advisable to ask her if she has had a henna treatment before perming her hair.

Health and safety in the salon

Protecting and promoting good health and safety is the responsibility of all who provide a service to the public. Hairdressers must follow the guidelines laid down by local bye laws as well as the Health and Safety at Work Act (1974) and the Office, Shops and Railway Premises Act (1963).

These Acts and bye laws are for the protection of the service suppliers as well as their customers.

It is important that you are aware of possible dangers and know how to deal with them. Various aspects of health and safety at work are covered throughout the units where relevant. First aid procedures and information on getting help in an emergency are covered in the Reception unit.

We have already dealt with clients suffering from infectious disorders of the hair and scalp, and the need for precautionary tests before certain treatments, in this unit.

We will now look at some of the other potential hazards which can present themselves in the salon.

Electrical equipment

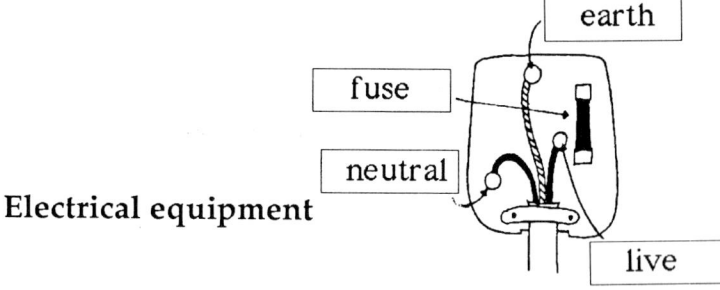

* Frayed flexes on electric equipment should be replaced immediately to remove the risk of fire and shock.

* Electric appliances should not be used near water, so keep them away form shampoo basins and do not clean by immersing in water. Never touch an electric appliance with wet hands.

* Make sure switches are not faulty, and switch off before inserting or removing a plug.

* Electric cables should not be left trailing on the floor as someone could trip over them.

Fire

Salons owners should always ask the fire authorities to check the premises for fire hazards and ensure that they meet the regulation standard of safety.

Always keep the recommended fire fighting equipment where it is easily accessible and in good condition. Check regularly to make sure they are working.

Every salon employee should know the procedure to be followed in case of fire which has been laid down by the management on the advice of the fire authorities.

Make sure any escape routes are not blocked.

Tools

Scissors, tail combs and other sharp implements should not be placed in the pockets of clothing or held in the mouth.

Always store dangerous tools such as razors and scissors out of the reach of children.

Steam and hot water

Always test the temperature of the steam before putting a client under a hot steamer. Similarly, test the temperature of tap water before wetting the client's head.

Chemicals

Always store chemicals in a safe place out of the reach of children.

Be careful not to spill any on the client or the surrounding area. Make sure the client's clothing is adequately protected at all times.

Always wear protective gloves and clothing when working with chemicals.

Chemical containers should be labelled clearly and correctly.

It is a good idea to have clear instructions for how to deal with spillage or other accidents with chemicals posted up in the salon.

Salon Hygiene

Hairdressers are obliged to keep their tools and premises in a hygienic condition.

Sterilisation procedures must be carried out to ensure that harmful bacteria and viruses are destroyed.

This is particularly important with the advent of Aids, although hairdressing is not considered to be a high risk occupation for the spreading this disease. Hairdressers are more likely to be infected by hepatitis, a sometimes fatal disease contracted by contaminated blood getting

into the blood stream of another person. It is therefore very important to keep even minor cuts well covered in case a client is cut during a service.

Pathogenic bacteria, that is bacteria which cause disease, must have favourable conditions in which to grow. These include heat, moisture and the absence of direct sunlight. A warm, busy salon is an ideal environment for bacteria to multiply and be passed from person to person.

Very often infections are spread in the air by coughing and sneezing. It is therefore important to have the salon well ventilated to keep fresh air coming in and stale, contaminated air going out.

Many diseases are passed on by direct contact with the source of infection. They can be transferred by contaminated food, cups, tools etcetera. It is therefore essential to keep all utensils and tools used in the salon scrupulously clean.

Any food preparation should be done hygienically in a separate kitchen and food stored in a covered container.

Always wash your hands before eating and preparing food, and after going to the toilet.

Sterilising tools used in the salon

There are three methods of sterilisation commonly used in salons.

* **Chemical sterilisation**
* **Steam sterilisation**
* **Ultra violet radiation**

Chemical sterilisation

Chemical sterilisation is carried out using either liquid disinfectants or sterilising vapours.

Disinfectants will kill bacteria if used correctly. Special containers are available for disinfecting salon tools. The tools can be placed in the container of liquid disinfectant after use and stored there until required for another client. Ordinary household bleach is very useful for sterilising many materials.

Formaldehyde vapour was commonly used in the past to sterilise tools but it is now thought to be carcinogenic and vapour sterilisation has become unpopular. However, alternative chemicals have been introduced to replace formaldehyde and this method may become popular again. A specially designed cabinet with perforated shelves is used for vapour sterilisation.

Steam sterilisation

Boiling water will kill most, if not all, bacteria.

Autoclaves are specially designed sterilising units which use steam produced under pressure to sterilise metal tools and other objects capable of withstanding a temperature of 121 degrees centigrade. They are a very efficient and effective method of sterilisation.

Ultra violet radiation

Cabinets with a mercury vapour lamp for producing ultra violet rays are very popular in hairdressing salons. Because the rays only sterilise the surface of the object where they touch it, this method is neither efficient nor very effective. Objects have to be turned over, and if they have an irregular surface some areas may be missed.

PRACTICAL SECTION

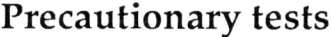

Precautionary tests

Porosity test

Take a few hairs and, holding them near the ends, run your fingers down towards the roots. Broken and raised cuticle scales will feel rough. The rougher the hair feels the more porous it will be. Sample hair from different parts of the head as the degree of porosity can vary.

Elasticity test

Take a dry hair, pull it gently between the fingers and then let it go at one end. Hair in good condition will not stretch much but will spring back immediately. If the hair stretches quite easily, does not return to its original length or breaks, its cortex is weak and the hair has little tensile strength.

Allergy test (skin test)

Requirements checklist

* Gown
* Towel
* Shampoo
* Gloves
* Cotton wool and buds
* Surgical spirit
* Colouring product
* Colour chart
* Client's record card

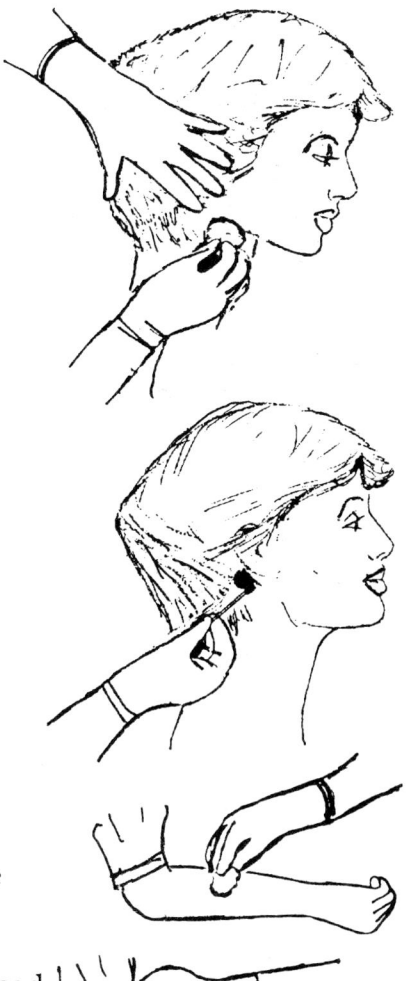

Procedure

1 Put a gown and towel round the client.

2 Clean a small area of skin behind the ear or on the inside of the elbow with cotton wool dipped in surgical spirit.

3 Wearing protective gloves, mix a small amount of the colour to be used according to the manufacturer's instructions.

4 Apply a small quantity of the colouring product to the cleaned area with a cotton bud and allow it to dry.

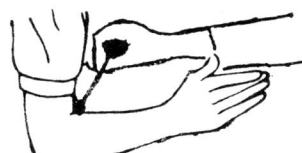

5   Cover dried patch with collodian which acts as an extra skin.

6   Ask the client to return to the salon after 24 to 48 hours. Advise her not to touch the patch unless it becomes irritated, in which case she should wash it off and apply a soothing lotion such as camomile.

7   When the client returns to the salon look for signs and symptoms of allergic reaction. The most obvious signs are redness due to irritation or swelling at the patch site. However, headache or nausea may also be symptoms of a positive reaction.

<u>If the test is positive you must not proceed with the treatment under any circumstances.</u>

8   Record the results on the client's record card.

Incompatibility test

Requirements checklist

* Gown
* Gloves
* Scissors
* Non-metallic container
* 6% hydrogen peroxide (not in cream form)
* Ammonium hydroxide
* Client's record card

Procedure

1   Cut a small strand of hair from below the crown area where it is less noticeable. You may need more than one sample if the hair seems to be affected in different areas.

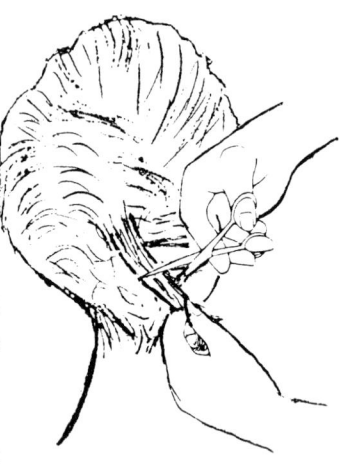

2   Wearing protective gloves, mix one part of ammonium hydroxide with 20 parts hydrogen peroxide in a non-metallic container.

3   Immerse the strand in the mixture and leave for thirty minutes.

   (To be completely certain the strand should be left in the solution for 24 hours.)

4   The presence of copper will make the solution bubble and the container will feel warm. Lead will change the colour of the hair.

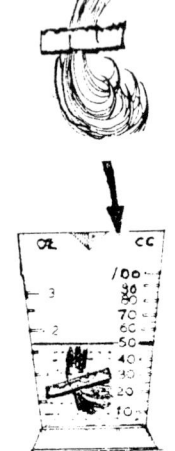

<u>If any of these reactions occur the test is positive and no perm or colouring treatment should be given which involves the use of hydrogen peroxide.</u>

5   Record the results on the client's record card.

Pre-perm test for residual curl

This is done by simply wetting the hair and examining it for signs of any remaining chemically induced curl, as opposed to natural curl. It is easily carried out after the hair has been shampooed.

Pre-perm test curl

Requirements checklist

* All the equipment required for a full perm

Procedure

1 Section off a small strand of hair below the crown where it is less noticable.

2 Apply a pre-perm buffer if necessary.

3 Wearing protective gloves, wind the strand and apply the perm lotion according to the manufacturer's instructions.

4 Repeat these three steps on other strands of hair as required using different sized rods and/or different perm lotions.

5 Test the processing every 3 or 4 minutes and when complete note the time taken for each strand.

6 Rinse the rods and apply the neutraliser according to the manufacturer's instructions.

7 When processing is complete rinse the neutraliser from the hair gently but thoroughly.

8 Examine the test curls and make your decision about how to proceed on the basis of your results.

9 Record the results on the client's record card.

Test cutting for colour

Requirements checklist

* All the equipment required for a full colour treatment apart from shampoo supplies and stain remover.

Procedure

1 Take a small strand of hair from the less noticable areas of the head and sellotape each at one end.

2 Mix small quantities of the colours you wish to test according to the manufacturer's instructions and label each one.

3 Immerse the samples in the colouring agents and process as instructed.

4 Rinse colour off when processing is complete, and dry the hair with a blow dryer.

5 Examine the samples in natural daylight.

6 Make your decision about how to proceed on the basis of your results.

7 Record the results on the client's record card.

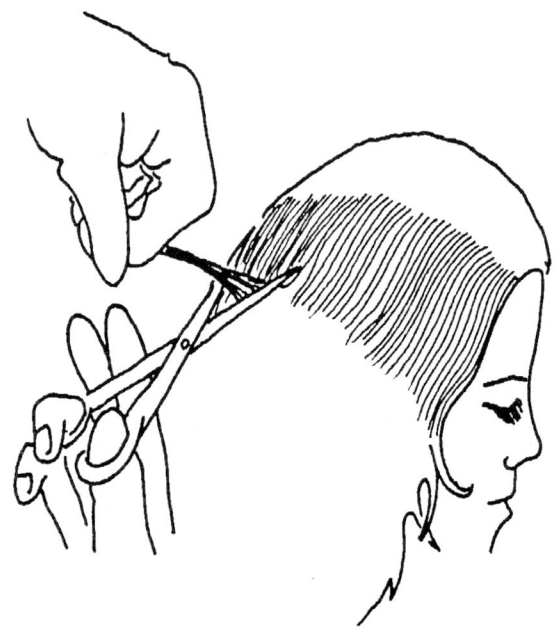

Consultation and diagnostics procedure

Requirements checklist

* Client's record card
* Protective gown
* Large toothed comb

Procedure

1 Place a protective gown over the clients shoulders and seat her comfortably.

2 Confirm with the client which services she requires. If she is not sure at this stage continue with the procedure and discuss at the end.

3 Consult the client's record card to see what treatments and results she has had previously and ask her about other treatments she may have had.

4 Comb the hair through and examine it and the scalp for any signs or symptoms of disease or abnormality. If any are present make a careful diagnosis. Get a second opinion if unsure. If an infectious condition is present stop working with the client immediately and explain tactfully why you cannot proceed.

5 Assess the condition of the hair. Carry out porosity and/or elasticity tests if necessary.

6 Shampoo the hair and condition if required.

7 When hair is wet analyse the client's hair growth patterns.

8 Determine the hair's natural movement, unless of course it has been permed in which case it will be the new movement that you see.

9 Determine the density and texture of the hair.

10 Consider the client's face shape, facial features, body shape and size.

11 Ask the client about her lifestyle if the type of style she is considering is difficult or time consuming to maintain.

12 If the client is having her hair coloured note her natural colouring, including hair, skin and eyes. Using the manufacturer's shade chart discuss which colours are suitable for her.

13 Taking all your findings into consideration, decide what treatments and types of styles are appropriate for the client.

14 Discuss your conclusions with the client and come to an agreement with her. If the services or products you recommend are more expensive than usual explain to client why you are recommending them. Make sure she understands exactly what you intend to do, and what the cost will be.

15 Carry out any precautionary tests if required.

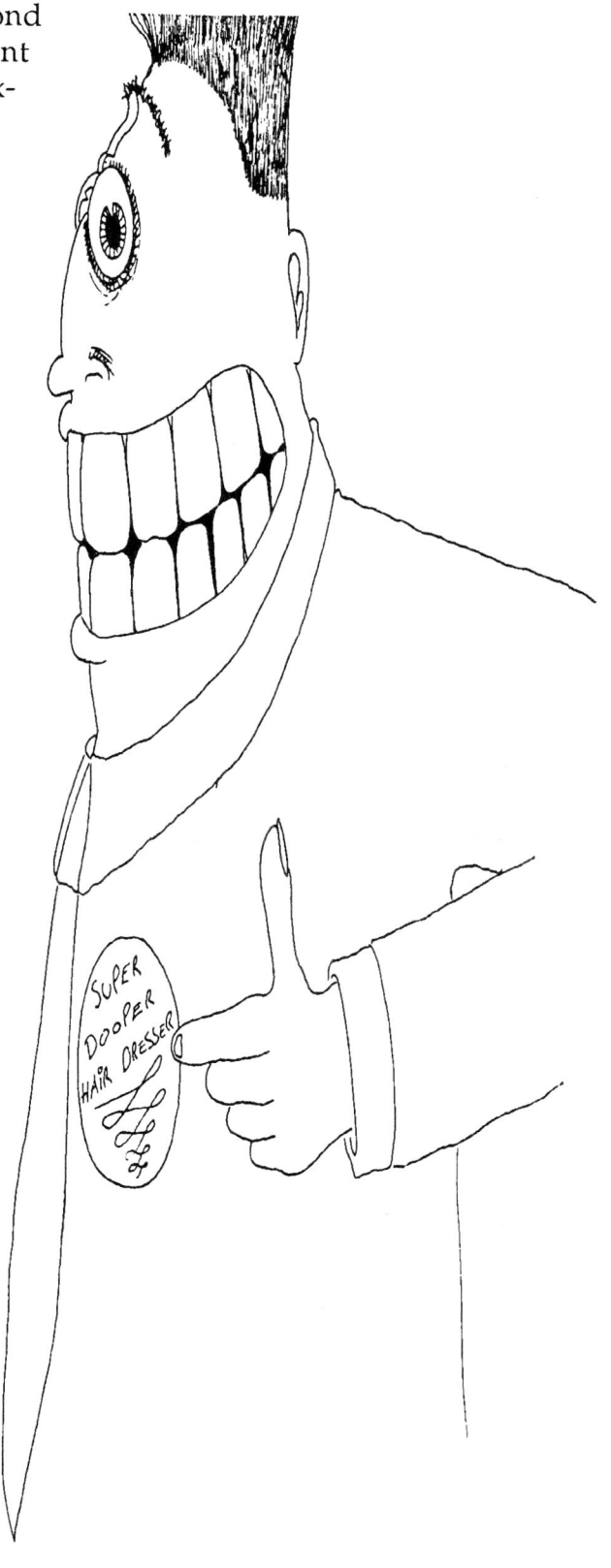

3 CONDITIONING HAIR AND SCALP

Before starting this unit it might be a good idea to remind yourself of what we discussed in the consultation and diagnostics unit regarding hair structure, hair and skin disorders and massage treatments.

Health and your hair

Some years ago our children brought home a stray dog. His coat was dry, dull and sparse and he looked ill. A visit to the vet confirmed that he was suffering from distemper, a sometimes fatal disease in dogs. With treatment and a balanced diet the improvement in his health was rapid. As his health improved so did his coat, although this took longer. It became thick and took on a healthy sheen.

Have you ever noticed the deterioration in the condition of your own hair after an illness, or even after taking a course of medicine?

The condition of our hair depends very much on the state of our health *while it is growing*.

The hair we see is actually dead so, although we can greatly improve the look of it temporarily, if it is in poor condition we cannot make the hair itself 'healthy'.

A balanced diet is the first step to healthy, shining hair. However, hair growth is affected by many physiological factors. Illness, drugs and hormone imbalances all have an adverse effect on the way hair develops.

Physical and chemical damage

After the hair has emerged through the scalp it can be damaged both physically and chemically. Too much sun, overbrushing, backcombing and blow drying are just a few ways in which the hair can be damaged by physical means.

Harsh alkaline shampoo, perming, bleaching and colouring can all cause chemical damage. (For more detailed information refer back to the Consultation and Diagnostics Unit)

Conditioners

To improve the look and feel of damaged hair we use conditioners.

Recent studies have shown that more women condition their hair today than at any time in the past, and are better informed about their hair and why conditioners are necessary.

It is also a fact that supermarkets and chemists sell far more shampoos and conditioners for home use than do hairdressing salons. Many salons neglect this lucrative market by failing to provide a range of professional conditioning treatments for home use as well as salon use.

A conditioner for your hair is like a moisturiser for your skin. Cleansing the skin removes some of the essential natural oil. Young skin replaces these oils quickly but as we grow older the skin becomes drier and needs the addition of a moisturiser. In the same way shampoo, especially alkaline shampoo, removes the hair's natural oil leaving it dry and unprotected from the elements. Conditioners can be used to replace this. Some people have greasy hair and do not need a conditioner for this purpose. However, conditioners have other functions than simply moisturising the hair.

Conditioners are used to

* reduce the effects of physical and chemical damage
* counteract dryness of the hair
* restore the natural pH value
* make the hair shine
* make the hair more manageable
* help prevent chemical damage

The scalp too can be easily damaged by incorrect use of high alkaline products such as perm lotions, and conditioners help to alleviate the effects of this.

The effective use of any hair conditioner depends on a thorough understanding of how it works.

When we know how the different conditioners work we will know which one to use in a given situation, when to use it and how to use it.

pH - what is it?

pH means 'potential hydrogen' and is a term used to identify the degree of acidity or alkalinity of a substance.

It is measured on a scale from **0 to 14.** Distilled water is neutral, that is neither acid nor alkaline, and has a pH value of **7** which is right in the centre of the scale.

pH values greater than **7** are alkaline. The more alkaline the substance the higher its pH value.

Acids on the other hand have pH values less than **7**. The more acidic they are the lower the pH value.

Very strong alkalies will burn the skin and hair, or dissolve them completely if left on too long. They are only used as hair relaxers or depilatories in the salon.

Very strong acids are also extremely dangerous and never used for hairdressing purposes.

Estimating pH value

One way to assess whether a liquid is alkaline or acidic is by immersing *litmus paper* in it. The paper will turn *red* if it is acidic or *blue* if it is alkaline.

To estimate its pH value you will need either *universal indicator* or an *electric pH meter*.

Universal indicator is impregnated on paper and changes colour according to the pH value of the liquid in which it is immersed. The colour change is compared to the colours on a chart and the pH value estimate accordingly. This method is sufficiently accurate for salon use.

For an exact reading use an electric pH meter. These are expensive and rarely used by salons.

Effects of heat and cold on the hair

If you compare the effects of acids and alkalies with those of *heat* and *cold* on the hair you will find that there is a basic similarity.

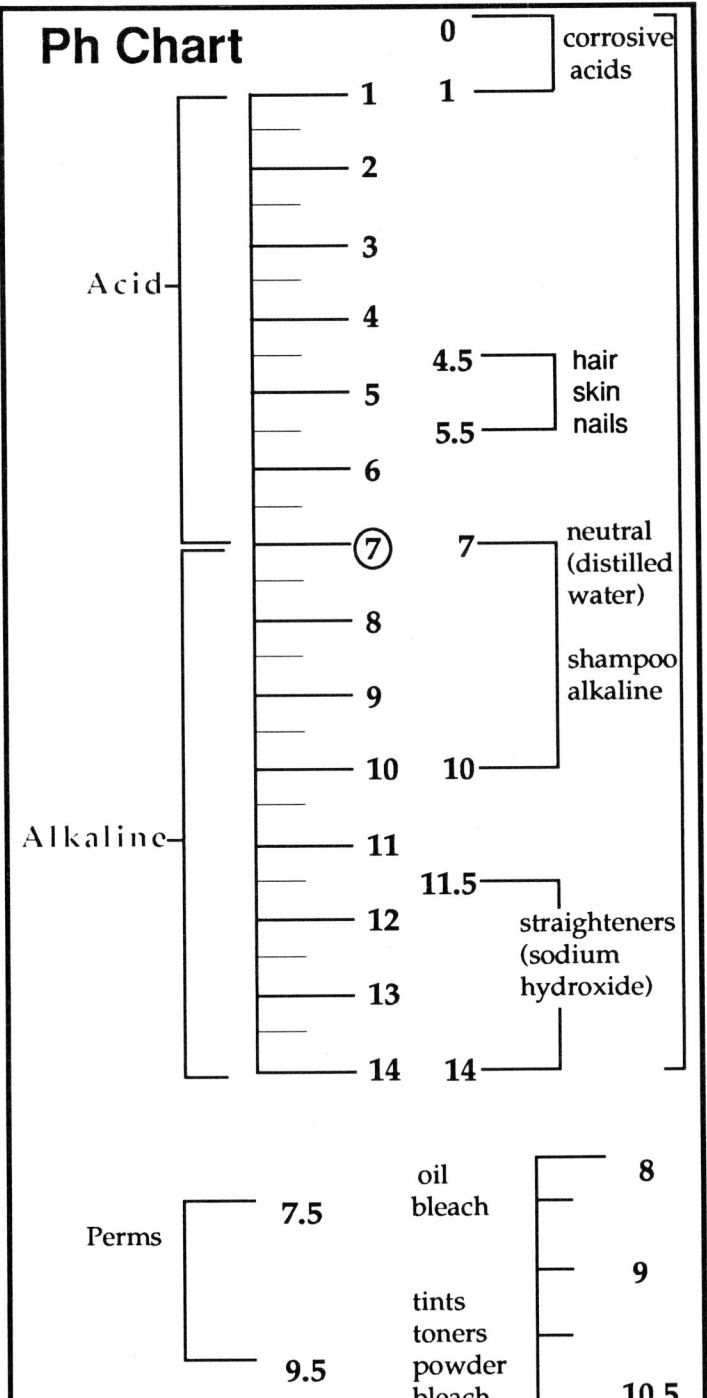

Cold causes contraction and tightens the cuticle as do acids.

Heat causes expansion and swells the cuticle as do alkalies.

Combining complementary forces during hairdressing processes enables us to achieve a *faster* and *stronger* result. For example, combining an acid conditioning treatment with cold rinsing leaves the cuticles as tight and flat as possible, although the client may not find the procedure too comfortable! Similarly, certain alkaline treatments can be *speeded up* by using a warm hairdryer. This must only be done according to the manufacturer's instructions or the hair could be damaged.

Porosity and Elasticity

The use of alkaline products causes the hair to swell and this in turn can have a detrimental effect on the hair's *porosity* and *elasticity*.

An understanding of these two concepts is the key to understanding many of the hair conditioning problems that you will encounter in the salon.

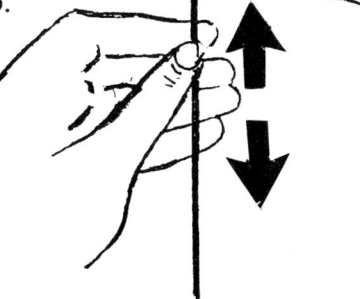

Porosity is measured by the amount of moisture hair can absorb.

Elasticity is measured by how much a hair can stretch under pressure and return to its original length when the tension is released.

If the hair is damaged its moisture content and its ability to stretch will be adversely affected.

Over-porous hair

* is brittle, dry and dull
* is easily broken
* is spongy and tends to mat when wet
* is difficult to manage
* does not hold a style
* absorbs too much of the chemicals used in perming and colouring treatments

Hair which has lost its elasticity

* is easily over-stretched
* breaks easily especially when wet
* has no bounce or spring

There are two basic types of conditioners

1 Those designed to treat superficial damage are SURFACE CONDITIONERS

2 Those designed to treat deep-seated damage are PENETRATING CONDITIONERS

Surface conditioners

Superficial damage is usually the result of harsh physical treatment and is restricted to the cuticle layers of the hair shaft.

Superficially damaged hair will look dry and dull but will not have lost its elasticity. Conditioners used to treat such damage work by replacing moisture and restoring the hair to its natural pH. Because they are acidic they tighten the cuticle layers leaving them smooth and the hair shiny and manageable.

These conditioners take effect immediately because they do not have to penetrate the cortex. They come as liquids, creams and waxes. Some are oil based.

Surface conditioners are also known as *normalising*, or *anti-oxidising* conditioners because they are used after chemical treatment with alkalies to stop oxidation by restoring the acid pH.

Before modern conditioners were introduced people used things like vinegar, egg white, beer, lemon juice, olive and almond oils, lanolin and various herbs to condition their hair. In their natural state these act as surface conditioners because the molecules are too large to penetrate the cortex.

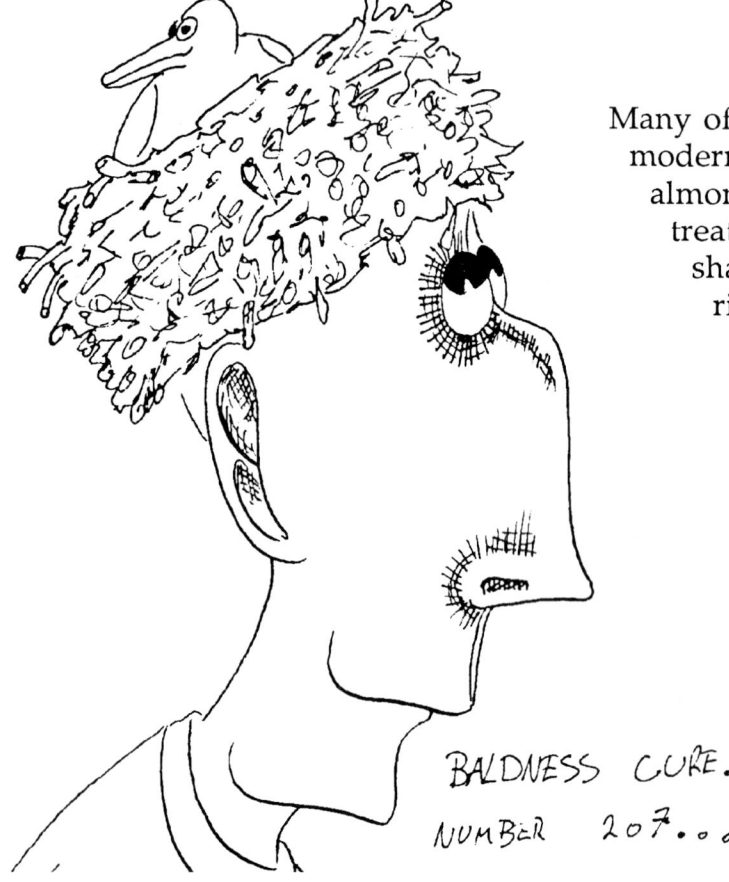

BALDNESS CURE.
NUMBER 207...

Many of these ingredients are incorporated into modern conditioners. In fact lanolin, olive and almond oils are still used today to give hot oil treatments. They are removed with an acid shampoo applied directly to the oil before rinsing. (Note that some people are allergic to lanolin.)

Conditioning creams and waxes contain synthetic silicones which coat the hair shaft with a polymer to improve elasticity and manageability. They should be well rinsed from the hair because the heavy cream, wax or silicone would interfere with styling.

Penetrating conditioners

Deep seated damage has occurred when the cortex of the hair is affected. The hair will be dry, dull and limp. When wet it may feel spongy and be difficult to comb.

This damage can be caused during the formation of the hair due to factors already mentioned such as illness and poor diet. It can also be caused by severe physical damage such as overheating, but is perhaps more often the result of harsh chemical treatment.

Deep seated damage affects the hair's porosity and elasticity. Only penetrating conditioners will help to reduce the effects of this. Penetrating conditioners are derived from either *vegetable* protein, such as henna, gingseng, soya, wheat germ and balsam, or *animal* protein from cattle tissue such as bones, horns and placenta.

The conditioning protein is processed until its molecules are small enough to penetrate the cortex easily. It replaces amino acids in the damaged polypeptide chains, reducing porosity and restoring elasticity. These conditioners also treat surface damage at the same time.

Penetrating conditioners derived from animal products, also known as *neucleic acid* conditioners are quite new on the market and superior to the vegetable based ones. They actually restructure the hair by rebuilding the polypeptide chains.

They are able to penetrate further into the cortex than any other conditioner, to strengthen the hair effectively without having side effects on any other chemical service, and to remain in the hair longer than any other conditioner.

These conditioners also protect the hair from highly alkaline chemical services such as tints, permanent waves, straighteners and bleaches.

They are the most expensive conditioners available and some clients do not agree with using animal products so keep these points in mind when recommending this type of conditioner.

CETRIMIDE, which is a *quaternary ammonium compound*, is also used as the base of some penetrating conditioners. It reduces static and softens the hair shaft, making the hair look good and easy to manage.

Conditioning the hair prior to a chemical service

Applying a conditioner prior to a chemical service is termed a BUFFER or FILLER treatment. It is used to even out over-porous hair. The conditioner fills the hair and temporarily equalises the porosity along the length of the shaft so that the chemical is absorbed uniformly. It also closes the cuticle so the hair will not absorb too much chemical.

Using heat during the conditioning process

Some conditioners require heat to aid penetration into the cortex. When the heat is applied it will raise the cuticle scales allowing deeper penetration of the conditioner.

Traditionally this was done by wrapping hot damp towels in turban fashion around the head but today most salons use equipment such as steamers, infra red accelerators, thermal caps or plastic bags in conjunction with warm driers.

Scalp treatments

It is true that a healthy scalp is indicative of healthy hair. Scalp conditioners are available which contain natural organic ingredients generally formulated without perfume, alcohol or artificial colour to avoid irritating sensitive skin.

Their main purpose is to help remove dandruff, moisturise the scalp and maintain a healthy acid mantle. They also help to condition the hair.

Scalp massage given in conjunction with a scalp treatment is thought to stimulates the nerves, muscles and glands in the scalp. It will also increase the blood supply which nourishes the scalp tissue and the hair papilla.

<u>Never give scalp massage before or immediately after a chemical service.</u>

Massage techniques

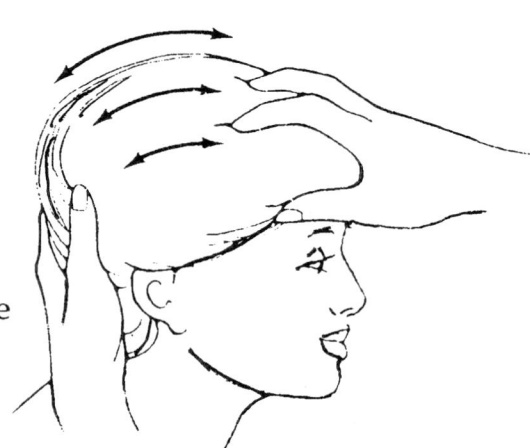

Effleurage

This is a smooth *stroking action* starting at the front hairline and moving towards the nape. It is done with a gentle but firm movement of the fingers. Effleurage massage is soothing to the nerves and allows the client to relax.

Petrissage

Petrissage is a *kneading movement* which stimulates the scalp. The scalp is moved by pressure from the pads of the fingers and will loosen up as the fat under it breaks down. Petrissage is also very relaxing.

Tapotement

This is a stimulating treatment consisting of *rapid tapping* with the fingers or sides of the hands, it is not normally applied to the scalp. It is used mainly on other parts of the body to break down fatty tissue.

Vibration

Vibration, as the name suggests, is a technique which produces a *shaking movement* in the scalp. It can be done with the hands but is usually performed by an electric vibratory machine, commonly known as a 'vibro'. It is used to stimulate the scalp tissues.

Conditioning the hair and scalp

Remember conditioners can hinder certain salon services.

Requirement checklist

* Client's record card and release form if appropriate
* Brush and tail comb
* Release form if appropriate
* Range of hair conditioning products

Applying a conditioner, oil or scalp treatment

Protect client's clothing with protective covering.

1 Brush hair and shampoo using an acid balanced shampoo.

2 Part the hair into four equal sections using a tail comb

3 Apply a small amount of conditioner directly from the container or use a tinting brush.

4 Apply from the crown area to the nape followed by the side sections, and comb through to ensure even distribution.

5 Massage the conditioner into the scalp with the cushions of the fingertips in a firm circular movement.

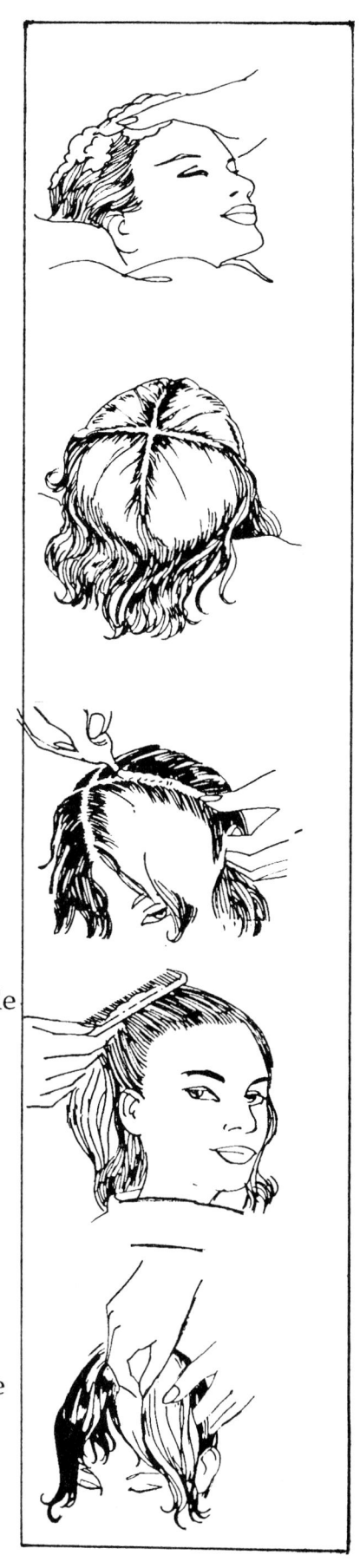

7   If additional heat is required use an appropriate source.

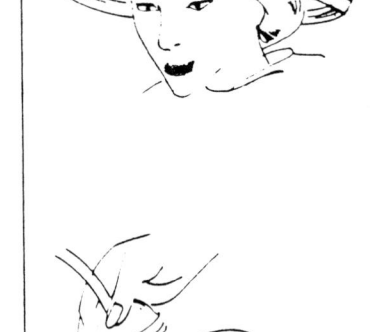

8   Leave conditioner on for time suggested by manufacturer.

9   Rinse hair thoroughly with tepid water, otherwise the hair will be sticky and unmanageable.

10 Shampoo again if instructed by manufacturer. Remember that oil treatments are removed by applying shampoo directly to hair *before* applying water.

11 Analyse results.

12 Record client's details on record card.

13 Recommend home care treatments.

14 Clean work area and equipment used.

4 SHAMPOOING

Because shampooing is a vital preliminary step for many hairdressing services it should be mastered early in training.

We shampoo the hair to

* cleanse the hair and scalp by removing dirt, grease, dead skin, hairdressing products etc.

* get the hair ready for further salon treatments

* treat certain hair and scalp conditions

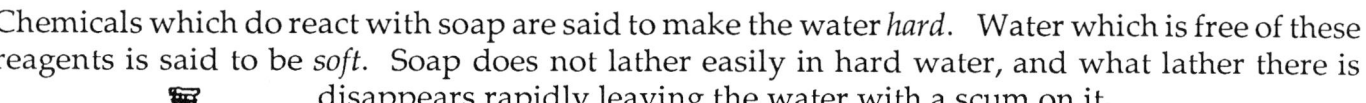

Shampoo and water

Pure water is composed of hydrogen and oxygen. However, the water we get from our taps contains many other chemical substances. Most of these do not react with soap and soap based products, but others do.

Chemicals which do react with soap are said to make the water *hard*. Water which is free of these reagents is said to be *soft*. Soap does not lather easily in hard water, and what lather there is disappears rapidly leaving the water with a scum on it.

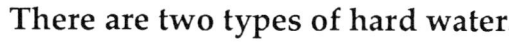

There are two types of hard water.

Temporary hard water contains calcium or magnesium bicarbonate. When heated the bicarbonate turns into a carbonate. This is a solid and it forms a white chalky deposit. Temporary hardness can be removed by boiling.

Permanently hard water contains calcium or magnesium sulphate. The deposit left by these chemicals cannot be removed by boiling and permanently hard water can only be softened by the addition of other chemicals.

Modern shampoos rarely contain soap so we rarely encounter the problem of clients emerging from the basin with a ring of scum round their heads! However, hard water can still present problems in the salon as it leaves deposits in pipes. It can block up the spray heads on the shampoo basin and the nozzles in steamers. The spray heads can be removed and cleared with a pin or chemical descaler such as is used in domestic kettles. It is advisable to use distilled water in steamers if the tap water is hard.

Soapless shampoos contain detergents such as *triethanolamine lauryl sulphate* (TLS) or *sodium lauryl sulphate* (SLS) which are made from vegetable oils treated with *sulphuric acid*. They invariably contain other ingredients which we will look at later.

Action of Shampoo

Shampooing involves both *physical* and *chemical* action.

* The *physical action* involves applying the shampoo and massaging it into the hair and scalp.

* The *chemical action* results from the shampoo's ability to act as a *wetting agent*.

Wetting agents break or lower the surface tension of water. This allows the detergent molecules to surrround the particles of dirt and other foreign substances which are attracted to a shampoo molecule. These are then emulsified and rinsed from the hair.

Try washing a greasy plate after a breakfast of bacon and egg by immersing it in hot water. The grease will lie in droplets on the surface. Add some washing up liquid and the grease will wash off easily. The washing up liquid has acted as a wetting agent.

Some hairdressers mistakenly think that if a shampoo lathers richly and makes the hair 'squeaky clean' it is a quality product. A good lather does not necessarily indicate a good shampoo. Many expensive, high quality shampoos do not lather well and still clean the hair thoroughly. 'Squeaky clean' hair has had all the natural oil stripped from it, usually by an alkaline in the shampoo, and could in fact be damaged

The Detergent Molecule

This can be illustrated by a head and a tail. The head is *hydrophilic*, that is water loving. The tail is *hydrophobic*, that is water hating and is attracted to grease. The tail surrounds the grease particle isolating it from the water. This chemical action, along with physical massage, allows the hair to be cleaned by emulsification.

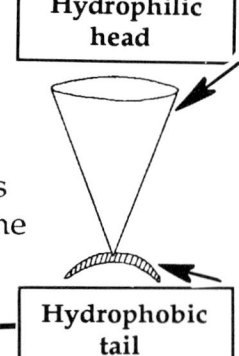

pH and shampoo

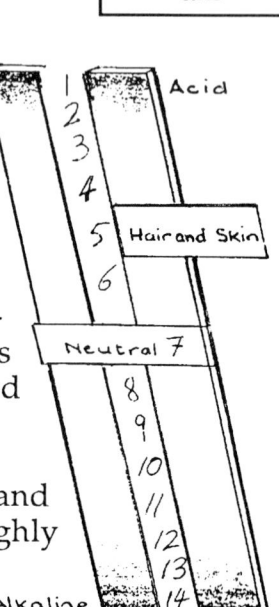

The pH scale

It is essential to understand how the pH value of a shampoo affects the hair and scalp so that you will know which product to use in a given situation. (pH is discussed fully in the conditioning unit.)

Skin and hair are naturally surrounded by an *'acid mantle'* due to the combination of sebum and sweat, and have a pH value between 4.5 and 5.5. This protects the skin against bacterial infection and also keeps the cuticle in good condition.

Acid-balanced shampoos have a pH value similar to that of the 'acid mantle' and help to replace the acid removed by washing or processing. They are highly recommended, especially if the client is having other treatment with alkaline products.

Some shampoos can have a pH value as high as **10**. Although alkaline shampoos are powerful cleansers they are not good for the hair. If an alkaline shampoo is used it should be neutralised with an acid rinse to bring the hair and scalp back to their natural pH. You should explain to the client why an acid rinse is essential in case she feels you are incurring unnecessary expense.

SHAMPOO TIPS

* Before perming use an acid balanced shampoo that contains no additives, and do not stimulate the scalp too much as this will make it sensitive.

* When removing an oil treatment apply shampoo directly to the hair before wetting it. This will emulsify the oil allowing it to be rinsed out of the hair.

* When removing a permanent colour, bleach or lightener select an acid shampoo to counteract the alkalinity of these services.

* Damaged hair tangles easily especially if it is long. So use a gentle stroking movement beginning at the front and work towards the nape.

* Use tepid water when shampooing damaged hair. In exceptional circumstances hot water and undue tension could break damaged hair.

* Before applying a semi-permanent colour to undamaged hair shampoo with a mildly alkaline shampoo to open the cuticle and allow the colour to penetrate into.

* For regular hairdressing services, such as a cut and blowdry, select a shampoo suitable for the individual's hair and scalp type.

SHAMPOO	pH	PURPOSE	COMMENT
Beer	Alkaline		Contains a high amount of soapless detergent (Only traces of beer)
Conditioning / Protein	Acid	Recommended for fine greasy hair. Said to give 'body' to the hair	Contains vegetable or animal protein. Effects are temporary
Coal Tar	Acid	To improve structurally damaged hair	Shampoo is left on the hair for a few minutes. Gives a good shine to the hair
Anti-Dandruff	Acid	For the prevention of dandruff. Over-use dries hair. Dulls blonde hair	Contains selenium sulphide or zincpyrithione. Some people are allergic to sulphur
Dry Powder	–	Designed for people who cannot wet their hair for medical reasons	Talcum powder is often used to absorb grease, and is then brushed out
Brightener	Acid/ Alkaline	To brighten the hair and bring out highlights. It is left on the hair for 5 to 10 minutes.	Can contain henna to add redness to brown hair, camomile to brighten blonde hair or peroxide (3%) to lighten the hair
Non-Stripping (Colour Fast)	Acid	Used after colourants. Will not fade the colour. Removes traces of the oxidation process	This shampoo has an acid pH which will reduce oxidation damage and restore the hair to its natural pH (4.5 - 5.5)
All - Purpose (Regular)	Acid	For general use. Will not interfere with sevices such as perms, tints, bleaches etc	This shampoo has a low pH so is kind to hair and skin
Egg	Acid	Recommended for dry, brittle, processed hair or sensitive scalps.	Contain a lower amount of soapless detergent than most shampoos. Contains oily and fatty substances. Only traces of egg are present
Oil	Acid	Recommended for dry hair and scalps.	Contains olive, coconut almond or lanolin oils **Note** some people are allergic to lanolin oil
Stabilising	Acid	Used after a hair relaxer (straightener)	The shampoo contains an oxidant which fixes the hair bonds in the new straight position permanently
Lemon	Alkaline	Recommended for greasy hair. Note. Lemon does not prevent greasy hair	Contains a high amount of soapless detergent. Overuse causes dry skin

PRACTICAL SECTION

You will have gone through a Consultation and Diagnostics procedure before beginning the hairdressing service of which shampooing forms a part. Use the appropriate shampoo for the treatment and condition of the hair.

Procedure for Shampooing

Requirements Checklist

* Shampoo gowns
* Towels
* Capes
* Clean combs and brushes
* Neck strip
* Range of shampoos and conditioners
* Record card and release form if used

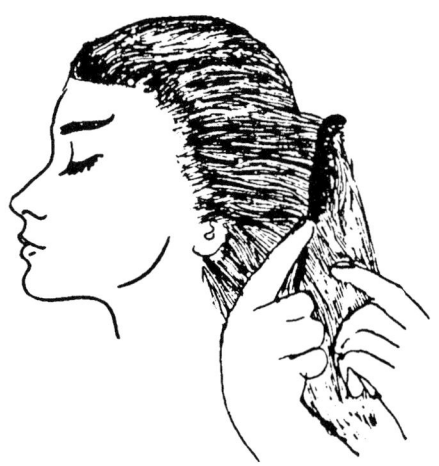

Procedure

1 Seat the client comfortably at the shampoo basin and protect her clothes with a protective gown and towel.

2 Remove grips, hair clasps etc.

3 Brush the hair carefully. (Avoid excessive brushing prior to permanent waving)

4 Lower the client's head gently over the shampoo basin.

5 Pick up the spray and direct the nozzle into the basin before turning the water tap on to avoid spraying the client and surrounding area.

6 Check the temperature and pressure of the water by spraying the back of your hand before applying to the client's head. When the water is at the right temperature and pressure, direct it on to the hair, keeping your hand in the spray to detect any change.

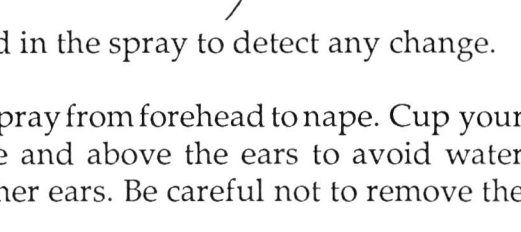

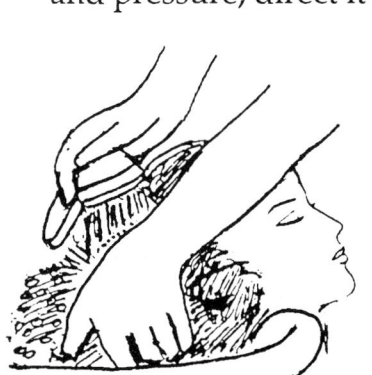

7 Saturate the hair, working the spray from forehead to nape. Cup your hand round the client's hairline and above the ears to avoid water running down her face or into her ears. Be careful not to remove the clients make-up if worn.

8 When the hair is completely saturated turn off the water and place the spray nozzle in its holder.

9 Put a measured amount of shampoo on the palm of the hand and distribute it evenly through the hair. If shampoo should accidentally get into the client's eyes, immediately blot them gently with a clean towel and rinse thoroughly in cool water.

10 Using both hands gently work the shampoo through the hair and scalp from the front hairline towards the back of the head. Use a stroking movement at the front hairline and a rotary movement on the rest of the head. Repeat this sequence at least four times.

11 With one hand supporting the client's head, massage around the ears and nape area.

12 Using warm water, rinse the hair thoroughly to remove all shampoo.

13 Apply more shampoo, repeating steps 9 to 12. Remember, do not shampoo vigorously prior to chemical services such as perms.

14 Rinse the hair thoroughly with tepid water. If a conditioner or cream rinse is to be applied, squeeze the hair gently to remove excess water and apply treatment according to the manufacturer's instructions. Rinse thoroughly again.

15 Squeeze the hair to remove excess water and wrap the client's head in a towel.

16 Place a dry towel round the client's shoulders.

17 Using a wide toothed comb, comb the hair through beginning at the ends of the hair. Start in the nape area.

18 Inform the stylist that client is ready for the next service.

19 Clean the shampoo basin and surrounding

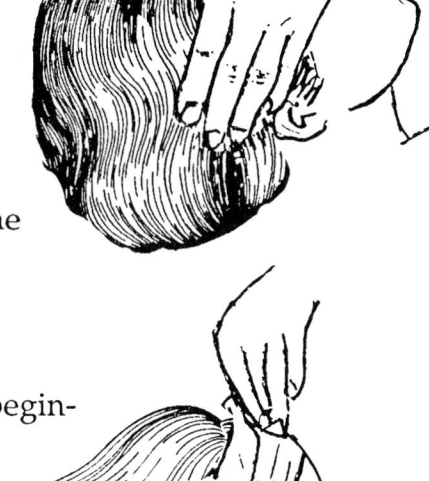

5 HAIRCUTTING

What is a good haircut?

Is a "good' haircut an expertly executed one with clear, clean lines or is it the artistic product of a creative mind?

The answer is both of these. You should regard yourself as an artist, otherwise you will simply be a technician churning out mass produced styles which will neither satisfy you nor discerning clients. Of course you are limited to some extent by the client's own preferences and hair type but if you regard this as a challenge rather than a restriction it will not hinder your creativity.

Artists must be able to use their tools competently and know all the techniques needed to produce their works of art. In this unit you will learn different cutting techniques and how to use the tools to carry these out. The creative aspect comes through a combination of experience, originality, initiative and an eye for shape and colour.

Sometimes trainee stylists feel apprehensive about cutting hair because it seems very complicated. However, there are only *three* basic types of cuts.

1 Bobbed
2 Graduated
3 Layered

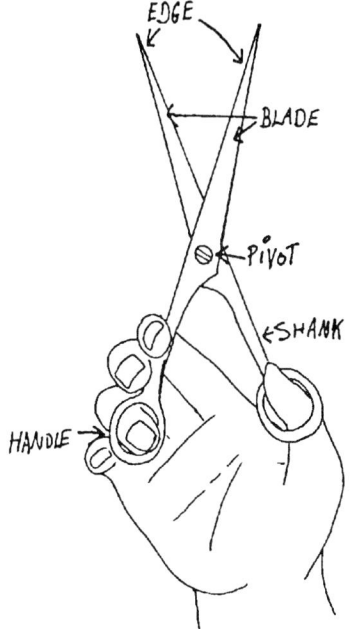

All modern styles are based on one or a combination of these cuts. Before we learn how to do the basic cuts we will look at the tools used to achieve them.

Tools used to cut hair

The tools used to cut hair are scissors, razors and clippers.

Scissors

Scissors vary in design, size and price. They should be comfortable to hold and must be very sharp. Choose the best quality you can afford. Good quality scissors will last you a long time if you look after them carefully. Never cut anything other than hair with them.

Razors

'Cut-throat' razors with fixed open blades are rarely used in ladies' hairdressing. Modern razors have disposable blades with a safety guard.

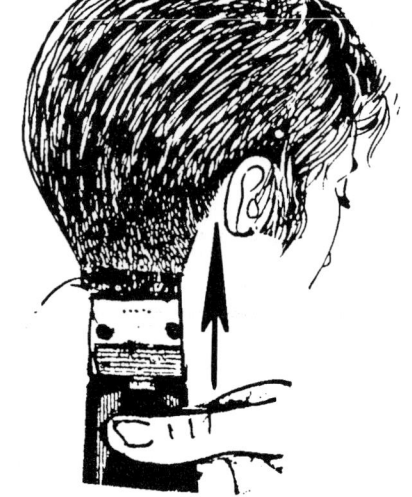

Clippers

Electric clippers are used for very short graduated styles.

Cutting techniques

All haircuts are achieved by using one or more of the three techniques listed below.

1 Club cutting with scissors

2 Tapering with scissors

3 Tapering with a razor

Wet or dry?

Hair can be cut wet or dry. However, with a few exceptions it is best to cut the hair **wet** for the following reasons.

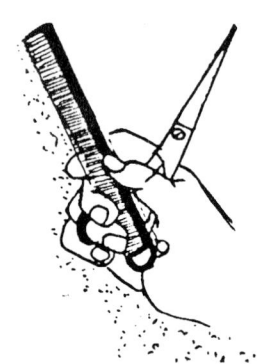

* The hair is easier to control.
* The head shape is easier to define.
* The hair falls into its natural growth pattern
* Shampooed hair is more hygiene to work with.

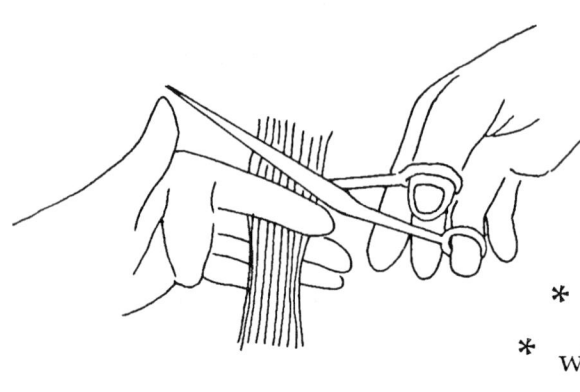

Exceptions to the above are:

* when cutting very curly hair which should be club cut dry
* when removing split ends
* when removing bulk with scissors
* when the client insists on a dry cut
* when cutting close graduated styles with clippers or scissors

Note Remember that hair will stretch more when wet and will return to its original length when dry. This will result in the hairstyle appearing shorter than when it was cut.

Club cutting with scissors

This technique is the one most frequently used today. The hair is cut straight across the section leaving the points even. This gives a well-defined blunt line. It can be used on wet or dry hair and is ideal for creating any of the basic types of cut. It encourages hair to lie straight because no weight has been removed from the ends of the hair.

A scissor-over-comb method of club cutting is commonly used to create the modern short graduated haircuts which follows the contours of the side and nape area of the head.

The degree of slope in the graduation depends on the angle at which the comb is held. (Many hairdressers prefer to use electric clippers fitted with various sizes of comb attachments instead of scissors as clippers make this type of graduation extremely easy to master)

Another form of this technique is known as *bevel* cutting. The hair is combed round the forefinger and the lower blade of the scissors slipped under the hair. The top blade slices through the hair at an angle. The result is a chiselled or bevelled shape at the hair ends giving a graduated effect.

Tapering with scissors

This technique is also known as *slithering* or *feathering*. The idea is to reduce some of the bulk from the hair ends without reducing the length. The hair is tapered into a point rather like a feather. This encourages hair movement or curl at the ends.

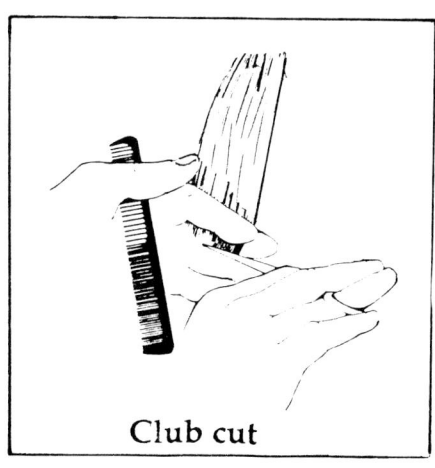

Club cut

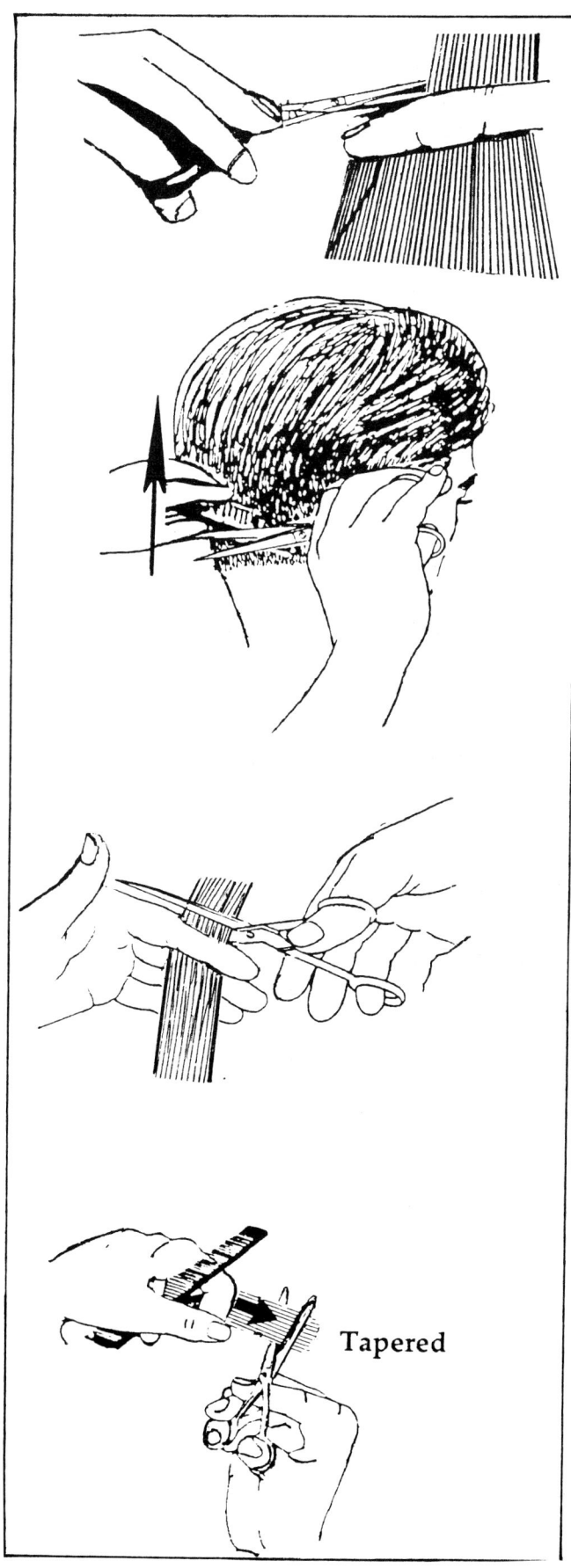

Tapered

Hold a section of hair between the index and middle fingers at the point you want the tapering to start. Backcomb gently then taper the hair with a slithering movement, that is, sliding the blades up and down.

Texturising or Point Tapering

This is a popular technique used to create softness at the perimeters of the hair, especially fringes. This is done by carefully 'biting' into selected strands of hair with the points of the scissor blades.

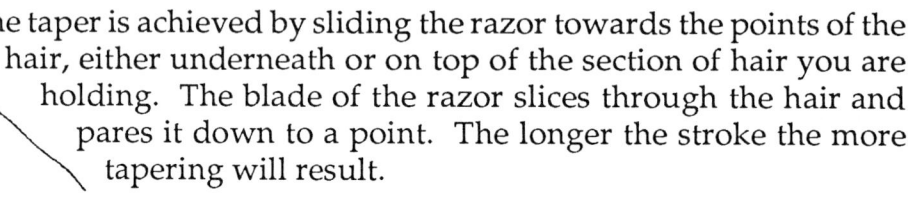

Tapering with a razor

Tapering with a razor achieves exactly the same effect as scissor tapering and is always carried out on wet hair. It can be used to reduce both weight and length from the hair.

The taper is achieved by sliding the razor towards the points of the hair, either underneath or on top of the section of hair you are holding. The blade of the razor slices through the hair and pares it down to a point. The longer the stroke the more tapering will result.

Thinning hair

Very thick hair can be thinned out to reduce its volume with special thinning scissors. Another method is to lif t meshes of hair twist as indicated and use regularscissors in a sliding motion to remove weight. The hair remains the same length. It is **not** a form of tapering. The hair is cut dry

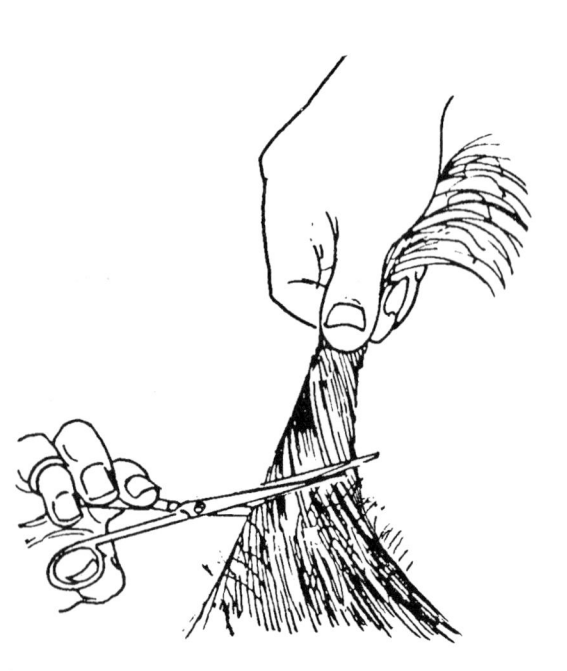

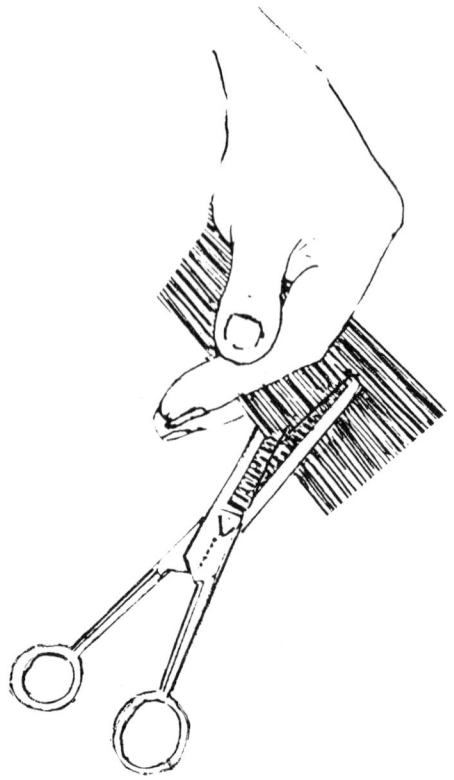

Angle Direction

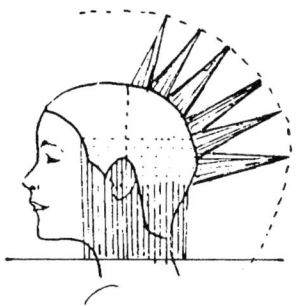

The length and shape of a hairstyle are determined by the **angle** at which it is cut.

The **two** angles you must consider are:

1 the angle at which the hair is *held* out from the head

2 the angle at which the cut is made *across* the hair section

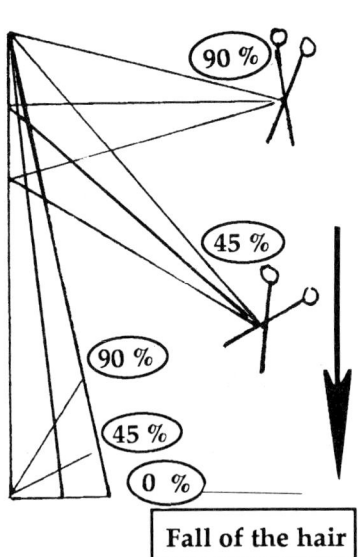

Fall of the hair

Variations in these two angles will create many different effects.

Establishing basic guidelines

Guidelines are sections of hair, cut to determine the *length* and *angle* of the cutting line to be followed.

The diagrams above and below show typical guidelines for layered and bob cuts.

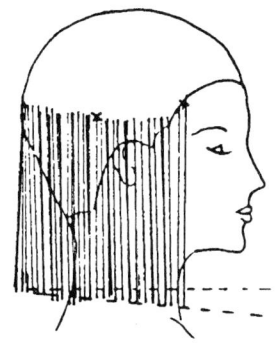 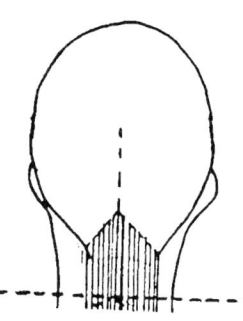 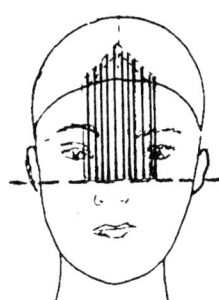 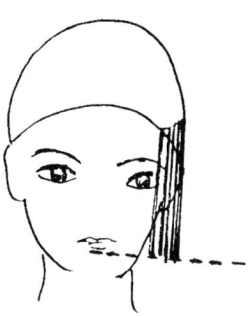

Sectioning

The hair is divided into sections so that guidelines can be established and the hair cut systematically.

The way hair is sectioned depends on the style you want to create as you will see when we go through step-by-step cutting procedures.

Points to Remember

* There is no set starting point to begin sectioning.
* Keep the initial idea of the finished effect you desire firmly in your mind while cutting.
* Always be systematic.

Let's look at the 3 basic cuts.

Bobbed cuts

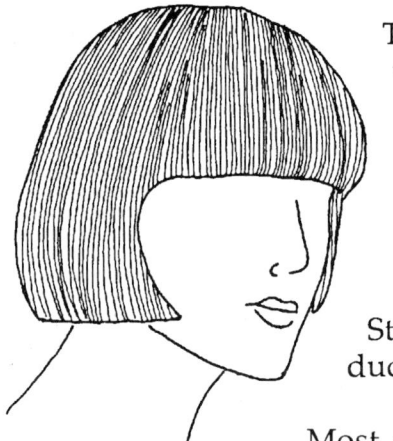

The 'bob' created a sensation when it was created in the 1920's. It was revived in the 1960's by Vidal Sassoon and has been popular to the present day.

The basic bob is a one length style with a straight, concave or convex base line. It is highly versatile and can be adapted to suit most hair types and facial shapes.

Straight hair allows a sleek sculptured look while curly hair produces a softer effect.

Most cuts combine straight and curved lines, but the bob consists entirely of *straight* lines and is one of the easiest cuts to do.

Graduated cuts

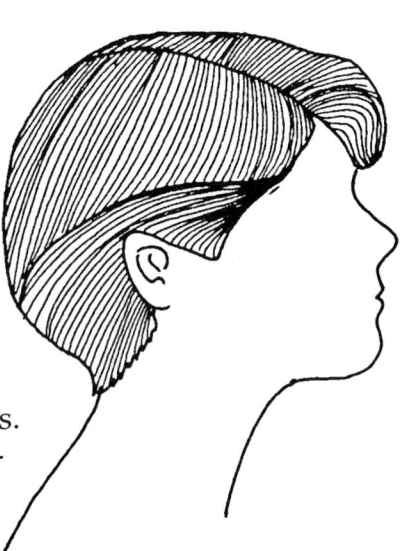

This type of cut became popular in the mid-seventies when Joanna Lumley wore a wedge style in the TV adventure series 'The Avengers'. This haircut is still popular today and there are many variations on this basic theme. By enhancing the strong graduated line with colour quite stunning effects can be achieved.

Graduation is a blending of longer length hair into shorter lengths. The *angle* at which the hair section is *held* while cutting determines the degree of graduation.

Layered Cuts

This cut is probably the most popular look today. It can be worn by any age group and is easily adapted to suit all hair lengths, types and face shapes. It can be worn short or long.

The basic layer cut is achieved by holding the hair sections at a *90 degree angle* to the contour of the head. This results in the hair *length* and *weight* being evenly distributed throughout the haircut. By varying the degree of the angle you hold the hair you will achieve different effects.

There is no rule to where you start this hair cut. However, most hairdressers commence sectioning at the front hairline at the *frontalis* bone or just above the crown at the *parietal* bone.

There are two types of graduation.

1 *Normal* graduation describes hair which is longer at the top of the head becoming progressively shorter towards the neck.

2 With *reverse* graduation the shorter layers are on the top of the head and the longer layers below.

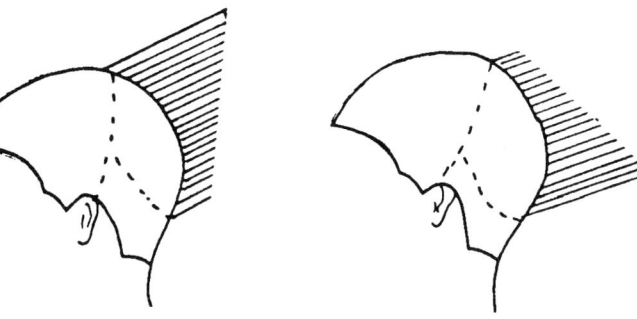

Choosing a style

The hairstylist should be able to advise the client on how to emphasise her best features and to create a style which compliments her personality, facial features, age, weight and height. For example long loose styles emphasise height, and full round styles emphasise width. It is also important to consider the client's lifestyle. Working women, for instance, usually want easily managed styles which require little time to keep in shape, whereas teenagers are often prepared to spend hours on theirs. Most clients have at least a vague idea of the style they would like, but some know exactly what they want. Unfortunately it is sometimes inadvisable, or even impossible, to give them the style requested. For example they may not have the right hair texture, their hair may be too long or too short, or the natural movement would prevent the hair lying correctly.

So how do you go about deciding the type of style you should advise a client to have? Let's look at some of the factors you will have to consider.

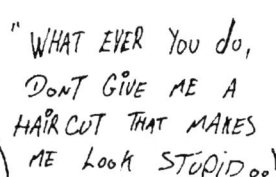

"WHAT EVER YOU do, DoNT GIVE ME A HAIR CUT THAT MAKES ME LOOK STUPID..!!"

Hair texture

The texture of the hair will help you decide which type of haircut to advise, and will also indicate which technique and tools you should use. Texture varies according to race. European hair is usually fine to medium, Oriental hair coarse, and Afro hair medium to coarse and wiry.

Fine textured hair
Fine hair does not hold a style well and is difficult to manage. The ideal technique for cutting this type of hair is club cutting with scissors. This gives the hair fullness and the style lasts longer.

Medium textured hair
Generally this type of hair can be layered, graduated or bobbed and any of the various haircutting techniques are suitable. It is the easiest hair to work with.

Coarse textured hair
A layered cut is often the most suitable for coarse hair. It can be tapered to reduce heaviness.

* *There are no hard and fast rules about which technique to select for different hair textures and the above are only basic guidelines.*

Natural growth pattern of hair

Hair grows from a natural position on the crown. Always consider the direction the hair grows from this point because working against this will result in a bad haircut.

The direction is easy to see when the hair is wet.

The angle at which the hair lies is dependent on the angle of the follicles under the scalp and dictates natural partings, cowlicks, crowns and double crowns, widow's peaks, fringe direction, low nape growth etcetera.

Double crowns, and hairlines which recede at the temples, should not be cut too short as the hair is inclined to stick out in these areas. Another area where hair growth should be considered is the nape of the neck. It is common for the hair to grow upwards into the centre of the nape, causing the hair to collide and stick out if cut too short.

"Cow's Lick"

"Double Crown"

"Nape Whorl"

Hair condition

Damaged hair with split ends is unsightly so try to design a style which entails removing as many of these as possible.

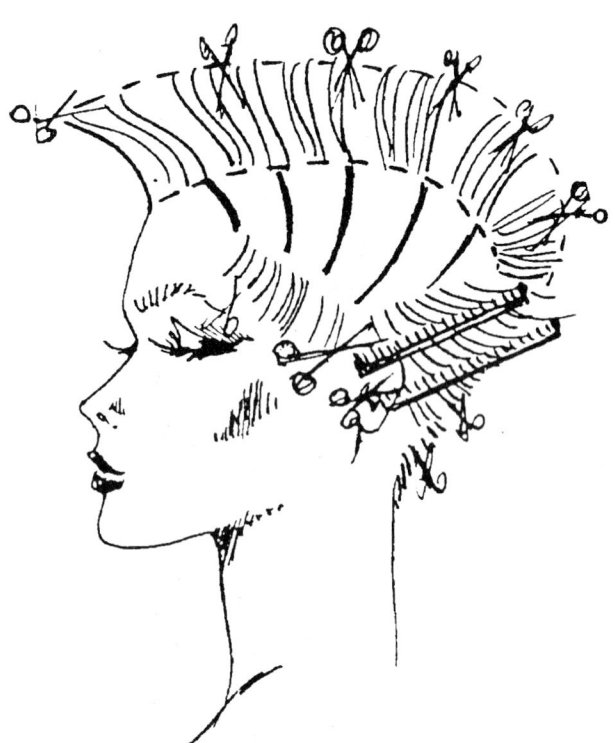

PRACTICAL SECTION

Never start cutting a client's hair without first going through a Consultation and Diagnostics procedure to determine what type of style is suitable for the client. You will learn how to do this in the unit of that name.

Cutting the hair

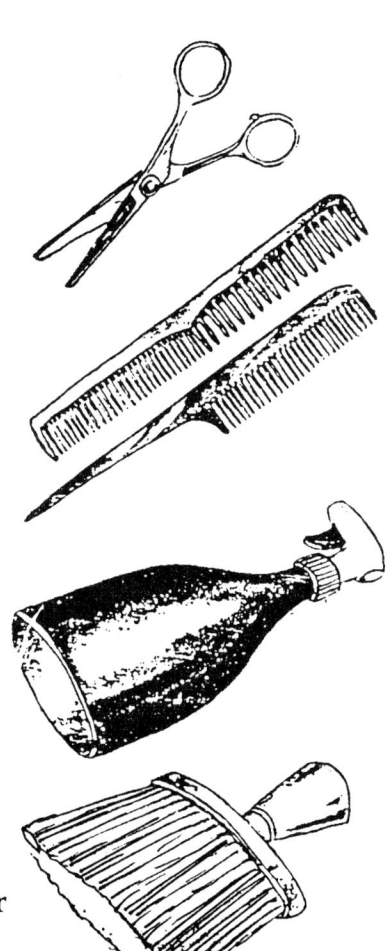

Requirements checklist

* Cutting tools
* Cutting cape
* Neck strips
* Water spray
* Cutting combs
* Section clips

Standard procedure for all cuts

1 Shampoo and towel dry hair if required.

2 Put cutting gown round client's shoulders.

3 Comb hair through.

4 Section hair as required by style.

5 Cut hair.

6 Remove all cut hair from client's neck, paying particular attention to any trapped under collars etcetera.

7 Proceed with any other service as required.

BOB CUT

1 Section the hair as indicated. Carve out a 2 cm horizontal section and comb the mesh on hair onto the skin, cut the hair to the desired length and angle.

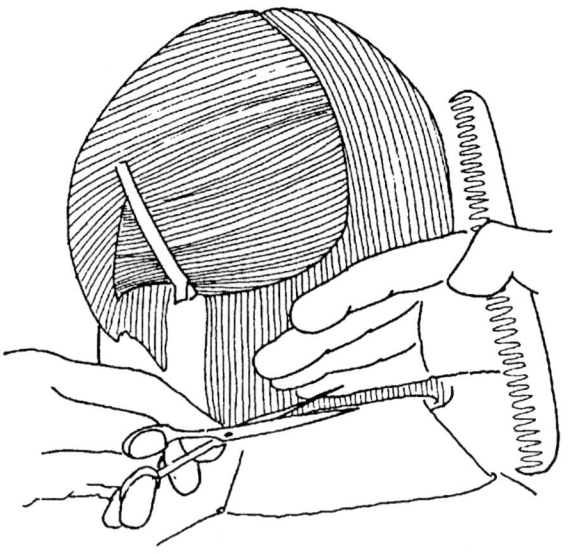

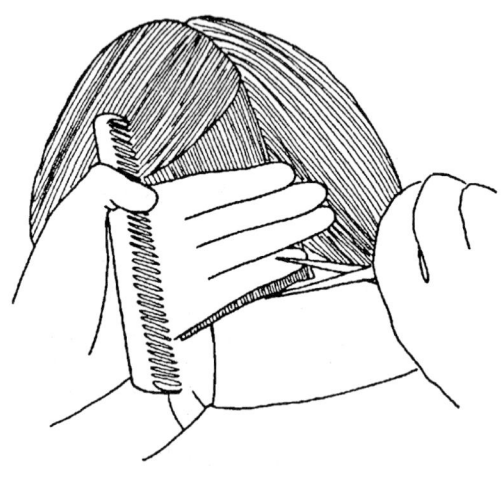

2 Take another horizontal parting above the first section and comb the hair firmly through the first mesh on to the skin. Using the first mesh as the cutting line cut along this line precisely.

3 Continue this sequence up to the crown area. (note the natural growth pattern at the crown)

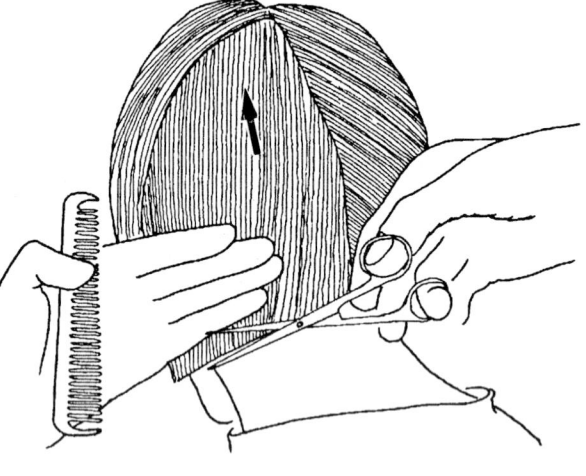

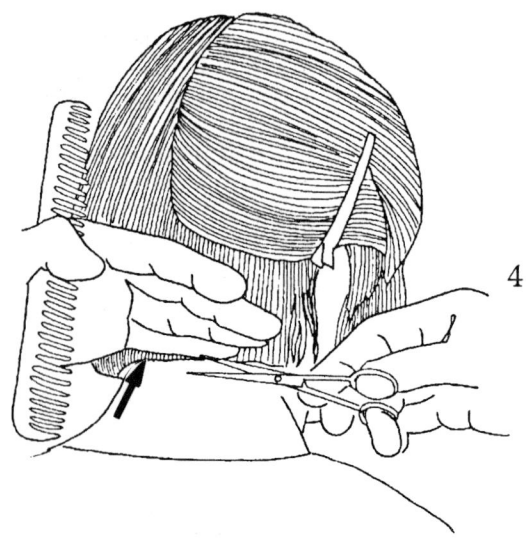

4 On the other side of the back section repeat step 2 using other section as a cutting guide to ensure cutting line is balanced.

5 At the sides carve out a 2 cm horizontal section taking a small mesh of hair from the back section to determine the cutting guideline.

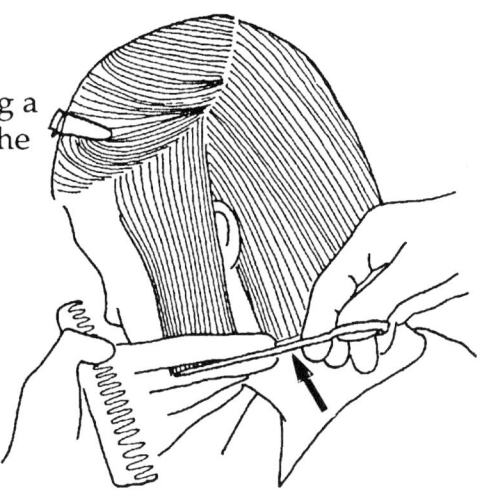

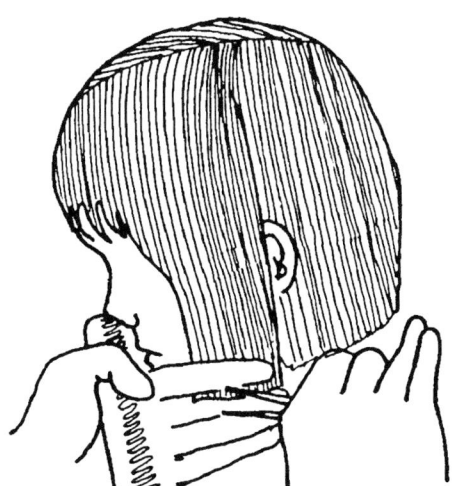

6 Hold the hair as indicated cut along the guideline. Repeat this sequence working up to the natural parting

7 Repeat sequence 6 on the other side.

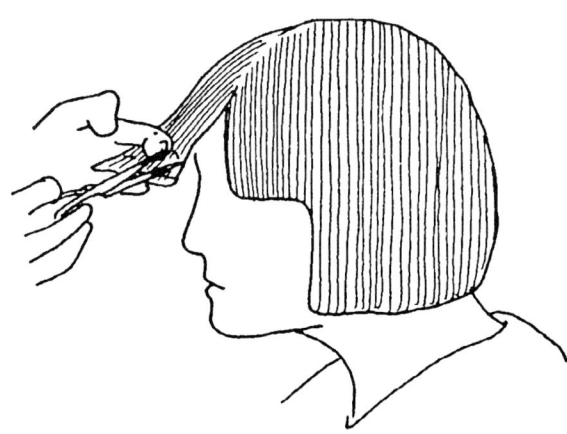

(remember the hair will be shorter when dry).

Comb the fringe into position, taking into consideration hair growth patterns.

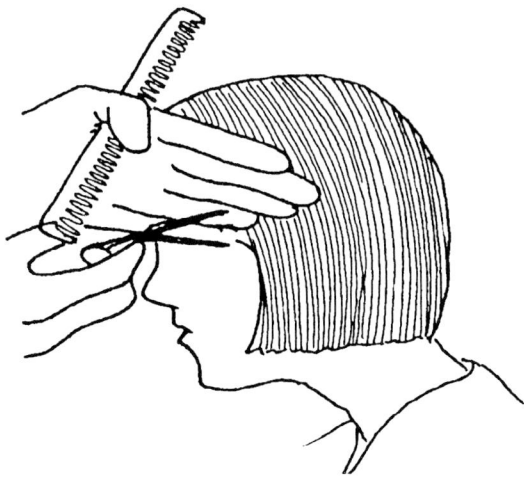

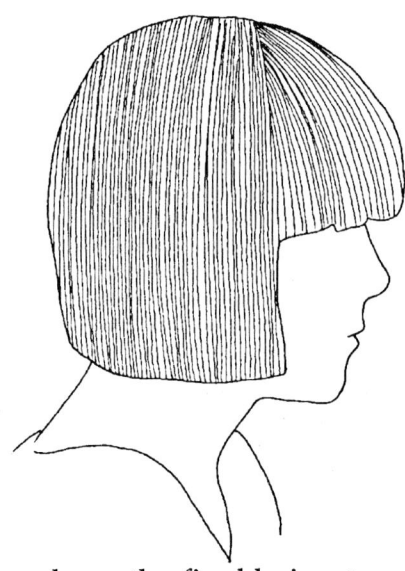

Here we have the final haircut.
Consult blow dry unit for Bob blow dry procedure.

GRADUATED (WEDGE) CUT

1 Carve out a mesh of hair by drawing an imaginary line from the ear to the top of the eyebrow as a guide

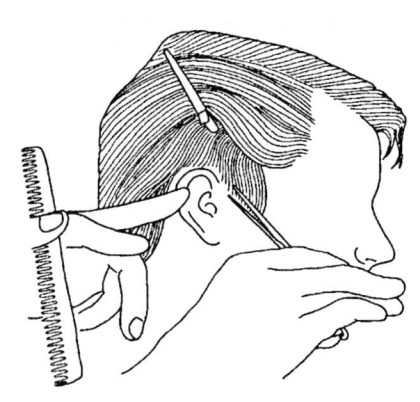

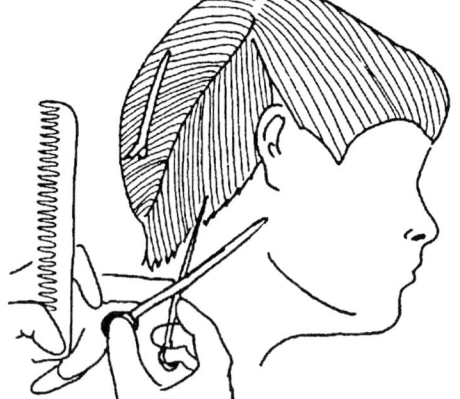

2 Hold the hair slightly away from the face between the fingers as indicated and cut the hair very precisely to the desired length.
 Carve out another section above the first mesh and comb it firmly through this mesh, cut the hair using the previously cut hair as your guideline.
Continue taking small sections working up to the parting

3 Take a small section from the top of the ear to the nape parallel to hairline and cut to desired length.

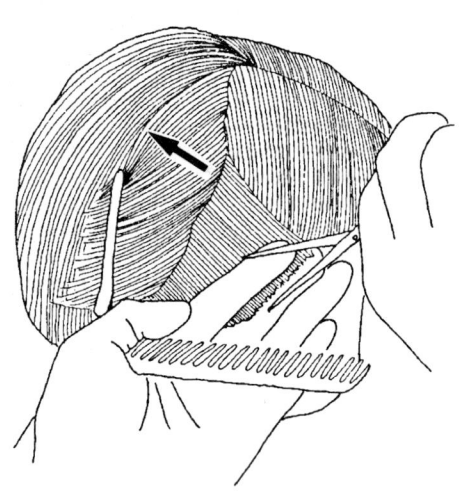

4 Continue taking small diagonal sections working towards the centre back of the head.

5 Cut the nape section to the desired length.

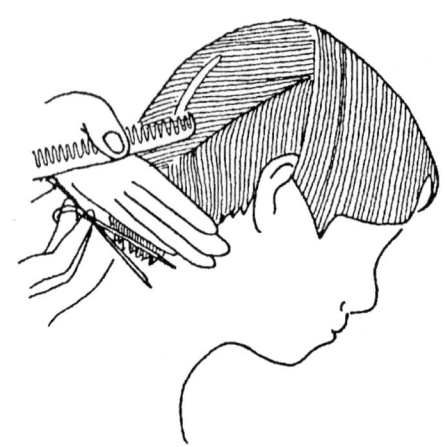

GRADUATED (WEDGE) CUT

5 At the other side repeat same process through **1 - 4**

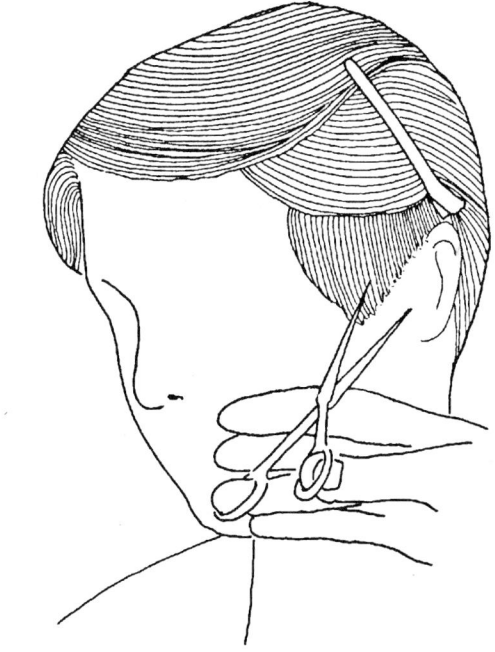

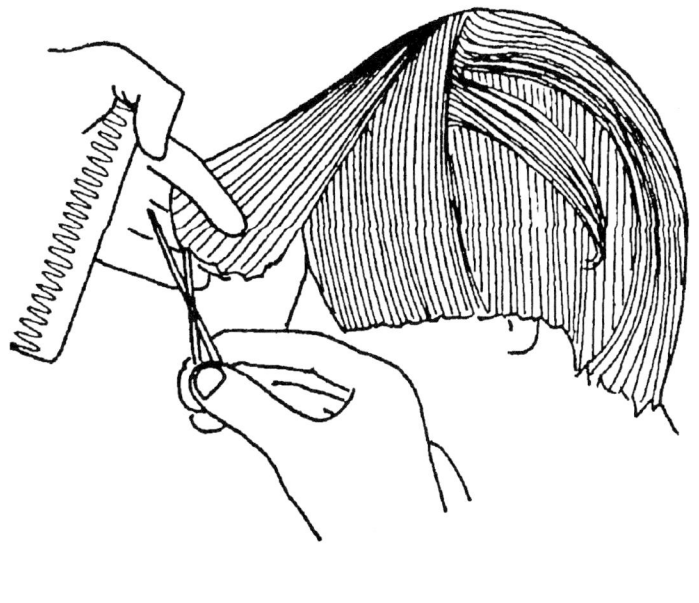

6/ 7 Continue up to the natural parting and through back section.

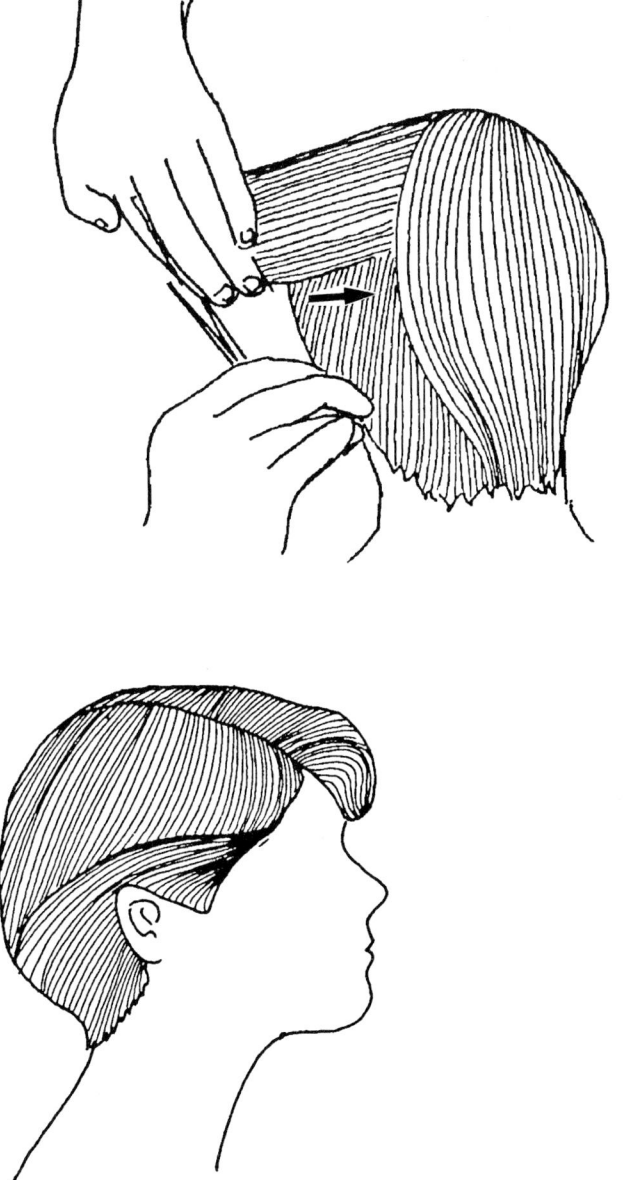

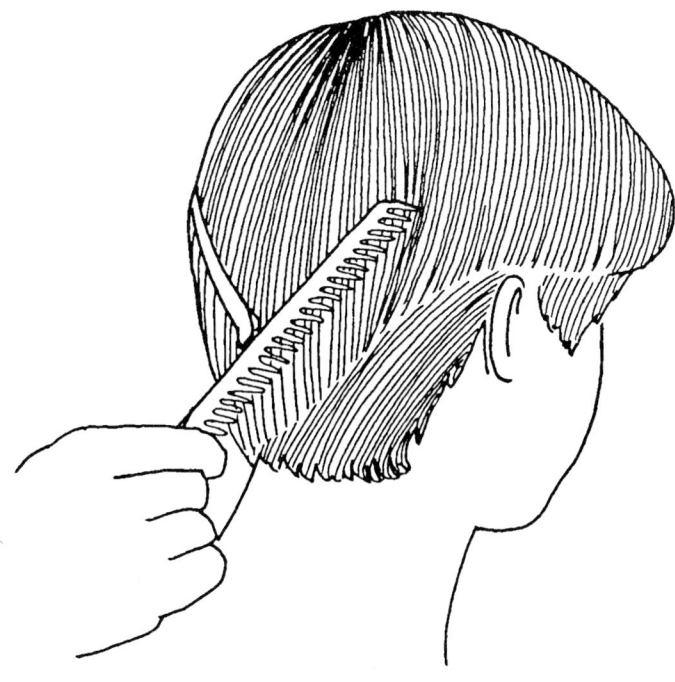

The haircut is now finished. To blowdry the graduated cut consult the Blowdry unit.

LAYERED CUT

The easiest method of layer cutting is to start by cutting a top centre section of hair and using the length of this section as a guide for cutting the sides and back.

1 Determine natural parting. Beginning at the front hairline take a 3cm mesh and hold at a 90% angle and cut as indicated. This is now the guideline for the entire cut.

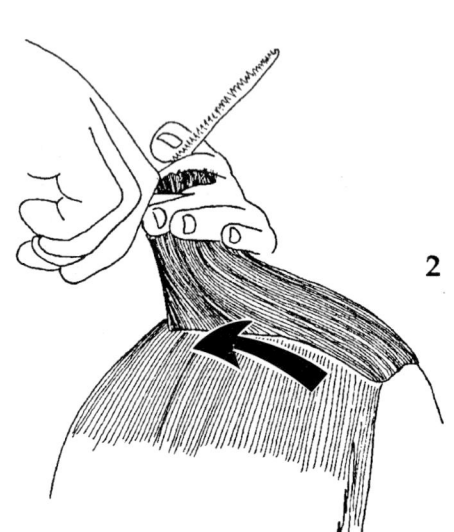

2 Continue working back towards the crown. Remember to hold at 90% and use previous cut mesh as a guide.

Guideline

3 The next section to be cut is to the right of the previous section. Comb part of the front top section into this section to give you a guideline for length.

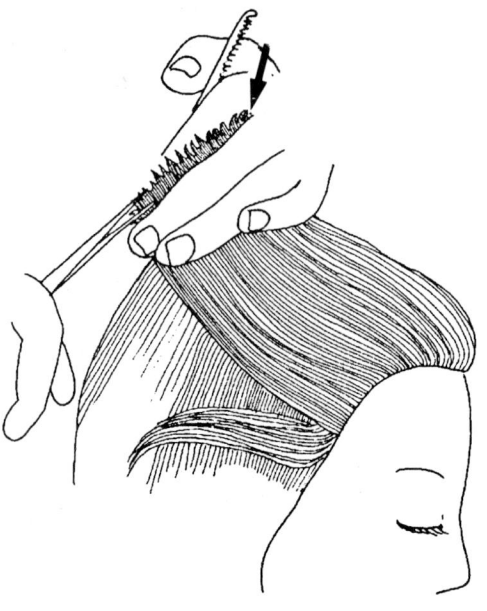

4 Continue in this way, using the previous mesh as a guideline for the following one, until the whole section is cut.

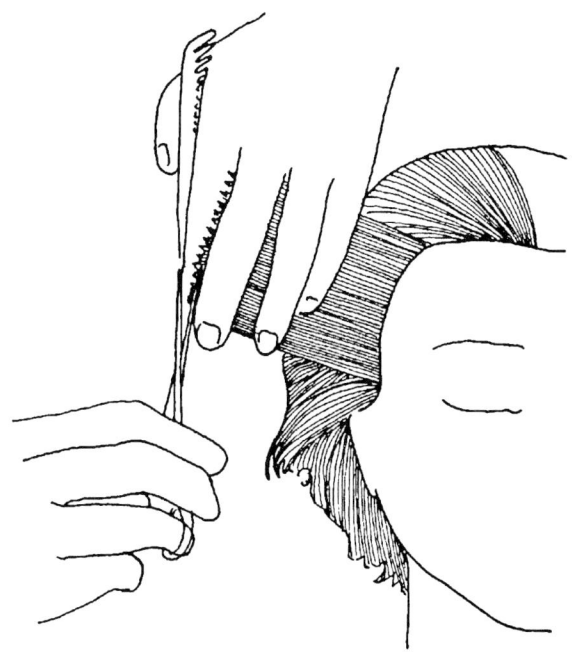

5 Cut the next section following the procedure in steps 1 - 4.

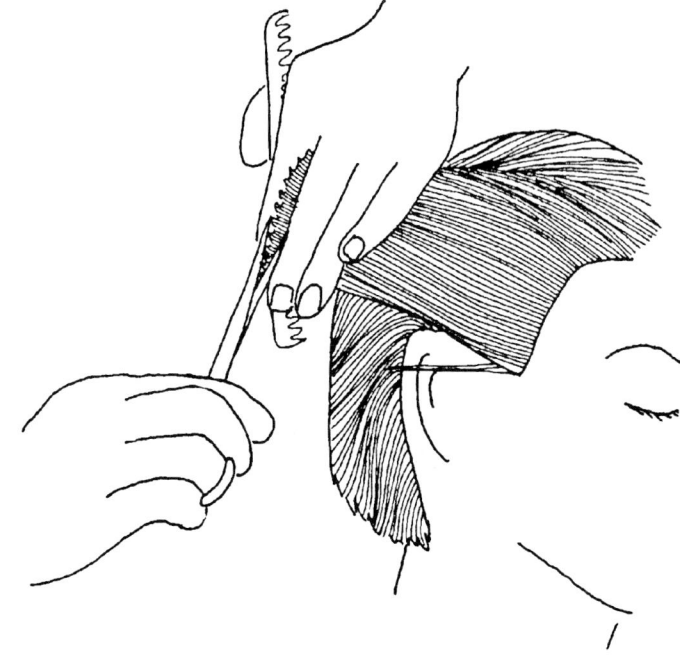

6 Work towards centre back. (See next illustration)

7 Centre back. Remember to follow guidelines. **Repeat above process on opposite side 1 - 7.**

8 Work towards centre back

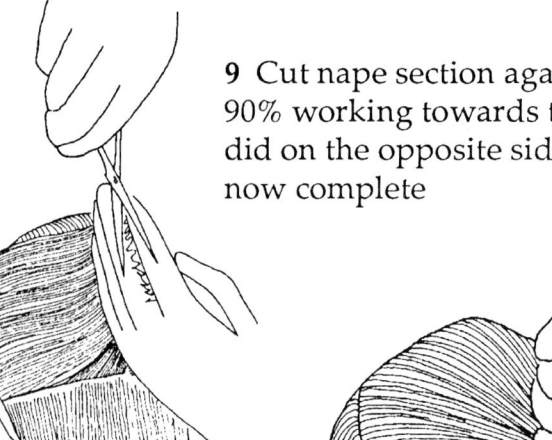

9 Cut nape section again holding at 90% working towards the centre as you did on the opposite side. The haircut is now complete

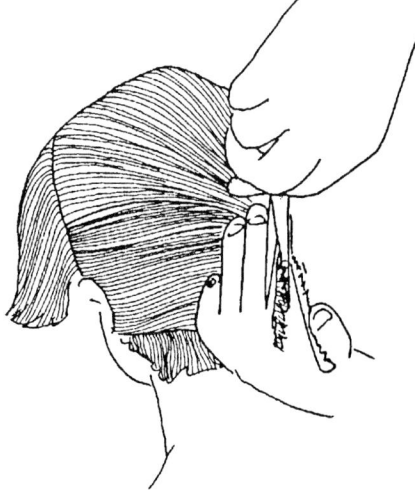

6 BLOWDRYING

Blow drying and **setting** are techniques employed to style the hair using heat instead of chemicals. Because the theory behind each technique and the consultation and diagnostics procedure followed are basically the same, we will consider these two units together.

We will also cover styling dry hair with tongs, hot brushes, heated rollers and crimpers.

The theory

The protein in hair in its natural unstretched state is referred to as **alpha keratin**.

When hair is wet the very weak hydrogen bonds between the polypeptide chains are broken by the action of water molecules. This allows the hair to be stretched slightly more than when dry, and to be moulded into a new shape, which it will keep if allowed to dry because the hydrogen bonds will reform in their new position. Protein in the now stretched hair is referred to as **beta keratin**.

The process of wetting the hair, stretching it into a new shape and drying it in that shape is termed **cohesive setting**. Although millions of hydrogen bonds are broken the new shape will not be permanent. As the hair absorbs moisture from the atmosphere the hydrogen bonds will start to break down again and the stronger, though less numerous, S-bonds will pull it back into its original shape. This will take place immediately if the hair is soaked with water, as when shampooing.

Hair must be in good condition before it will blow dry or set well. If the hair has lost its elasticity too many hydrogen bonds have been damaged and the hair will not retain its new shape

Styling dry hair is different from cohesive setting in that the hair is stretched while heat is applied. It is the combination of heat and tension which breaks the hydrogen bonds in this case. As the hair cools in its stretched position new bonds form and the new shape is retained. Styles shaped in this way will come out with warm water.

The first step in any hairdressing service is finding out exactly what the client wants. Unfortunately, that is sometimes impossible to achieve and for various reasons. Perhaps the hair is too short or the texture too fine for a style the client would like. Sometimes a style goes against the natural movement and direction of the hair, making it difficult to achieve, and as the hair tends to return to its natural direction it will not last. On occasion you may consider a style unsuitable for other reasons.

This is why you must go through a **consultation** and **diagnostics** procedure, as outlined in the unit of that name, before attempting to begin styling. You must know about the different types and texture of hair, the patterns of hair growth, the natural movement of the hair and how to tell if it is in good condition.

Styling aids for both blow drying and setting

Setting lotions, blow-dry lotions and hairspray fixatives protect the hair from atmospheric moisture by coating it with a transparent waterproof film made of plastic polymers and resins such as *polyvinyl pryrolidone* (PVP). Plasticisers such as *polyetheleneglycols* and *silicones* are incorporated to keep the plastic film soft, flexible and more water resistant.

Mousse

Mousse adds body to the hair. It is especially effective when scrunch drying the hair and comes in regular or firm hold varieties.

Gel

Gel is generally used on shorter styles to give a spiky effect, or to keep the hair 'slicked' down.

Moulding Creams

These creams are ideal for shaping the hair in any direction. Can be used for blow, scrunch or natural drying.

Glazes

Glazes are stronger than gels and creams and set hard. They are particularly effective for slicking back the hair.

Setting lotions

These increase the life of the style and in some cases condition the hair. They are used for conventional styling.

Blow-drying lotions

These are not as strong as setting lotions and allow the hair to be dried without getting sticky. They help to control static and add body and shine.

Hairspray

Hair sprays put a finishing protective coat on styled hair. They come in various strengths from soft hold to firm hold and are easily removed by shampooing the hair.

SAFETY NOTES

Setting lotions, mousses, foams, gels, glazes and hairsprays all contain solvents which are flammable so should not be used near any naked flame.

Keep them away from the client's eyes and skin with a face shield. Accidental splashes in eyes or on skin should be rinsed away immediately. If irritation persists in the eyes seek medical advice immediately.

Hairsprays can cause breathlessness so avoid inhalation. If breathlessness does occur move the client into fresh air. If it persists seek medical advice immediately.

If any product is swallowed give two or three glasses of water or milk to drink and seek medical advice immediately.

* For application of styling aids see the practical section at the end of BLOW DRYING 6.

BLOWDRYING THE HAIR

Blow drying became popular in the '70s. Before that the vast majority of ladies' hairdressers could not blow-dry and the most popular way to style the hair was by setting it with rollers or pin-curls. At first some hairdressers thought blow-drying was just a passing phase but they were wrong. It has become an essential technique which every competent stylist must master.

Tools used to blow dry

Blow dryer

A powerful, high quality, professional hairdryer is essential for everyday salon use. Make sure it meets standard safety requirements.

Combs

Good quality combs made of hard rubber or strong plastic should be used. Metal combs heat up, making them impossible to hold.

Brushes

A good variety of flat, circular and semi circular brushes is required in different sizes. Bristle and hard plastic types are most heat resistant.

Blow drying techniques

Blow drying with brushes

This is the most used blow-drying technique. Meshes of hair are held round a brush and dried into the position in which it is held. Different types of brushes are used to produce various effects.

Flat brushes with round ends and nylon bristles set in a rubber pad are popular for creating gentle curved movements and encouraging natural smoothness. They are easily taken apart for cleaning.

Flat brushes with vents to allow easier penetration of the hot air are particularly useful when working with naturally curly or long hair.

Round brushes of various sizes are required to mould hair into curls or soft turns. They are a bit like rollers in that the diameter of the brush determines to a large extent how curly the result will be; the larger the diameter of the brush used, the softer the curl.

Using a small round brush helps to give body to fine textured hair but this technique is not suitable for creating much movement on long hair because the hair will become tangled round the brush.

Finger drying

One of the simplest ways of styling short layered hair is by running your fingers through the client's hair using a dryer at a low setting. Diffuser attachments jet over the end of the dryer to soften and spread the air flow.

Scrunch drying

Scrunch drying is a blow drying technique using the fingers instead of brushes to mould the hair into style. It is used to create soft, casual styles.

Styling dry hair

Tools used to style dry hair include curling tongs, hot brushes, crimpers and heated rollers.

Curling tongs and hot brushes.

These tools create soft movements, waves and curls and are easy to use.

Crimpers

These produce a crinkled effect and are very popular with young people. They work the same way as tongs and hot brushes.

Heated Rollers

These are used in much the same way as ordinary rollers, but on dry hair. They are made of a special heat retaining material and fit on to a stand which transfers heat to the rollers. The hair is wound round the hot rollers and allowed to cool. The effect achieved is soft and will not last as long as a wet set.

NOTE

* Excessive use of tongs, hot brushes, crimpers or heated rollers can damage the hair.

* Chemically processed hair should not be styled dry because it is too easily damaged.

PRACTICAL PROCEDURES FOR BLOW DRYING

HINTS ON BLOW DRYING

* Make sure the hair is shampooed and rinsed thoroughly as any residues of dirt and grease will make it impossible to style.

* Always direct the air from the dryer towards the ends of the hair to ensure maximum shine and bounce.

* Section the hair if it is long or difficult to control.

* Do not try to force the hair to go against the natural growth direction.

* Comb or mould the wet hair in the direction of the finished style before blow-drying. This gives a general idea of how the hair will look and helps you to dry the hair in the correct direction.

* Work systematically and keep a general plan for the style in mind.

* Use appropriate styling aids as required.

Applying styling aids

Most styling aids are applied to towel dried hair. If the hair is too wet the styling aid will be diluted and its holding power weakened. Make sure the product is distributed evenly over the whole head.

Mousse

To apply, shake the can and squeeze a quantity about the size of an egg on to the palm of the hand. Smooth evenly over towel dried hair with the finger tips and comb through. (Mousse can be reactivated by spraying lightly with water).

Gel

Apply with the fingertips to the roots of towel dried hair. Gel can be reactivated by spraying lightly with water and adding a little more.

Moulding creams

Apply with the palm of the hand and massage evenly through towel dried or dry hair.

Glazes

Apply to towel dried hair with the palm of the hands, avoiding contact with the roots.

Setting and blow-drying lotions

Sprinkle the lotion throughout towel dried hair and comb through to ensure even coverage.

Hairspray

Hairspray is usually used after the hair has been styled although it can be used to give added control and extra body during styling. Extra firm sprays are good for spiky or backcombed styles.

Give the client a protective shield to hold in front of her face and spray approximately twelve inches from the hair to avoid clogging the hair.

Never attempt to comb the hair directly after spraying with hair spray. Wait until it dries or the hair will become stringy and stiff.

Blow drying different styles

Requirements checklist

* Hand dryer
* Selection of brushes
* Hair spray
* Styling aids
* Combs
* Section clips

Before starting to blow dry prepare the client for styling by shampooing the hair well, rinsing thoroughly and towel drying the hair. Place a clean dry towel round her shoulders

Classic and Graduated Bobs

Procedure

1 Divide the hair into two sections from centre front hairline to centre back nape.
Lift a mesh at the nape area and blow dry with gentle heat using a semi circular or Denman brush, moving it through the hair from roots to ends.
Make sure that each section is thoroughly dry before moving onto the next section.
Determine natural parting if appropriate.

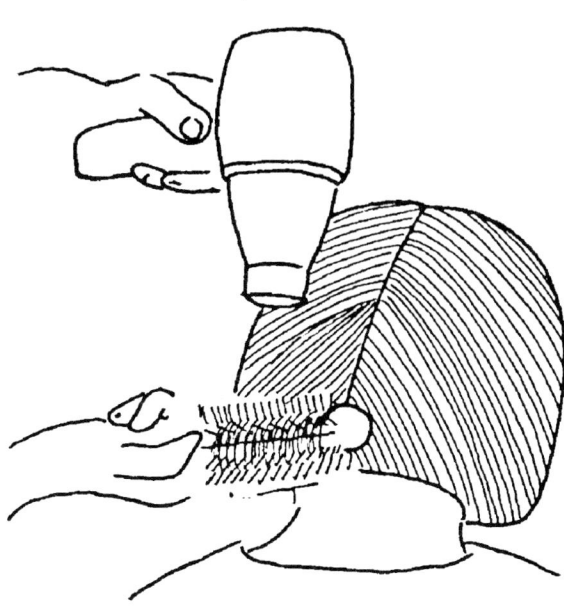
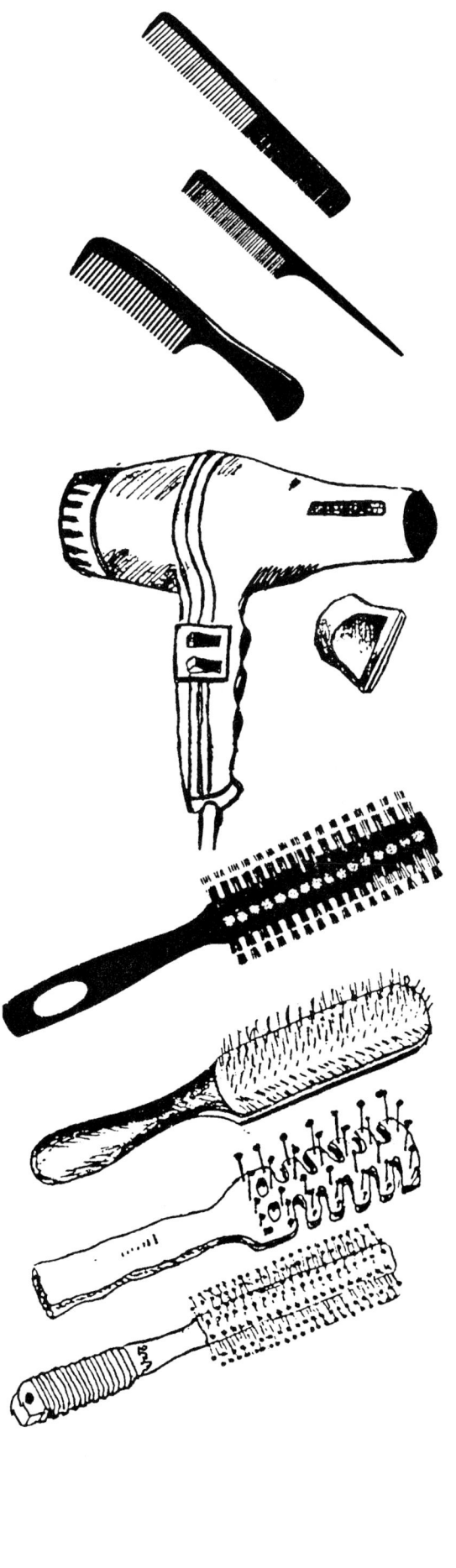

2 Continue taking horizontal sections, work up to to crown area.

3 Repeat this procedure at the sides.

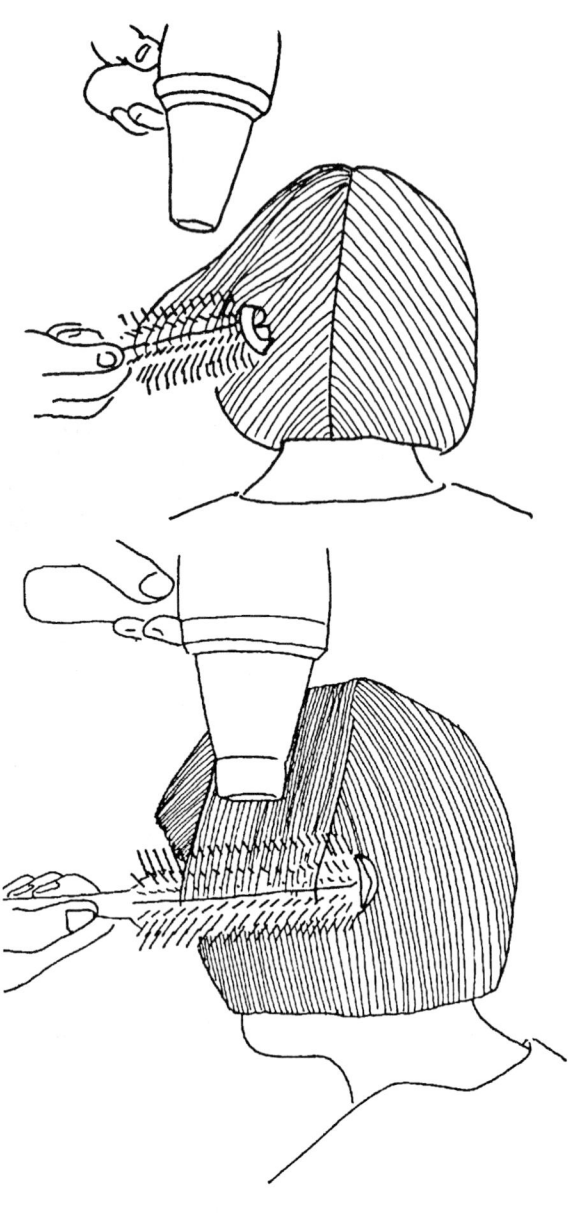

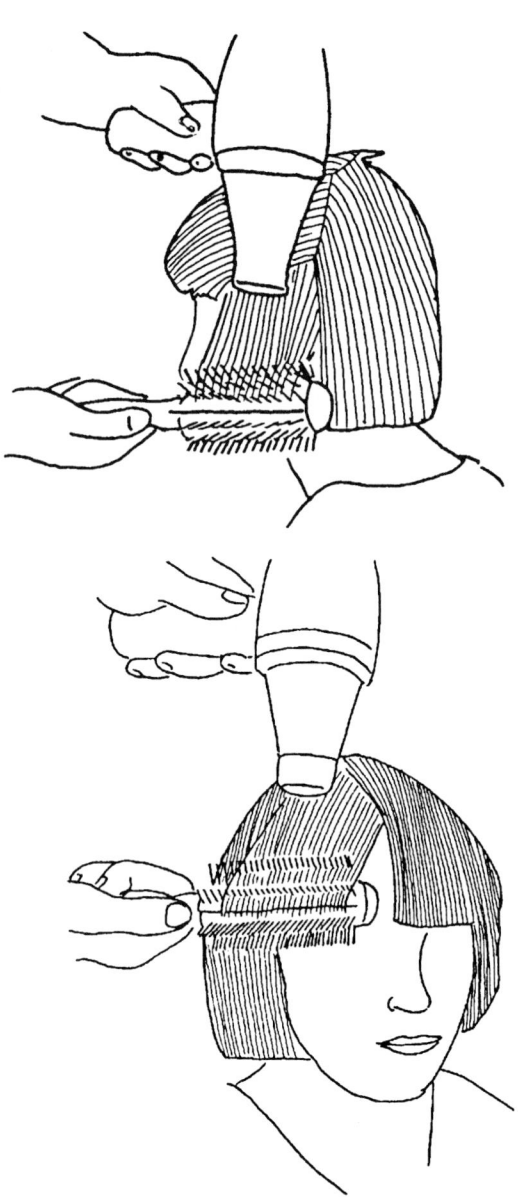

4 A round brush is popular when drying the fringe. Keep turning the brush as you dry the hair

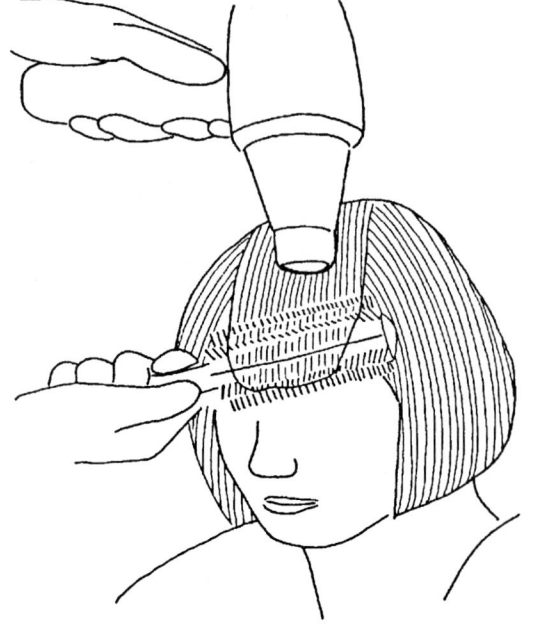

Wedge Style

Procedure

1 Use the natural parting to divide the hair into two sections.

2 The hair should be kept taut and blow dried forward and then brushed backwards into a wedge. shape.

3 At the nape blowdry as indicated.

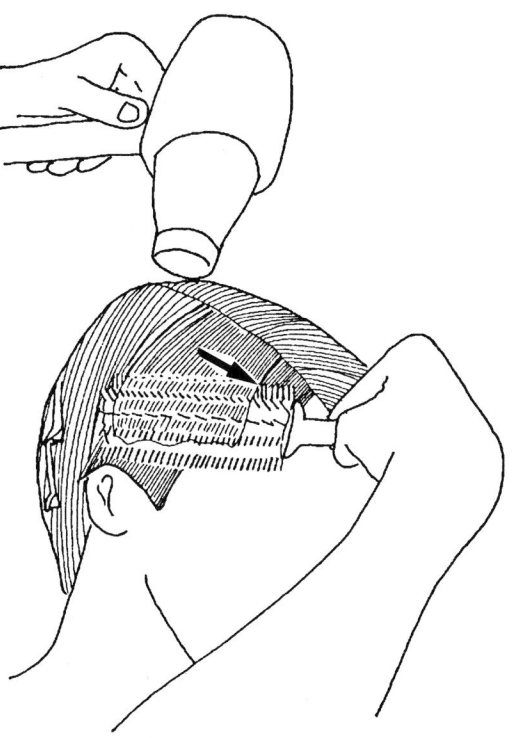
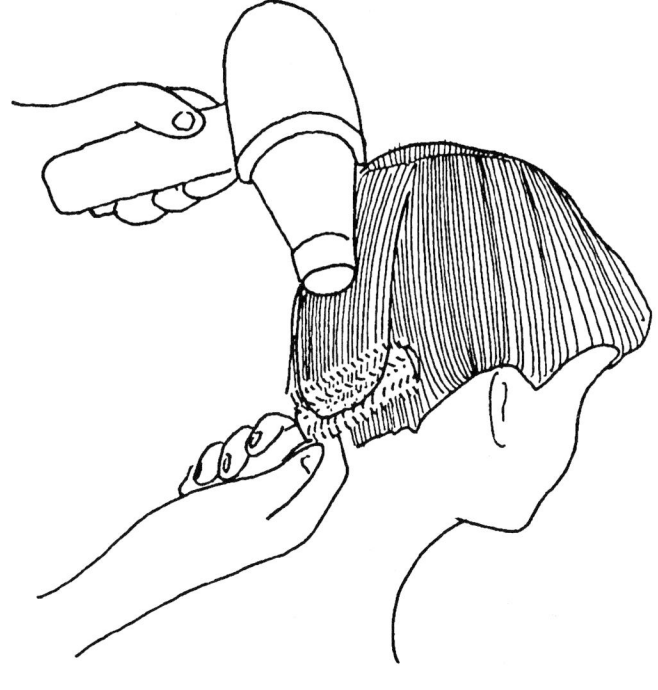

Direct the air jet from roots to ends

5 The fringe shoud be dry towards the face

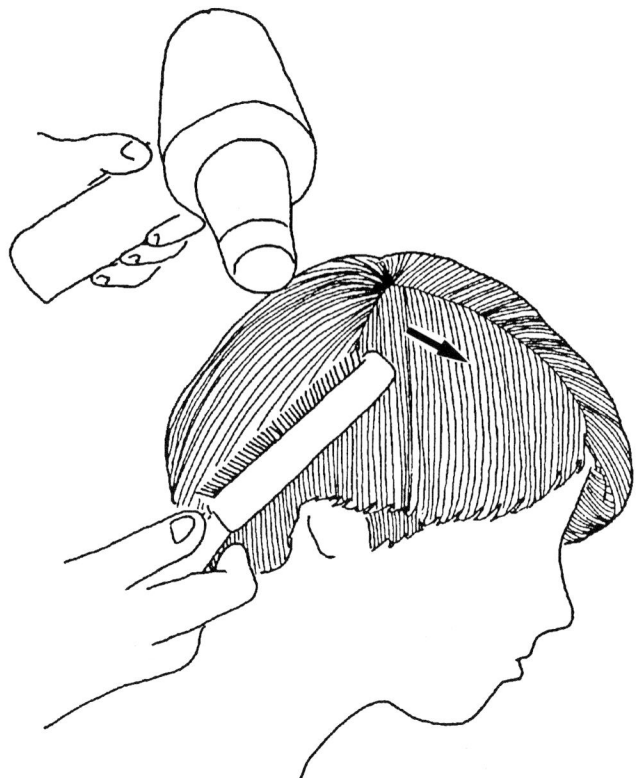
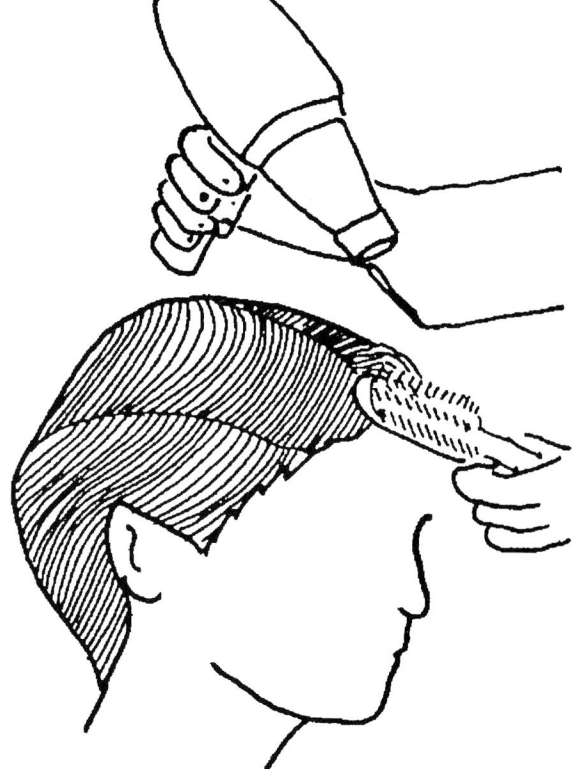

Wedge Blowdry

On the other side repeat the same procedure.

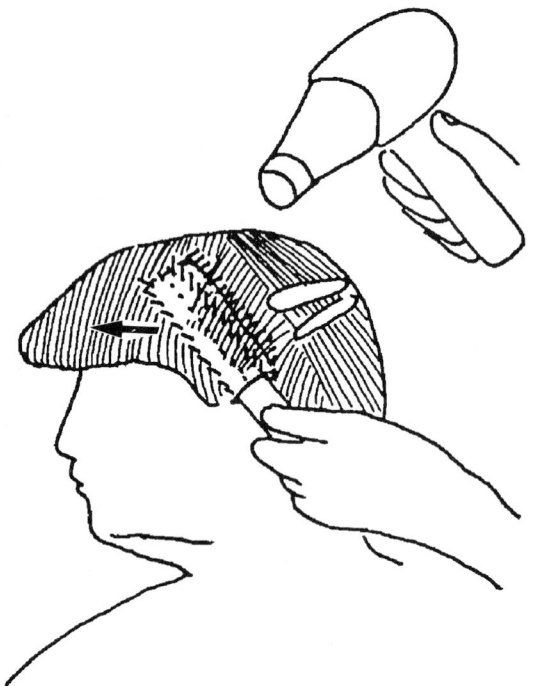

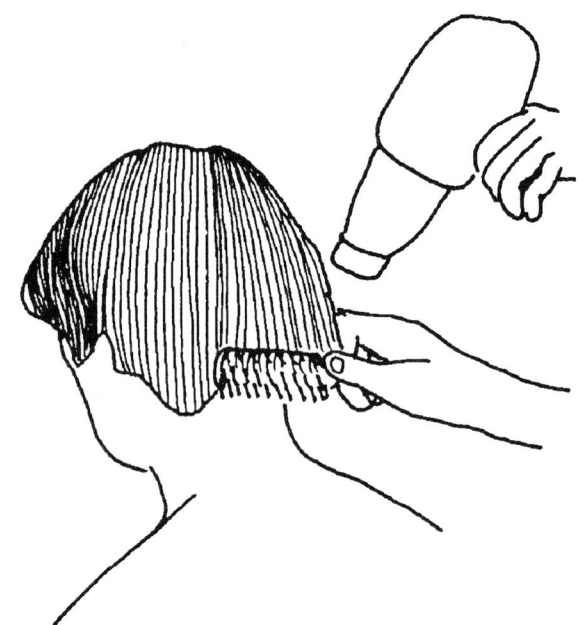

To finish brush the hair away from the face and direct the jet of air as indicated

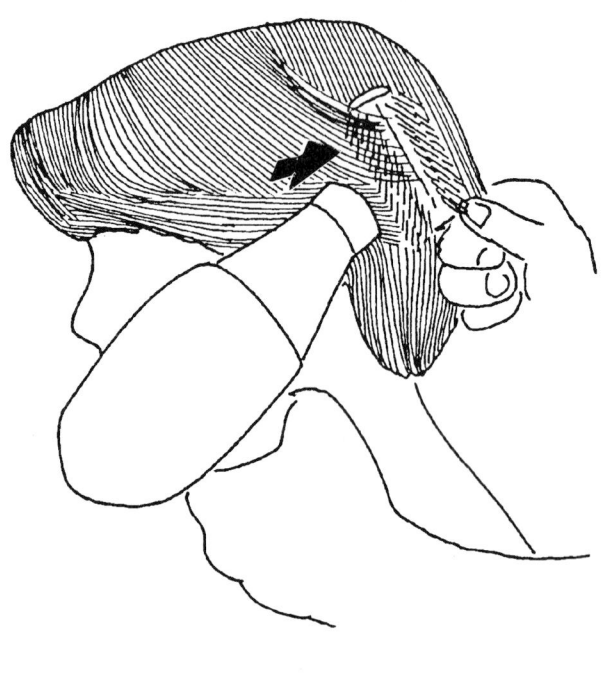

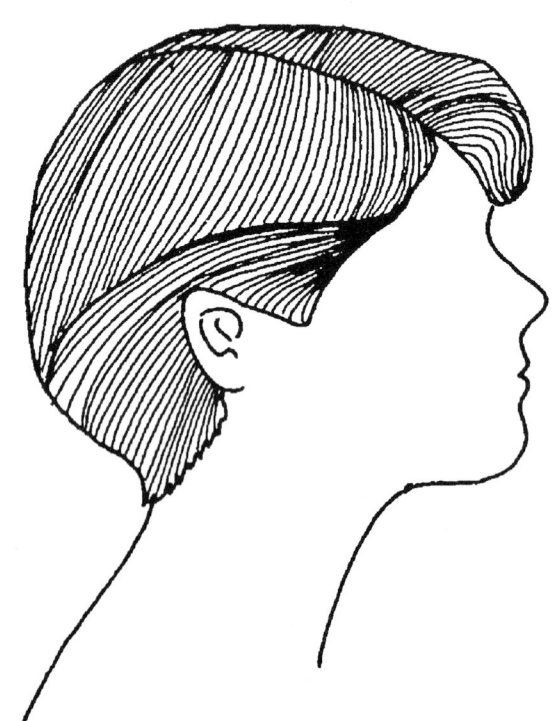

The finished style

Layered Style

Layered cuts can be dried in many different ways depending on the style required and the preferences of the stylist. Some stylists like to use round brushes, others vent or Denman brushes. Some styles are better finger or scrunch dried. (See below) Flat brushes are usually used for straighter style with a bit of movement
Here we show how to use a Deman drush to dry a layered cut.

Procedure

1 Make a parting from the front centre of the head to the nape.

2 At the nape area take a horizontal section of hair equivalent to the diameter of the brush you are using.

3 Place the brush onto the scalp gently rotate with a wrist action so that the tufts are facing outwards from the scalp. Keeping the hair taut but not over tight, direct the air jet from the roots to the ends of the hair, this keeps the cuticle smooth and encourages the hair to shine. Move the dryer up and down the hair to prevent burning the hair or scalp. Lift the hair away from the scalp to achieve movement and to avoid tangling the hair.

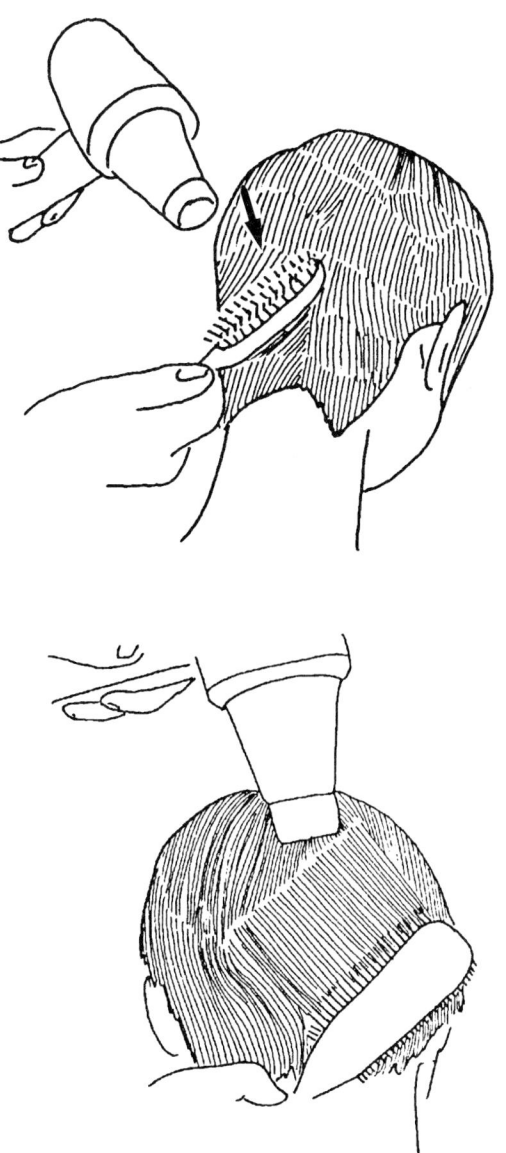
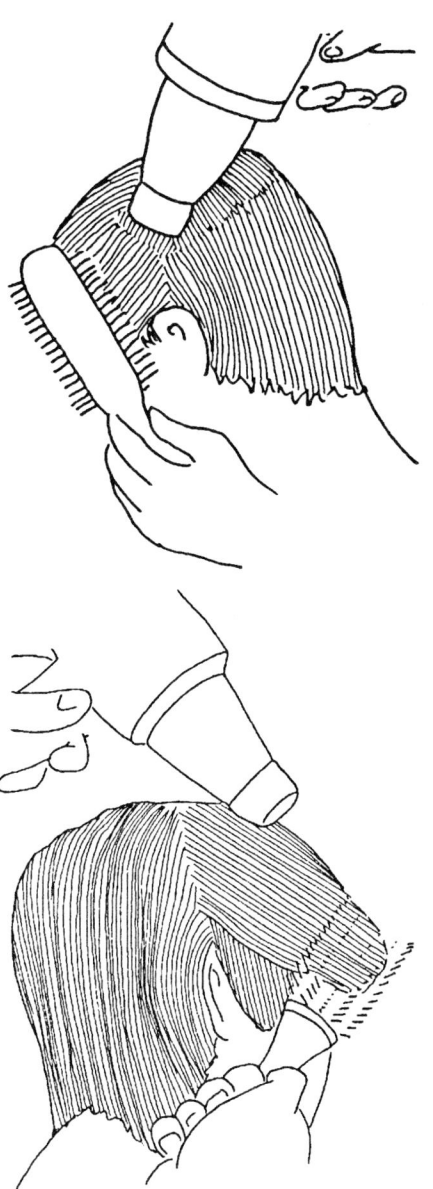

Layered Style

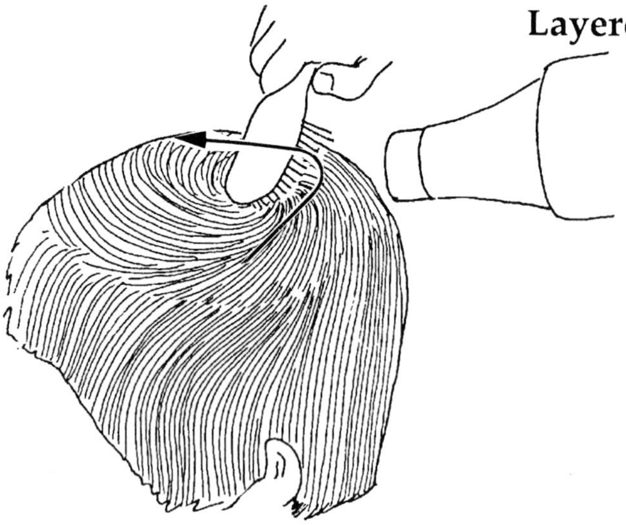

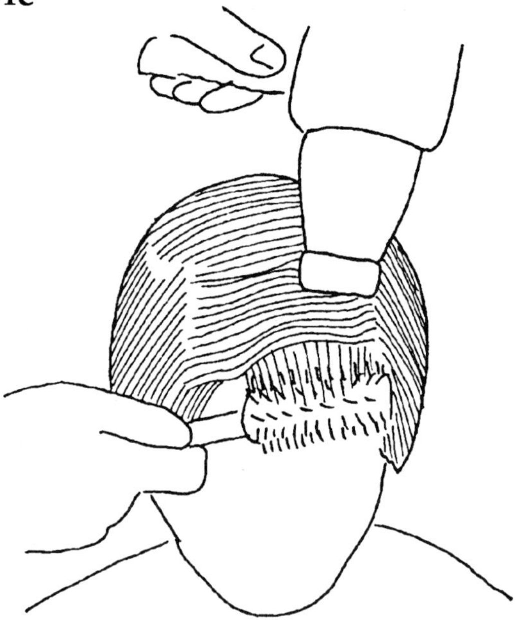

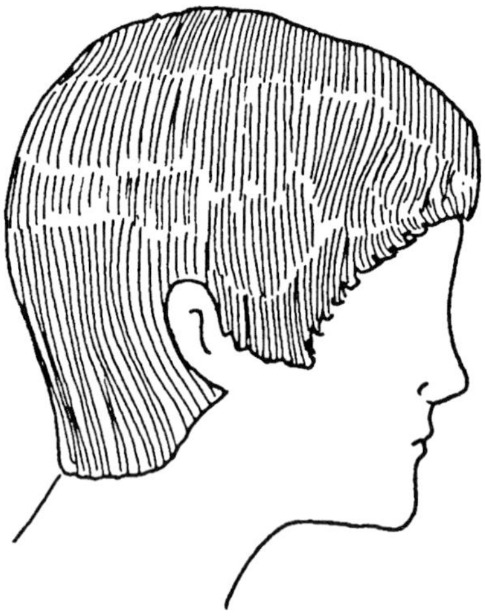

Finished Style

Finger Drying

Procedure

1 Towel dry the hair until slightly damp.

2 Apply a generous amount of setting mousse.

3 Attach a diffuser to the blow dryer.

4 Run your fingers through the hair, lifting it at the roots to give body. At the same time move the dryer up and down the hair you are working with.

To get more body at the roots ask the client to bend her head down and direct the warm air under the hair at the nape of the neck.

5 Mould the hair into the desired shape with your fingers as it dries.

Scrunch Drying

Procedure

1. Towel dry hair and remove as much moisture as possible.

2. Apply a generous amount of setting mousse.

3. Attach an air diffuser to the blow dryer.

4. Take handfuls of hair and squeeze or scrunch the hair gently, directing the diffuser into the palm of the hand. At the same time lift the hair up from the scalp.

5. As your scrunch the hair, gently rub it with your fingers to remove all the moisture.

Styling Dry Hair with Curling Tongs or a Hot Brush

Procedure

1 Take a mesh of hair and clip the rest up out of the way. There is no general rule about where to commence.

2 Place the ends of the hair smoothly and evenly over the brush or tongs and wind down towards the head.

3 If winding close to the scalp place a comb between the scalp and tongs to prevent burning the skin.

4 Leave for a few seconds before unwinding.

5 Repeat this process until all the hair is curled.

6 Allow the hair to cool before brushing or combing out.

Crimping
Procedure

1 Take a mesh of hair and clip the rest up out of the way.

2 Commencing at the roots, place the crimpers over the hair and squeeze the grips.

3 Leave for a few seconds then remove.

4 Continue to crimp the rest of the mesh, working towards the ends.

5 Repeat this process until all the hair is crimped.

6 Crimped hair is not usually brushed or combed but, if you want to do either, allow the hair to cool first.

7 SETTING THE HAIR

Setting can be done using various combinations of *rollers, pincurls,* and *fingerwaves*.

It is important to know exactly what you want to achieve before starting so that you can choose the best technique for the style. If using rollers you must decide which size of rollers you will need and how to place them.

As with other hairdressing techniques, the more you practice the more skilled you will become, and the more you experiment the more creative you can be.

Rollers

Types of rollers available

Rollers are either cone shaped or cylindrical and come in various sizes. Conical rollers however are rarely used, and very few salons keep them so we will not discuss them further.

Rollers are usually made of nylon or plastic, although wire mesh brush rollers were popular for a while. The latter are not recommended as they are difficult to clean and can damage the hair cuticles. Plastic rollers have a tendency to warp if washed in hot water and are rather clumsy to use. Nylon rollers have a magnetic attraction for wet hair causing it to cling firmly in spite of the roller's smooth surface. They are less clumsy than plastic ones.

Choosing the correct size

The size of rollers used depends on the effect you want to create. The smaller the diameter of the roller the tighter the curl will be.

As a general guide, if the hair is wound **less than one turn**, the result will be a soft half wave; **two turns** will create a wavy effect; **more than two turns** will produce curls.

If the hair is long the use of small rollers will result in the ends being curly and the roots soft because the diameter of the curl increases with the number of times the hair is wound.

To give long hair an over all curl use large rollers. (**See following page diagram**)

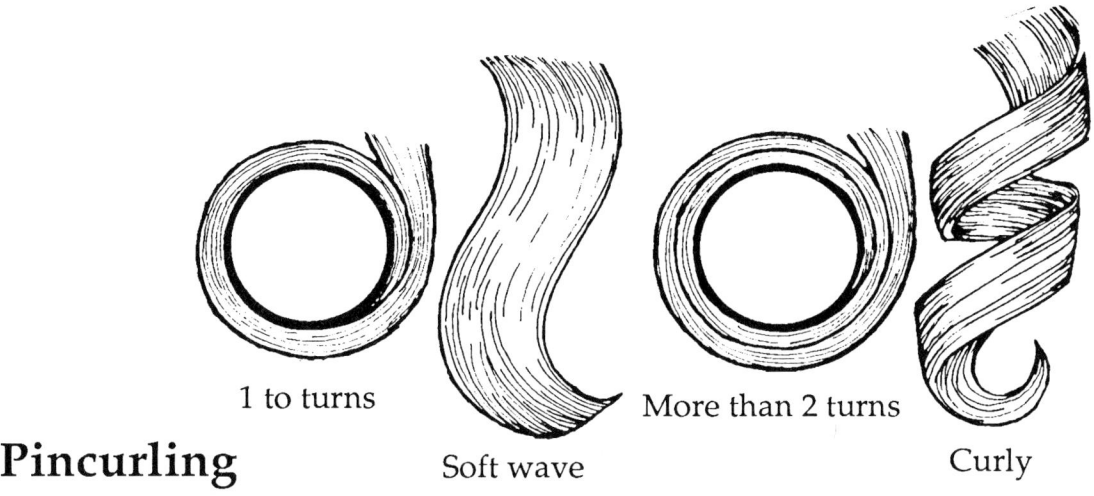

1 to turns
Soft wave

More than 2 turns
Curly

Pincurling

Pincurling is a technique used to achieve curl, wave or body by winding the hair in coils and securing it with pins. There are different types of pincurls.

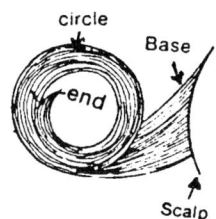

Closed pincurls (Clockspring)

This type of curl is closed at the centre and resembles a clock spring. They were used originally to produce the tight *cork-screw curls* at the nape area of old fashioned styles and are seldom used today. The curl produced is tight at the ends, gradually softening towards the roots where the diameter of the pincurl was greatest.

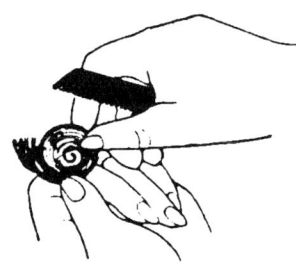

Open pincurls (Barrelspring)

The centre of the barrelspring is open at the centre, giving a similar effect to that obtained with rollers. This type of curl can either be flat or standing up.

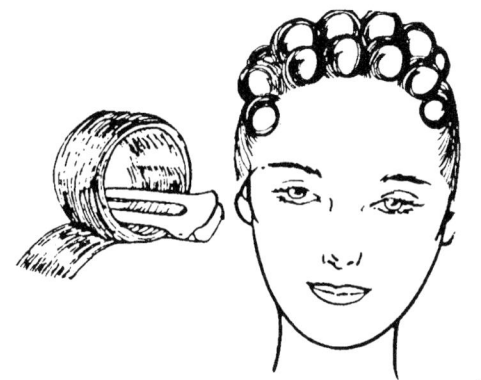

Flat curls are used to form movements that lie close to the head, usually in the form of waves.

To achieve a wave effect, pin-curls must be arranged in rows with the curls facing the opposite direction in each row. This technique is known as *reverse pincurling*.

Flat pincurls are useful for producing plenty of movement without volume at the roots.

Stand-up pincurls are used for volumous sweeping movements. They are formed by combing the hair away from the scalp and winding it down from the ends towards the roots as in roller winding.

Cotton wool is normally placed in the centre of the curl to support the open centre and avoid buckling.

Placement of Rollers and Pincurls

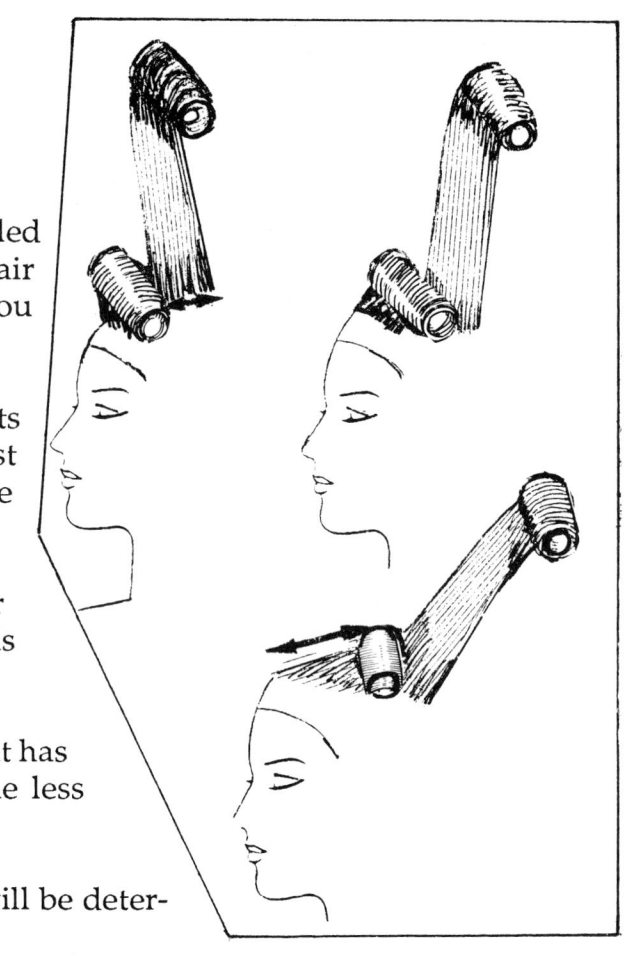

The area of scalp covered by the roots of a hair mesh is called the base. The amount of movement at the root of the hair after roller setting or pincurling depends on whether you use on-base, half-base or off-base placement.

On-base placement means that the roller or pincurl sits directly on top of its own base. This placement gives most lift and volume at the roots. How much depends on the size of roller or pincurl used.

Half-base placement means that only half the roller or pincurl is on top of the base area and less movement is produced.

When the roller or pincurl does not touch the base at all it has been placed *off-base,* and the further off-base it is the less movement there will be at the roots.

The volume and lasting quality of the finished style will be determined by the number of rollers or pin-curls used.

Methods of sectioning for roller setting and pin-curls

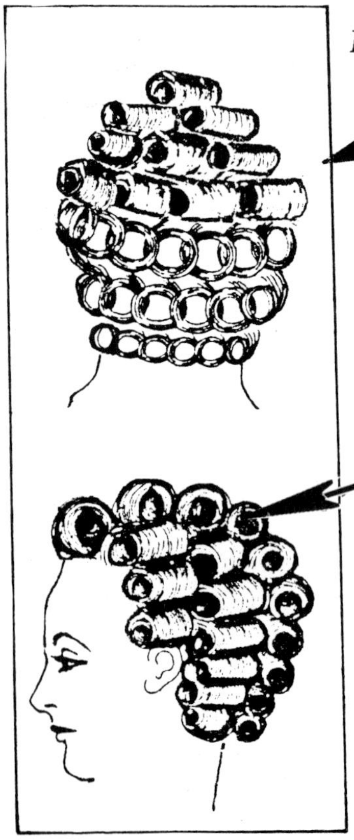

Brick sectioning safeguards against ugly gaps and partings in the finished hairstyle.

Channel sectioning is the most popular method because it is easy to do. It is inclined to cause unwanted vertical partings due to the unbroken straight lines.

Directional sectioning indicates some planning has gone into the design as the rollers or pincurls are placed to achieve a specific effect.

Finger Waving

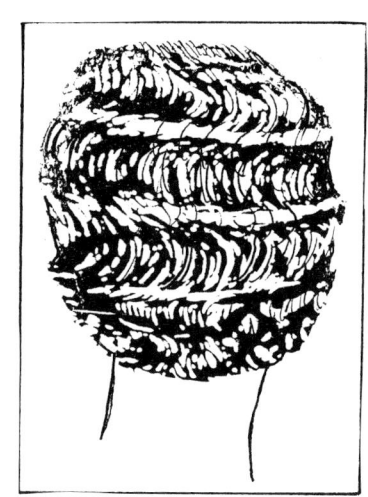

Finger waving is the process of forming *S-shaped* waves in wet hair using the fingers and a comb. It was a very popular technique before rollers came on the market, and has recently enjoyed a come-back, being used by top stylists to create high fashion designs.

Drying to set the hair

Place the client's head under a preheated dryer taking care not to disturb rollers, pincurls or finger waves. Most hair dryers require a hair-net to be placed over rollers to keep them in position.

Make sure the temperature is comfortable for the client.

Never comb out damp hair as the set will fall out immediately.

Dressing out a hairstyle

It is vitally important that the hair is completely dry before dressing out, and allowed to cool otherwise the life of the set will be shortened.

Brush the hair in the direction it was set, starting at the nape and working towards the front of the head. Brushing blends the hair together without gaps.

Tightly set hair requires quite a lot of firm but gentle brushing but be careful not to over-brush, especially if hair is fine or soft textured, as this will remove most of the curl.

Practice brushing various hair types so that you will be able to judge how much is required.

Moulding the hair

Mould the hair into shape as you brush. Always use the dress out mirror to check the progress and balance of your style. A competent hairdresser will be able to complete the dressing out without much combing.

Extra height, volume or support can be obtained by back-combing or brushing. Back-brushing does not give as stiff a finish as combing because the hair is not pushed tightly into the roots. Backbrushing and combing should always be done in the direction you want the hair to lie.

Plaiting the Hair   (Braiding)

Long hair can be plaited to create many sophisticated and attractive styles. Very often plaits are enhanced by weaving ribbons through them, or by adding beads.

Mastering the various types of plaiting takes practice. The easiest technique to learn is the three-strand English plait. The French plait is a slightly more difficult variation of the English one. 'Plaiting round the hairline' is a combination of these two techniques.

The procedures followed to achieve these plaits are in the practical section at the end of the unit.

PRACTICAL PROCEDURES FOR SETTING

When setting hair lift the mesh by directing the point of the tail comb carefully through the hair and lifting as much hair as needed to suit the size of the pincurl or roller. Over large meshes will result in the roots being dragged. All partings made should be clean and straight.

HINTS ON ROLLER SETTING

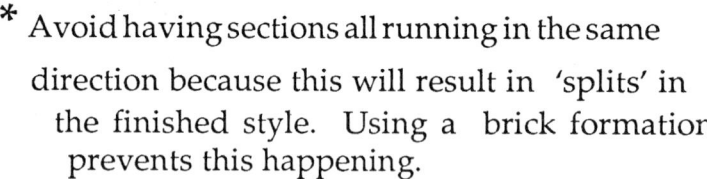

* Avoid having sections all running in the same direction because this will result in 'splits' in the finished style. Using a brick formation prevents this happening.

* Avoid making sections too big as they will drag the roots causing ugly gaps in the finished style.

* If the sections are too narrow you will have difficulty placing enough rollers. This will cause distortion at the roots.

* Wind the ends carefully to avoid frizz.

* Do not wind rollers too tightly as tension will be put on the roots and the client will be uncomfortable.

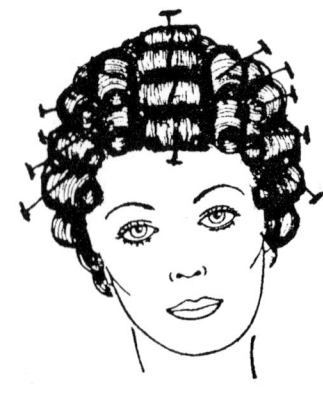

Roller setting

Procedure

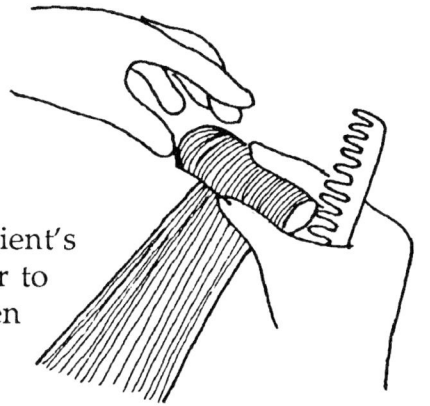
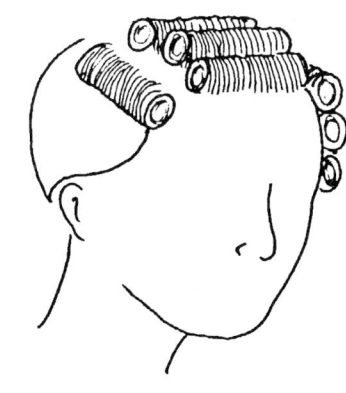

1 Position yourself behind the client's head and section off a mesh of hair to suit roller size. Hold mesh between middle and index finger and comb through from roots to ends

2 Keeping the mesh tense, mould the ends evenly round the roller and windtowards the scalp.

3 Secure the roller with a pin or clip, making sure the pin is not pressing into the client's skin.

Setting and Dressing out Pin- Curls

Requirement Checklist

* Tail comb and styling comb
* Bristle brush
* Setting lotion
* Water spray
* Towels
* Section clips
* Single or double prong clips

Procedure for reverse pin-curling

Shampoo the hair and find the natural growth pattern by pushing the hair toward the roots. This will determine which direction the first row of pin-curls should lie.

1 Carve out a section 2 x 3cm and comb the hair from roots to points into the direction in which the finished style is to be dressed.

2 The stem of the pin-curl is held between the forefinger and thumb.

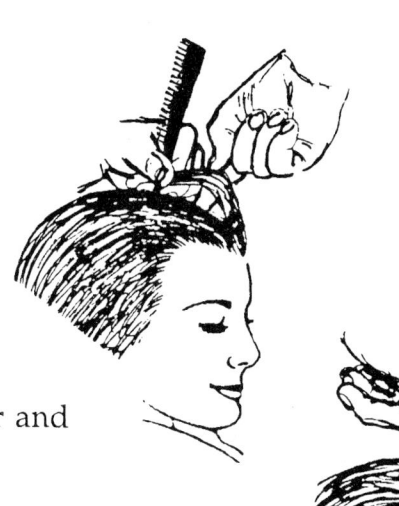

3 The hair is wound round the finger of the other hand careful not to twist the strand of hair.

4 The tail comb is used to push the base of the pin-curl to the side as you place or point your finger onto the scalp.

5 Push the pin-curl off your finger carefully and secure with a clip.

6 Complete a row of pin-curls going in the same direction.

7 In the next row, change the direction. Repeat this reverse sequence until all the hair has been wound.

8 Dry the hair under a hood dryer.

9 Brush the hair when cool with a medium lifted bristle brush firmly but gently.

10 Waves will appear as you continue brushing.

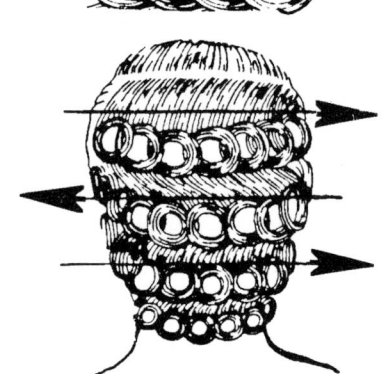

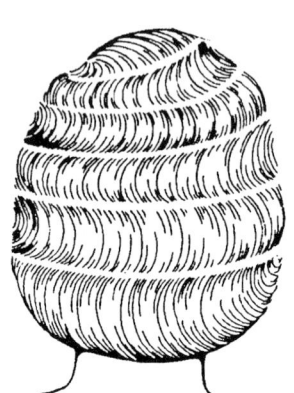

HINTS ON FINGER WAVING

* Always make sure the hair is thoroughly clean.

* Deep 'S' waves are made by pressing the ridges of the wave.

* The average width of 'S' waves is 1. to 1. 1/2 inches.

* Keep the hair thoroughly wet during waving.

Forming Finger Waves

Requirements checklist

* Styling combs
* Styling aid
* Towels
* Water spray
* Section clips

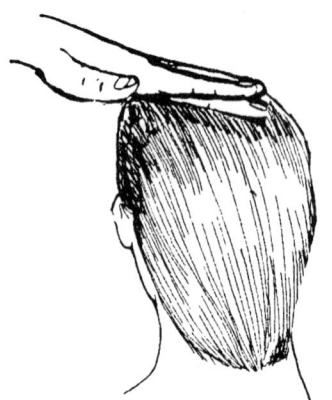

Procedure

1 Prepare the client for styling.

2 Apply setting gel and comb the hair evenly away from the natural parting.

3 Place the index finger of the left hand firmly on the strip of hair.

4 With the right hand, place the tail of the comb firmly against the index finger and comb or mould the hair into an **S**-wave two or three times about one inch from the index finger. Do not move the comb from this position.

5 Flick the comb downwards but do not move the teeth of the comb from the shifted position.

6 Move the middle finger of the left hand to the position held by the index finger of your left hand. This will produce the ridge of the wave.

7 Turn the comb to a flat position and place the index finger of the left hand across the lower half of the comb towards the head.

8 Push against the head with your index and middle finger, then move the comb in the opposite position combing through to the ends of the hair.

9 Repeat this procedure across the top of the head to form the first wave ridge.

10 Repeat the procedure keeping the **S** formation in the next row until the whole head is waved.

11 Secure waves by using hair setting tape and dry the hair under a hood dryer.

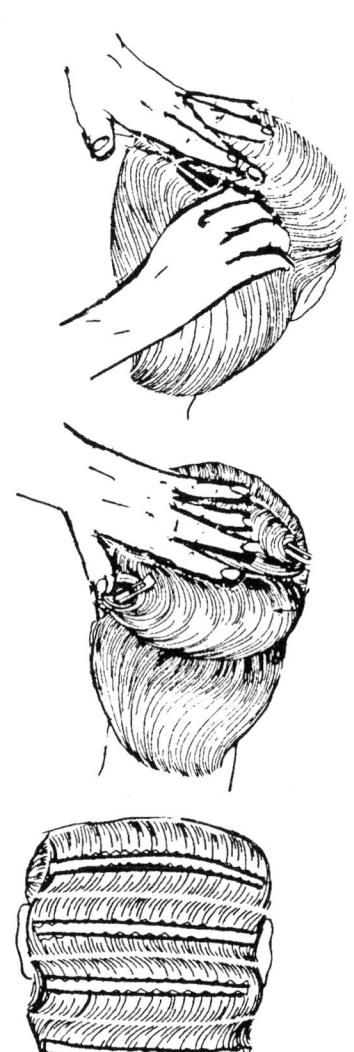

Backbrushing and Backcombing

Backbrushing

Procedure

1 Commencing at the nape, hold a strand of hair firmly in one hand and place the brush on top or underneath the strand of hair near the points.

2 Rotating the brush with a turn of the wrist, push the hair down towards the head.

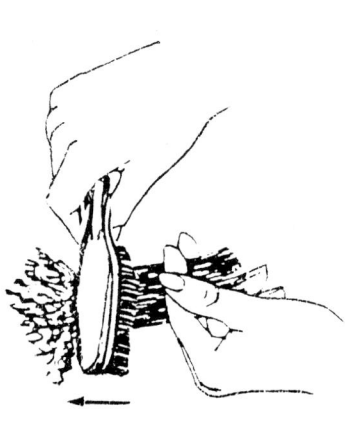

3 Repeat this procedure working towards the front of the head.

4 When the hair is completely back brushed, smooth gently and mould into shape using a brush or comb.

Backcombing

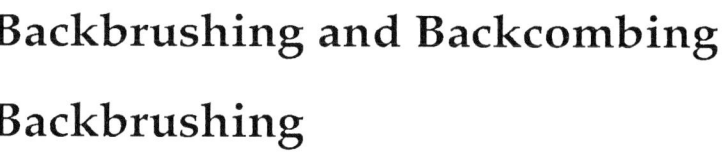

Procedure

1 Starting at the front of the head take a mesh of hair no deeper than the length of the teeth of the comb you are using.

2 Hold the mesh firmly at the angle you want the hair to lie.

3 Place the comb on the mesh and push the hair down towards the roots and repeat until you have the fulness required.

4 Continue until all the hair has been backcombed.

PLAITING — English Braid

Requirements checklist

* Tail comb
* Brush
* Elastic band, ribbon or clip for securing ends

Procedure

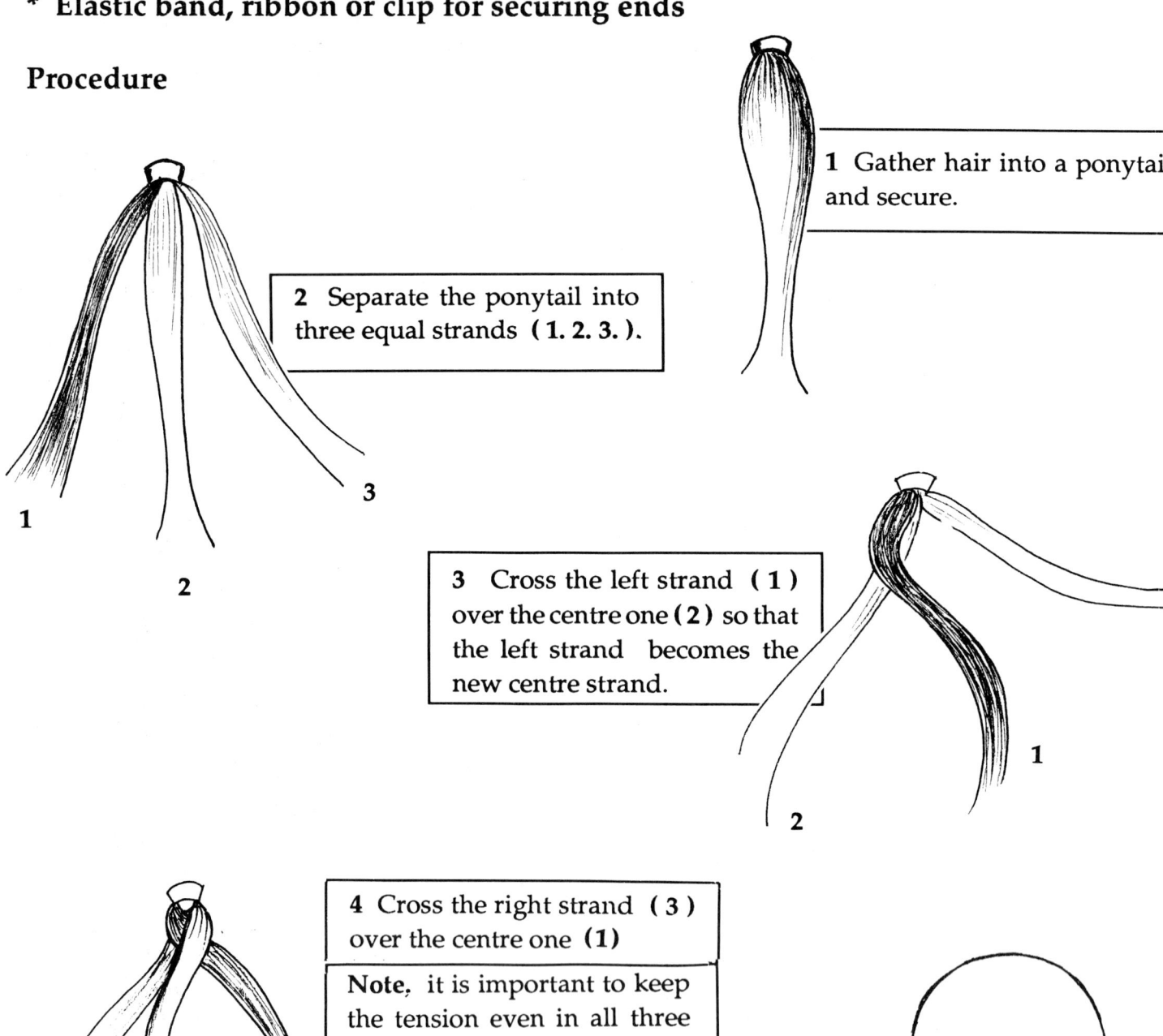

1 Gather hair into a ponytail and secure.

2 Separate the ponytail into three equal strands (1. 2. 3.).

3 Cross the left strand (1) over the centre one (2) so that the left strand becomes the new centre strand.

4 Cross the right strand (3) over the centre one (1)

Note. it is important to keep the tension even in all three strands throughout.

5 Repeat steps 3 and 4 until you reach the end of the hair. Secure with a band or clip.

PLAITING   French Plait

Requirements checklist

* Tail comb
* Brush
* Elastic band, ribbon or clip for securing ends

Procedure

1 Gather together the hair on the crown of the head above the ears and separate into three equal strands.

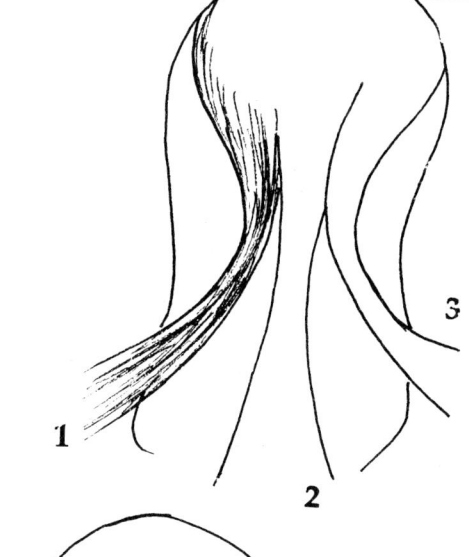

2 Cross the left strand (**1**) over the centre one (**2**) so that the left strand becomes the new centre strand.

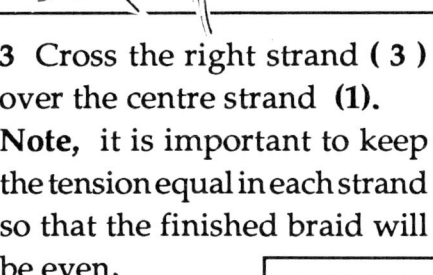

3 Cross the right strand (**3**) over the centre strand (**1**). **Note,** it is important to keep the tension equal in each strand so that the finished braid will be even.

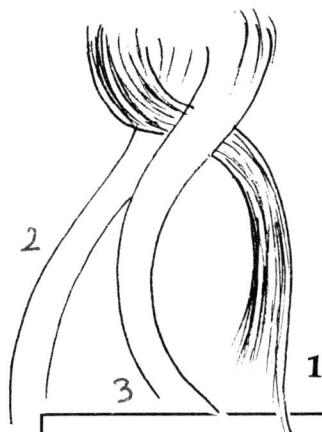

4 Holding the braid with the right hand, gather extra hair from the left front hairline, about half the thickness of one strand, and add it to the left strand (**2**). Cross this increased strand over the centre strand (**3**).

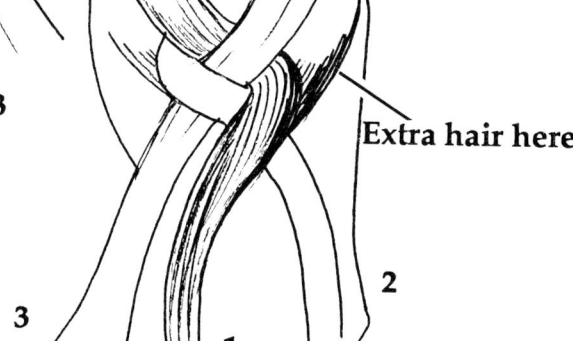

5 Repeat step **4** but hold the braid with the left hand and gather the extra hair from the right. Add it to the right strand (**1**) and pass this new increased strand over the centre strand (**2**).

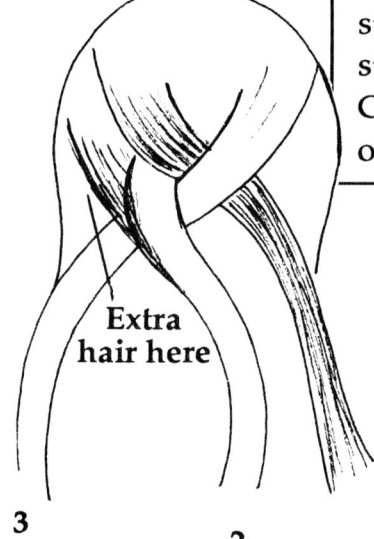

6 Repeat steps **4** and **5** until there is no loose hair at the hairline. Plait the remainder of the three strands as for an English Braid and secure the ends with a clip or band.

95

PLAITING   Plaiting around the hairline

(Braided face frame)

Requirements checklist

* Tail comb
* Brush
* Elastic band, ribbon or clip for securing ends

Procedure

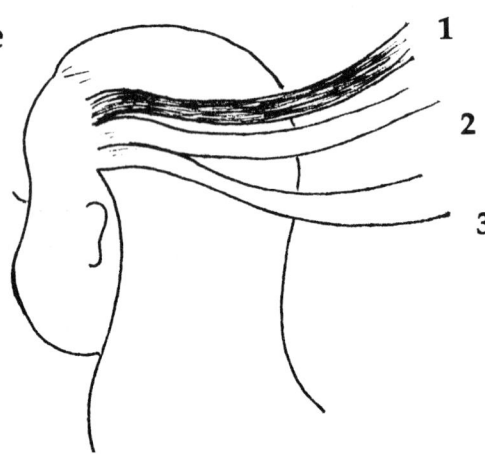

1 Starting at the left temple area, section off three narrow strands of hair at the hairline. (1 . 2 . 3 .)

2 Holding the three strands taut in the direction of the hairline, cross the top right strand (1) over the centre one (2) so that it becomes the new centre strand.

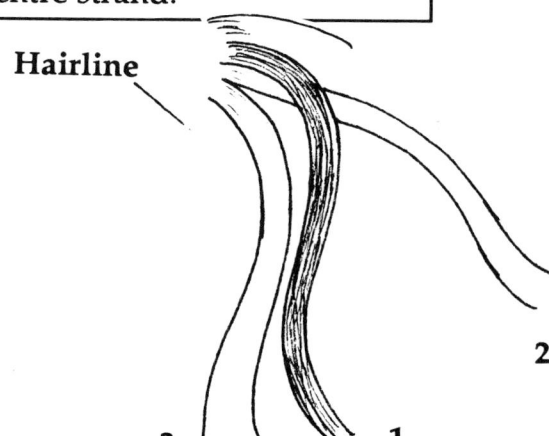

3 Cross the lower left strand (3) over the new centre strand (1).
Note. it is important to keep the tension even in all three strands throughout.

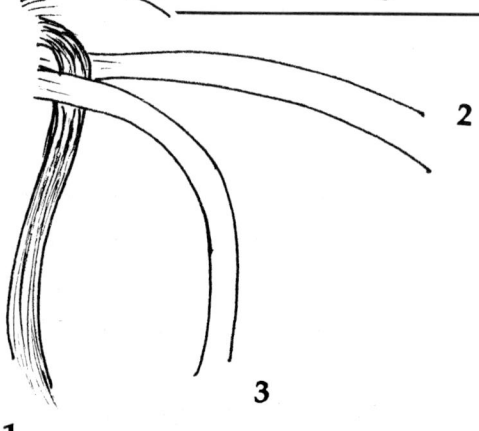

4 Lift a small section from the loose hair at the side of the top strand (2) and incorporate it into this strand. Cross this increased strand (2) over the centre strand (3).

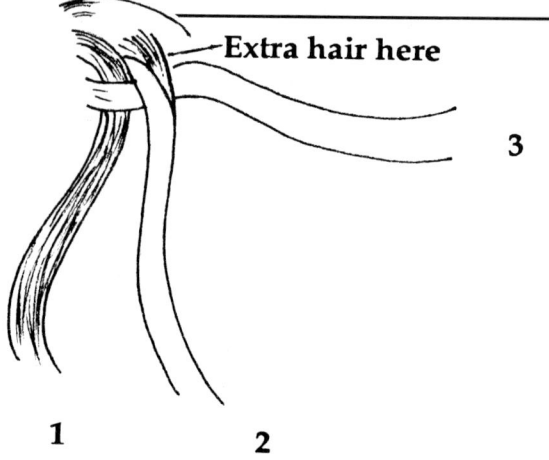

PLAITING   Plaiting around hairline

5 Lift a small section from the hairline under the bottom strand (**1**) and incorporate the extra hair into this strand. Cross this increased strand (**1**) over the centre strand (**2**).

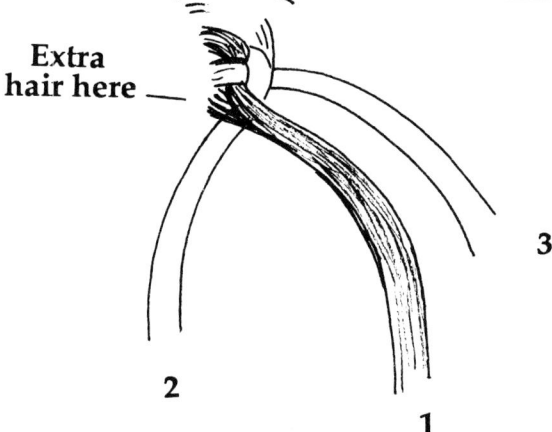

Extra hair here

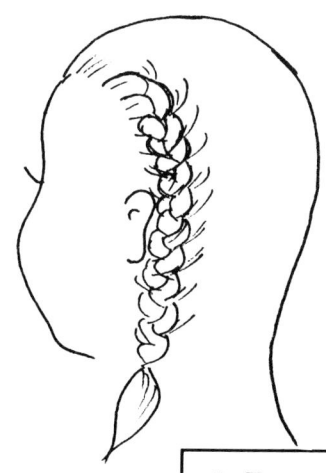

6 Repeat steps **4** and **5** right down the hairline to the nape of the neck and secure temporarily with a clip or band.

7 Repeat steps **1** to **6** on the right side of the head.
Remove the clips or bands from the two braids, holding them securely so that they do not unravel. These two braids plus the loose hair left between them now become three strands for a traditional English Braid.

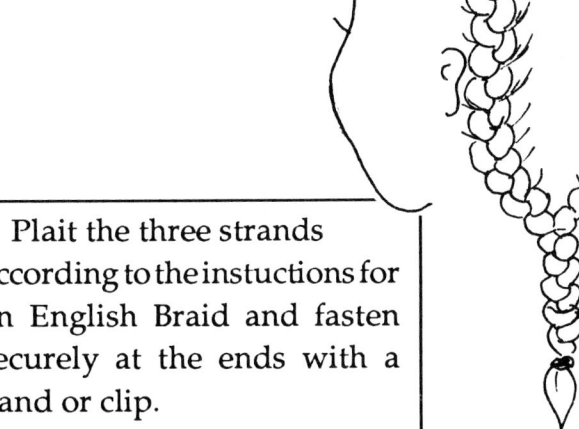

8 Plait the three strands according to the instuctions for an English Braid and fasten securely at the ends with a band or clip.

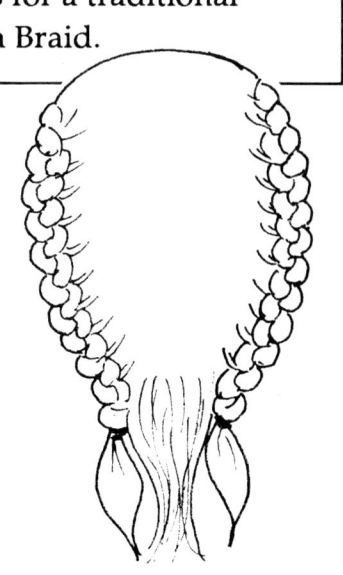

Note: Some stylists prefer to braid the Face Braid using sections lifted from the hairline side of the braid only. This is perfectly acceptable but the finished braid will be slightly uneven.

Styling Chart

Styling Tools	Description	Application	Selection	Comments
Brushes	Denman brushes Vent brushes Bristle brushes	For blowdrying For blowdrying Dressing hair	Use professional brand names. Cheap brushes can scrape the scalp	Always wash brushes after use Sterilise daily
Combs	Tail combs Straight comb large tooth comb rake combs	For sectioning. For cutting, waving and dressing hair. Disentangling hair	Choose professional combs. Metal combs can damage the hair and scalp	Wash and sterilise tools regulary. Never use combs with missing teeth
Crimpers	Electric appliance plates which presses hair	Produces crimped uniform pattern in the hair	Choose crimpers with safety features and light weight	Can damage the hair if used often. Do not use on processed hair
Curling tongs	Cylindrical irons electrically or gas heated.	For curling dry hair quickly. comes in various sizes	Pick professional tongs with 2 heat settings	Do not over use as they can dry up the hair.
Heated rollers	Rollers which are heated in a special holder before using.	Setting dry hair quickly. Gives a softer effect than setting wet hair	Avoid sharp spiky rollers. Made mainly for the domestic market	Over-use may result in dry hair.
Heated brush	Electrically heated radial brush	For curling hair quickly and adding a finish to blow-dried hair	Choose professional products Avoid sharp bristles	Do not use too often as they can dry the hair
Heated styling rods	Come in a special container. Styling rod are electically heated	For curling hair quickly	Make sure they are flexible- covered good quality foam or rubber	Easy to use do not need clips to secure rods
Hairdryers	Hand held electric hair dryer	For blowdrying	Choose professional dryer with several heat settings and nossle attachment	Use lower heat setting and hold at least 10cm from the hair
Rollers	Made in plastic and nylon. Come in two shapes cylindrial and conoid (cone)	For setting the hair	Spiky rollers damage hair. Sponge rollers are unhygienic	Always keep clean and free of hairs Autoclave will melt rollers
Styling rods	Sometimes called Molton Browners. Flexible foam Covered wire flex	For styling wet or dry hair. Also used to perm hair	Choose good quality flexible ones tha can withstand heat	Very popular as they create softer effects than rollers
Straighteners	Hand held electric flat plates between which hair is pressed	For straightening wavy hair easy to handle	Choose professionl light weight straighteners	Can damage porous or processed hair. Do not use often or brush or comb hair after straightening hair

8/10

PERMING and NEUTRALISING

Before starting this unit it is a good idea to remind yourself of what we discussed in the Consultation and Diagnostics unit regarding hair structure, hair condition and skin and hair disorders.

Perming is the name given to the process of curling hair by chemically altering its internal structure.

Neutralising is the term used to describe the chemical process which fixes the hair in a new position after it has been altered by the action of perm lotion. It is sometimes referred to as *oxidising* or *normalising*.

Although perming and neutralising are sometimes viewed as two distinct processes, neutralising is really just one stage in the perming process. Hair cannot be permed without being neutralised, and the theoretical basis of neutralising cannot be understood without first understanding how perm lotion alters the structure of the hair. For this reason perming and neutralising are considered together.

* *Instructions for carrying out perming and neutralising procedures are covered separately in the practical section at the end of the unit.*

The History of Perming

The ancient Egyptian pharaohs curled their hair by wrapping it round wooden sticks, bones or pieces of ivory and covering it with mud. The mud was left to dry, the sticks were removed, and the hair brushed out into curls - the original permanent wave!

It was not until the 1920's that the first real permanent wave was introduced. An Englishman by the name of Charles Nessler used a combination of his knowledge of using hot alcohol in wigmaking, and the Marcel technique of waving the hair by the use of heat, to create a method of permanently curling hair. He did this by applying an alkaline solution to hair wrapped round rods and heating it.

1939 saw the introduction of the original cold wave. The structure of the hair was altered by the action of *thioglycollic acid* which was applied to hair which had been wrapped around rods. It was a long slow process as the non-chemical neutralising action went on overnight.

By the **1940's** a new chemical neutralising agent, *hydrogen peroxide,* had been introduced which speeded up the process considerably.

This is basically the same process we use today although we now have a choice of perm lotions and neutralisers.

Some perm lotions used today are acidic. Although these are kinder to the hair, penetration of the cortex is much slower because the cuticle scales are not raised by acids. To compensate for this it is usual to apply some form of heat.

The neutralising procedure is the same for both an acid and an alkaline perm.

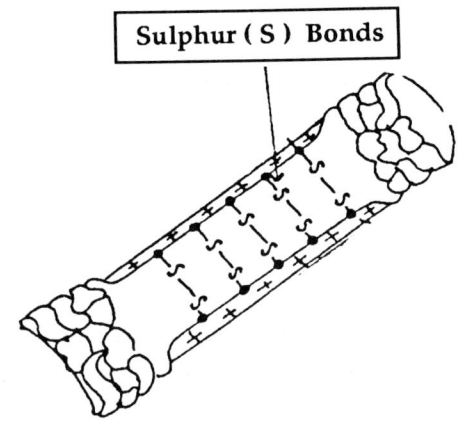

Sulphur (S) Bonds

Chemical Action
Ammonium Thioglycollate (perm lotion) is rich in Hydrogen (H) atoms which break sulphur bonds (di-sulphide bonds)

How do perms work?

Perming involves *two* stages.

1 The **reduction** stage

2 The **oxidation** stage (Also known as the *neutralising* or *normalising* stage.)

Hair as you know is made up of three layers. The cortex, or middle layer, is made up of *polypeptide chains* which are held together by *cross linkages,* the strongest of which are known as *disulphide bonds* or *S-bonds*.

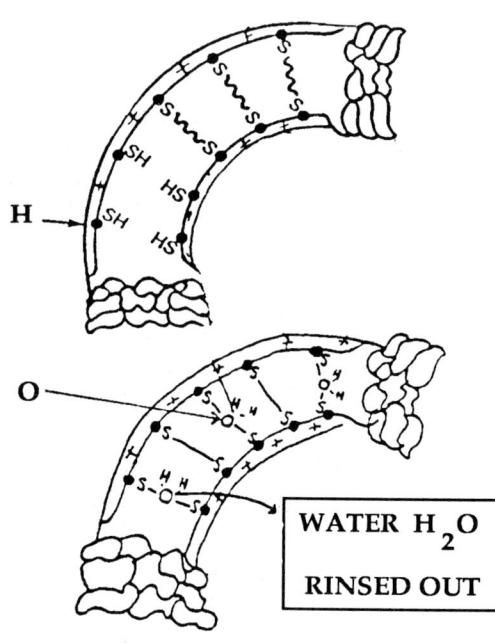

WATER H_2O RINSED OUT

NEUTRALISATION STAGE

The hydrogen peroxide H_2O_2 has active oxygen (O) which when released has a strong attraction for Hydrogen (H) atoms. This bridges the gap between the previously broken Sulphur (S) bonds.

The reduction stage

Perm lotion penetrates the outside layer of the hair, that is the cuticle, and **deposits** hydrogen in the cortex. This hydrogen breaks down the S-bonds by a process of reduction. When hair is wrapped round a rod the polypeptide chains are physically stretched. If perm lotion is applied to hair in this position the broken cross-linkages will leave the hair soft so that it relaxes into its stretched position.

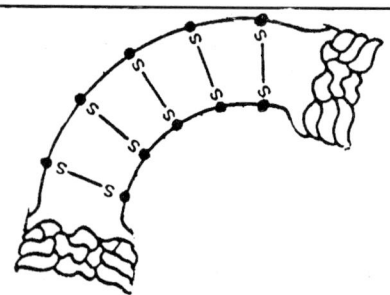

The oxidation stage

Neutralising **removes** the hydrogen from the cortex by uniting it with oxygen to form water. This oxidation process joins up cross-linkages and fixes the hair permanently in its new position.

Perm lotions

The active ingredient in most perm lotions is an alkali called *ammonium thioglycollate*, with a pH value of between **8.5** and **9.5**.

It is not a stable substance and will readily extract oxygen from the air. This of course is what makes it a powerful reducing agent. To prevent this happening before it is used buffering agents are added which slow down the rate of reduction.

It is important to make sure the tops of perm lotion bottles are replaced immediately, and lotion which has been exposed to the air should never be poured back into a bottle. If cheap 'bulk' lotions are not well buffered they will become progressively weaker each time they are used.

Lotions for resistant, normal and tinted hair vary in strength. This variation is governed by the percentage of ammonium thioglycollate present. Resistant hair requires a stronger lotion than normal or tinted hair.

Note that even the weakest of lotions can cause considerable damage to the hair if left to process for long periods of time. Fine hair is easily damaged and will require a mild strength lotion. Coarse hair can take stronger lotion unless it is also porous.

Acid perms contain *glycerol thioglycollate* and have a pH value between **5** and **6.5**. They do not break as many bonds as alkaline perms, but are better for the hair. They are recommended for fine, tinted and bleached hair. Acid perms are more expensive than alkaline perms and cannot be bought in bulk form.

SAFETY NOTES

Avoid perm lotion and neutralsers coming in contact with eyes, face and surrounding area. Accidental splashes in eyes or on skin should be rinsed away immediately. If irritation persists in the eyes seek medical advice immediately.

If any product is swallowed give two or three glasses of water or milk to drink and seek medical advice immediately.

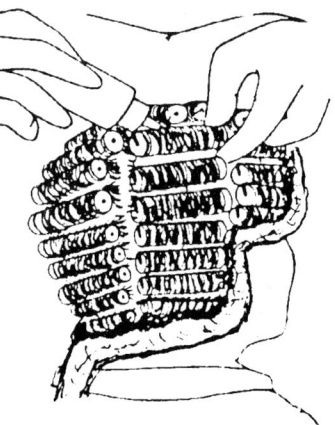

Wetting Agents

Usually perm lotions are improved by the addition of wetting agents and conditioners. Perfume is also added to mask the unpleasant odour of perm lotion.

The purpose of a wetting agent is to ensure a quick and even penetration of lotion into the cortex. It is a non-foaming cleansing product.

Conditioners

These will replace the natural oils removed from the hair by the alkaline solution and help th to retain a satisfactory moisture content.

Protein conditioners, such as protein hydrolysate, are used in some lotions to even porosity.

Rod Size

The size of rods used determines the size of wave or curl. As the length of hair increases, so should the diameter of the rod.

Small rods on long hair do not give tight curls because the diameter of curl increases as the rod approaches the root of the hair. The result is tight ends and poor root to mid length curl. Also, the use of small rods on long hair leaves the hair too thickly wound for perm lotion to penetrate properly and to allow adequate rinsing. Larger rods give a more uniform diameter of curl throughout on long hair.

On very long hair it is advisable to use spiral winding or other techniques which are discussed later.

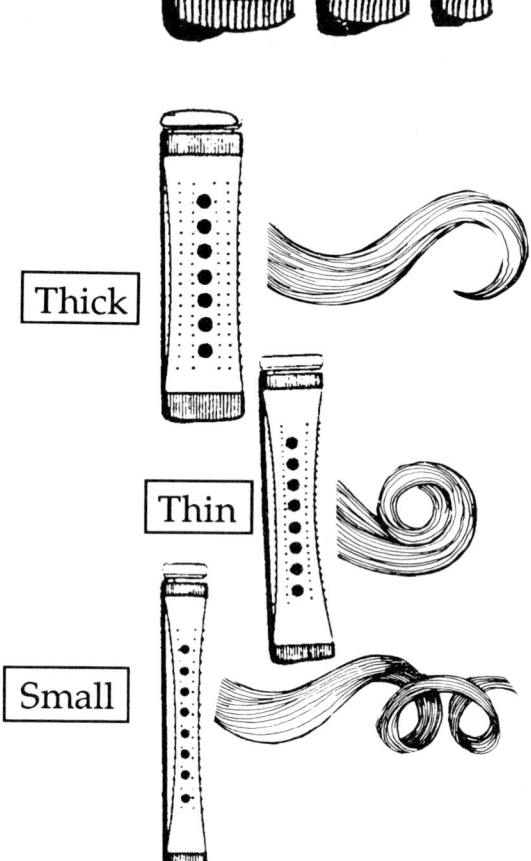

General guide

If the rod is rotated **2 to 3 times** the result should be a **soft** perm.

If the rod is rotated **3 to 4 times** the result should be **wavy** rather than curly.

If the rod is rotated more than **4 times** the result should be a **curly** perm.

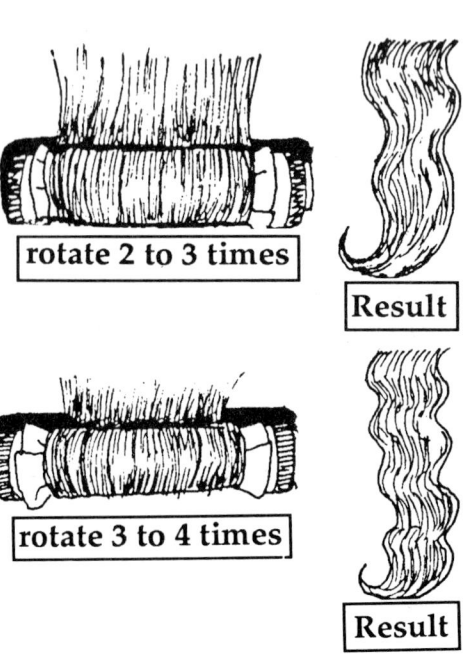

Winding

Before winding consider the *density* of the hair. If the hair is thick take smaller meshes than you would with thin hair.

Check hair ends to determine if they have been razor or scissor cut. If the hair has been razor cut the ends may be too feathery and could frizz if they are not first club-cut to give more weight.

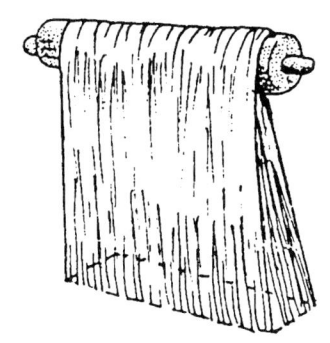

Hair is usually wound at an angle of ninety degrees from the scalp to give optimum lift at the root area and to minimise the possibility of rubber band damage. If the angle of wind is lower, it will result in fewer rods being put in the hair, which can mean overall poor root lift and a weak perm.

There are exceptions to the above rule, two of which are the stack and spiral winding techniques mentioned below.

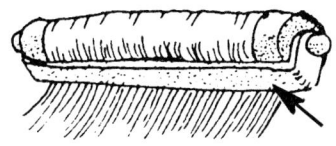

Sometimes, because the root hair does not show a good wave formation, the hair is left to process for longer than the recommended time resulting in damage to the hair ends.

When the hair is wound on to the perming rods it must be wound evenly to produce an even curl pattern, and under sufficient pressure to alter the keratin chains but not over-stretch them as this causes frizziness and damage to the scalp.

If the tension is too slack, the curl formation will be weak. Again, this could lead to the solution being left on the hair too long causing structural damage to the hair and loss of wave and elasticity.

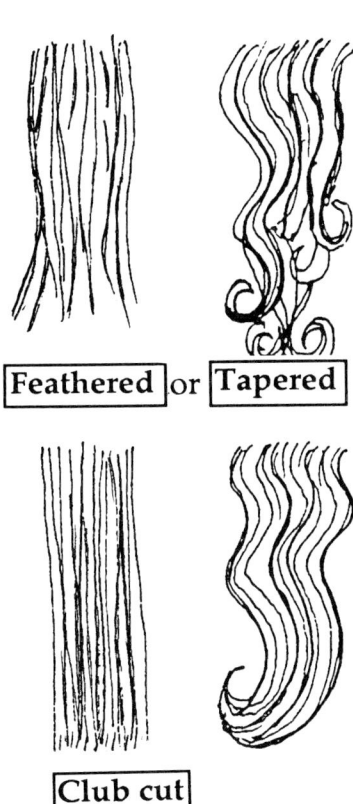

To ensure the correct tension is being applied look for the following signs.

* Hair pulling at the scalp - the tension is too tight.
* Rods easily pulled from the hair - the tension is too loose.

Winding techniques

Directional winding

The perm rods are wound to follow the specific lines of the style you want to achieve. Using perm rods, or Molton Brown permers, of different diameters will produce a more natural effect.

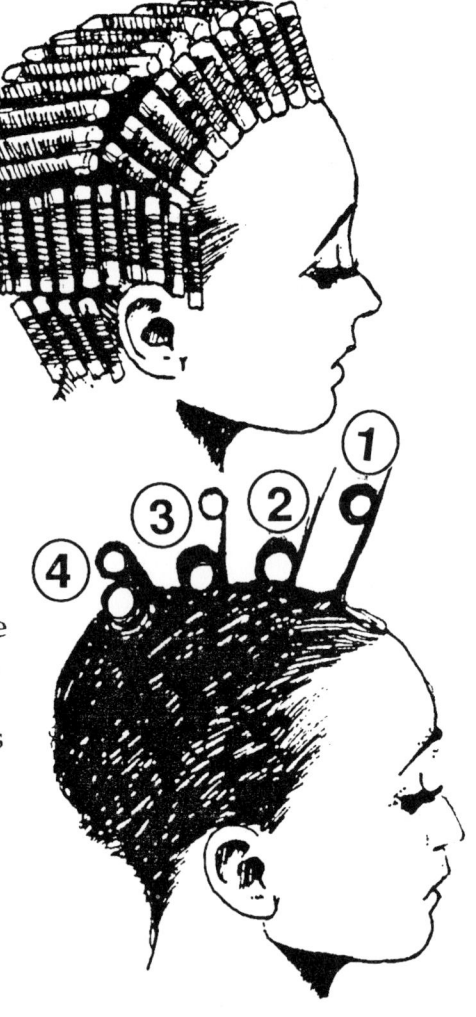

Piggy-back winding

This technique gives lots of body and volume to long hair.

Take a section of hair the same width as the rods. Place the first rod half way down the hair length and wind to the scalp.

The remaining hair is wound around another rod which is positioned on top of the lower rod, piggy-back fashion.

Stack winding

This technique was very popular in the early seventies and is still very useful for many styles in fashion today.

The hair is wound close to the scalp commencing at nape. With each subsequent sub-section the rod is wound to lie directly on top of the previous rod.

The effect is almost triangular with lots of supportive curl underneath and the top sub-sections are curled at the ends only.

Root perming

Suitable method when you only want to add supportive body but no movement at the ends. The technique is to wind as normal but use barrier cream on the ends or wind them with cling film instead of end papers.

Post-damping with perm lotion is normally recommended.

Many companies also produce root perms with thick gels instead of lotion. These are applied to the wound rods and because of their thick consistency do not penetrate into the ends of the hair.

Brick winding

The rods are positioned in much the same way as a brick wall is constructed. Using a section of hair the same width as the selected rods commence winding at the centre front hairline. Continue to build up the brick formation from this point.

By winding this way you can avoid unwanted gaps or partings in the hair which could occur in channel winding.

Ideal technique for creating short styles that are to be left to dry naturally.

Channel winding

For this technique the rods are wound in rows.

It is inclined to restrict the amount of movement that can be achieved but is the most popular method used today because it is quick and relatively easy to do.

This method is used by beginners and is the one described in the practical section at the end of this unit.

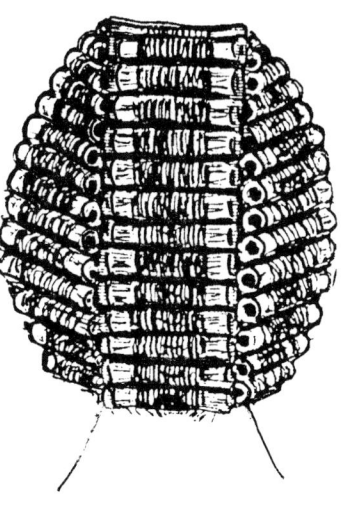

Molton Permers

This is a popular technique today. (produced by Wella Ltd) It is an alternative to traditional rods, which allows the possibility of creating softer effect using flexible rods. The rods are made of foam covering thin wire allowing the rod to be bent into desired positions

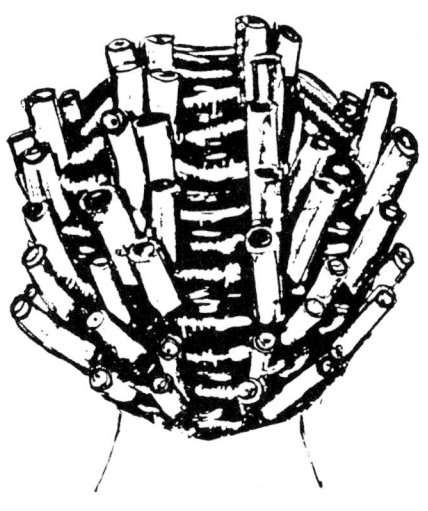

Application of Perm Lotion

Perm lotion can be applied in two ways.

* **Pre-damping** is the technique of applying the lotion while winding.
* **Post-damping** is the technique of applying the lotion after winding has been completed.

Important
The manufacturer's instructions must be followed as to whether or not the lotion being used is for pre-damping or post-damping.

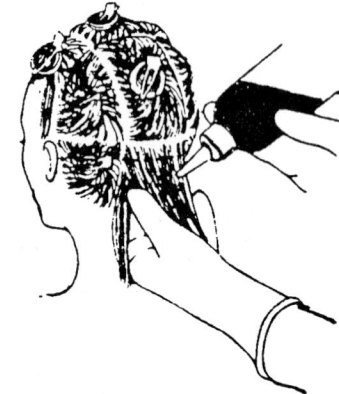

Pre-damping

The lotion is applied to each individual mesh of hair, a section at a time, before the end tissue is put on. This means the first rods of hair are processing while the others are being wound. It is an old fashioned method and not often used now.

Post-damping

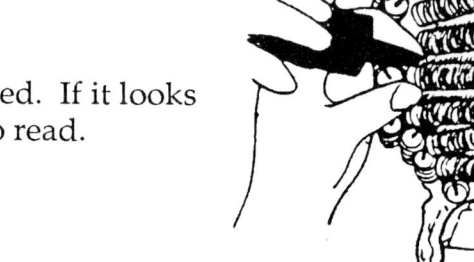

Because the lotion is applied after the rods have been wound the chemical process commences at the same time all over the head, which makes timing easier. It also eliminates the need to wear gloves while winding the rods.

The hair should glisten after the lotion has been applied. If it looks wet it is too saturated and test curls will be difficult to read.

Processing time

Manufacturers' instructions **must** be followed about the time perm lotion should be left to develop.

Heat speeds up the processing stage and you may be told to cover the rods with a plastic cap. This traps body heat and acts as an insulator. A warm atmosphere in the salon will also speed things up.

Sometimes external heat is applied with a hooded drier or a steamer. Computerised driers are now available which are able to work out when processing has been completed.

IMPORTANT

<u>When perming bleached, tinted or porous hair never use a perm which requires additional external heat to accelerate the processing time as the hair will be in danger of being overprocessed.</u>

10 NEUTRALISING

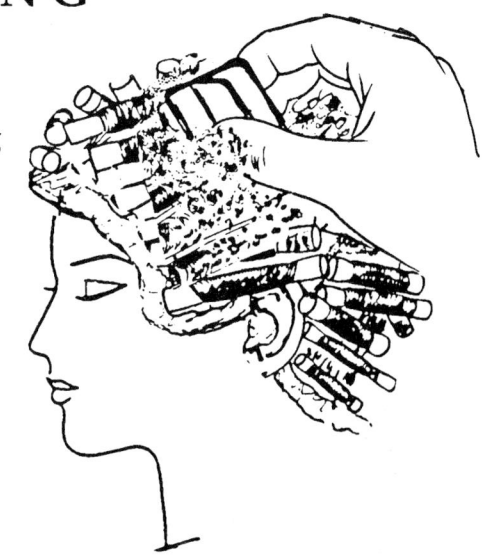

Perm lotion alters the chemical structure of the hair, allowing it to be moulded into a new shape. The hair is permanently fixed into the new shape by the action of an oxidising agent, known to hairdressers as a neutraliser. This was noted earlier when we discussed the reduction and oxidation stages in perming.

Neutralising must be carried out very carefully or the perm will be unsuccessful.

The active ingredient in neutralisers is usually either *hydrogen peroxide* or *sodium bromate*. The latter is commonly used in home perms and is less likely to irritate the skin.

Relatively weak dilutions of these reagents are used in most neutralisers; usually 6% solutions of hydrogen peroxide and 5% solutions of sodium bromate. Stronger solutions could result in some colour loss because of their bleaching action on the hair's pigment. They are also liable to cause further damage to porous hair.

'Instant' neutralisers, which are removed immediately after being applied, contain a strong solution of hydrogen peroxide and are not popular for the above reasons.

Neutralisers generally come ready to use, but a few require to be mixed with water. Ready to use ones come either in applicating bottles and can be applied directly to the hair, or in larger containers when they are measured into a bowl and applied with a sponge.

If neutraliser is not completely removed from the hair when the development time is up oxidation will continue slowly for the next few days, allowing the S-bonds to *'slip'* and be reformed in a straighter position. This is known as *'creeping' oxidation*.

Common problem in perming and possible causes

Problem	Cause
Perm too soft	Rods too large
Perm too tight	Rods too small
No root lift / wave	Insufficient number of rods used
Straight roots	Bad angle of wind
Weak curl formation	Insufficient lotion applied
Scalp damage (Pull Burn)	Tight winding plus excess lotion
Development time too long	Cap not used when recommened
Slow development	Room temperature too low
Not processed in areas	Uneven application of perm lotion
Over processed	Lotion left on too long
Under processed	Lotion not left on long enough

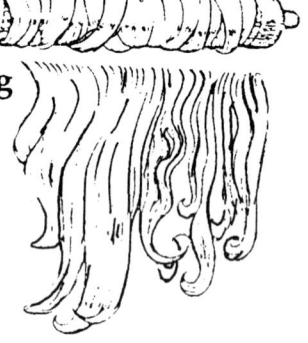

Uneven winding

Tight winding

Broken hair and straight frizz

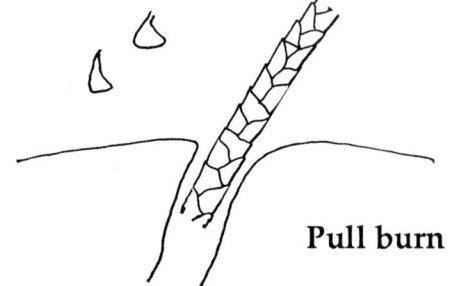

Excessive lotion

Pull burn

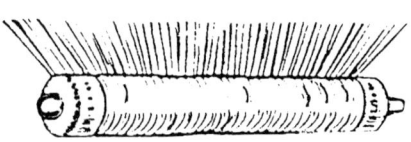

Section too big

PRACTICAL SECTION

Perming the Hair

Before carrying out a perm it is essential that you first carry out the Consultation and Diagnostics procedure found in the practical section of the unit of that name.

Make sure you carry out any precautionary tests recommended before perming the hair.

Requirements checklist

* Client's record card
* Release form if used
* Operator's protective apron
* Gown, cape, towels and neck strips
* Shampoo
* Conditioners
* Section clips
* Protective barrier cream
* Wide toothed and tail combs
* Perm rods
* Bowl and sponge if required.
* Perm lotion
* Neutraliser
* Perm papers
* Cotton wool and tissues
* Timer

There are seven different procedures involved in perming the hair.

1 Preparing the hair
2 Winding the rods
3 Applying the perm lotion
4 Testing curl formation
5 Removing perm lotion
6 Neutralising
7 Conditioning

Preparing the hair for perming

Procedure

1 Study the manufacturer's instructions

2 Shampoo hair with a good quality acid balanced shampoo. Do not over-stimulate the scalp by vigorous rubbing.

3 Cut the hair if the client wants it restyled. (Sometimes cutting is carried out after perming.)

4 If the hair is porous apply a pre-perm treatment to equal out the porosity.

Winding

Pre-dampening was the original method of applying perm lotion and winding was always started in the nape section of the hair, the reason being that the hair is not usually as porous in this area and less damage was likely to be caused by the extra processing time.

Traditions die hard and winding is still started at the nape area for both pre- and post-dampening techniques, unless the style demands otherwise.

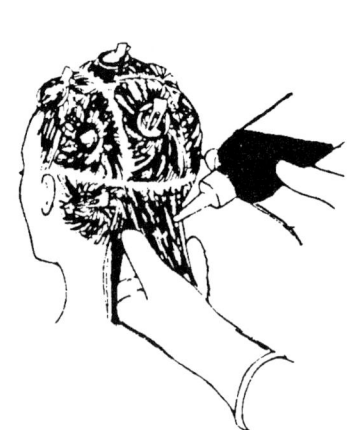

* If using a pre-dampening technique refer to the procedure for this first, under the heading 'Applying the perm lotion'.

Procedure for Channel Winding

1 Draw a parting from just behind one ear to the other, over the top of the head.

2 Place a rod on the centre of the crown area and use the length of rod as a guide to make two further partings from the crown forward, one to the forehead and another from the crown to the nape. Hold sections with section clips.

3 Make another section from the top of one ear to the top of the other ear round the back of the head and separate with section clips.

4 Starting at the nape section (1) of the hair lift a mesh of hair with a tail comb, using the size of the selected rod to determine the size of the mesh. The width of the mesh should be slightly smaller than the length of the rod, and its depth the same as the width of the rod.

5 Hold the mesh of hair at right angles and comb it with a tail comb along the inside of the mesh. Place end paper around the points of the hair. End papers protect porous ends and reduce the risk of the ends buckling. They also assist the winding process.

6 To wind the hair mesh, hold the rod parallel to the head and place it below the mesh against the end paper. Wind the hair evenly towards you, paying particular attention to the ends which should be wrapped smoothly round the rod. Do not use too much tension as this could hinder the success of the perm.

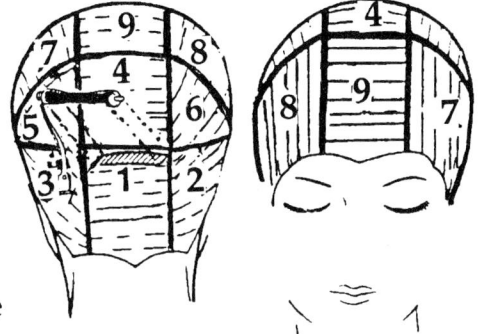

7 Secure the rod by hooking the elastic band over the end, making sure it does not mark the hair by pressing against the hair roots.

8 Completely wrap the middle nape section.

9 Wind the other sections following the numbered sequence.

10 When winding is completed and checked, apply a length of cotton wool around the client's hairline.

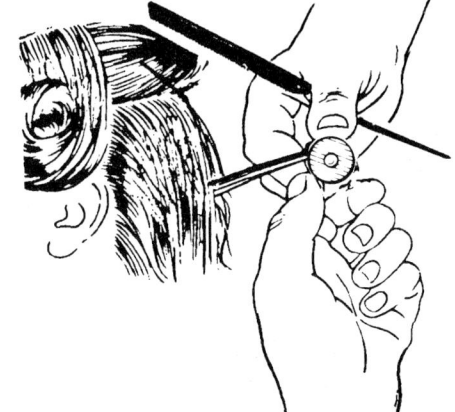

Applying the perm lotion

Using a pre-dampening technique

Procedure

<u>Wear gloves throughout the winding procedure to avoid skin irritaion.</u>

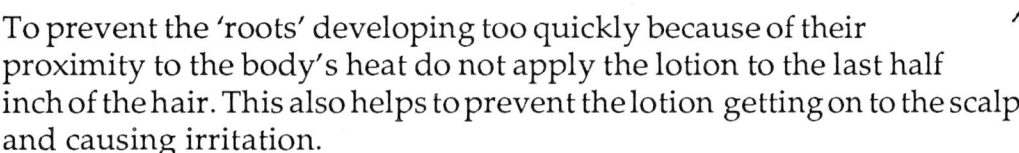

1 Starting at the nape area, apply the lotion to each mesh of hair, combing it through before winding on the rod.

To prevent the 'roots' developing too quickly because of their proximity to the body's heat do not apply the lotion to the last half inch of the hair. This also helps to prevent the lotion getting on to the scalp and causing irritation.

2 As soon as you have finished winding the whole head, start testing at the first mesh wound to see if it has been processed sufficiently.

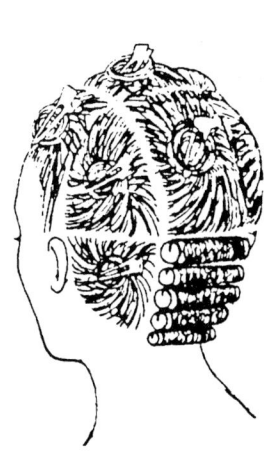

Using a post-dampening technique

Procedure

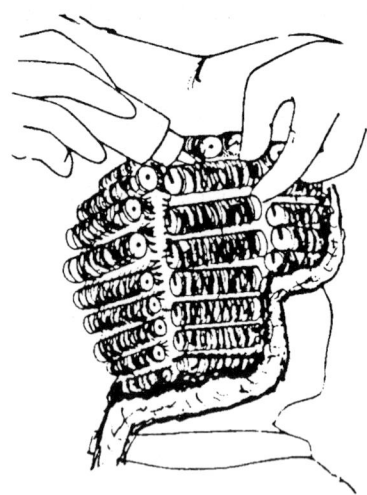

1 Beginning at the nape section and continuing in sequence according to the numbers shown, saturate the hair on the rods with the waving lotion, directing the nozzle first to the top and then the bottom of the rod.

Keep the lotion from running on to the scalp. Remove excess lotion by blotting with cotton wool.

2 Remove cotton wool wrapped round the hairline. Cotton wool saturated with lotion will cause a chemical burn if left in contact with the skin.

3 Leave to process for recommended time then test.

Assessing curl formation (curl test)

1 Test curls in the front, nape and side areas by loosening the rod and unwinding about 2 rotations, at the same time pushing the rod in the direction of the scalp.

Look for a well-defined S-formation equal to the diameter of the rod.

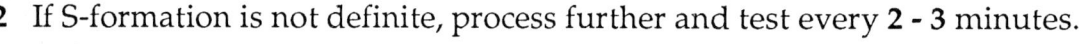

2 If S-formation is not definite, process further and test every **2 - 3** minutes.

Remember that air and body temperature will affect the speed of the process.

Do not exceed the manufacturer's recommended processing times by more than twenty percent. Always consult your supervisor if unsure.

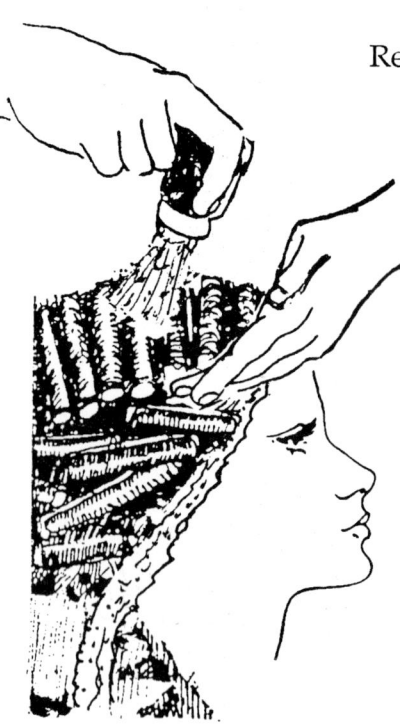

3 When the test curls show a strong S- formation processing is complete and the hair is now thoroughly rinsed with warm water.

Removing the perm lotion

Procedure

1 Seat the client comfortably at the basin. A back basin is recommended to lessen the risk of neutraliser running on to the client's face.

2 Make sure the client's clothing is properly protected as neutralisers can damage fabric.

3 Rinse the hair with tepid water for the time recommended by the manufacturer, usually five minutes.

Particular attention should be paid to the nape area when a back wash is being used as it tends to get missed.

4 After rinsing, the hair should be gently but thoroughly blotted with a towel to remove all excess water which would otherwise dilute the neutraliser.

The hair is now soft, fragile and swollen so be very careful not to rub hard. Rocking the rods can damage the hair by distorting the root.

Neutralising and Conditioning

Procedure

1   Place cotton wool around the hair line to absorb any excess neutraliser.

2 Follow the same section sequence used when applying the perm lotion. Wearing protective gloves apply two thirds of the neutraliser across the top and bottom of each rod.

 It is a good idea to go over each rod more than once to ensure the hair is thoroughly saturated, and that no rods have been missed.

3 Leave for the recommended processing time then remove the rods carefully.

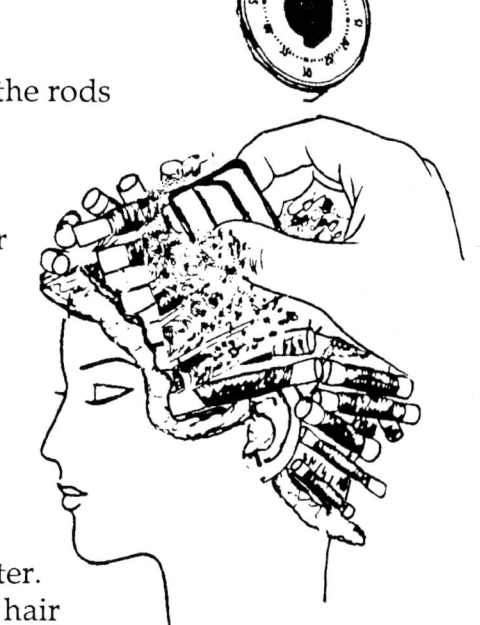

4   Apply the remaining third of the neutraliser and leave for further development time as instructed by the manufacturer.

The perm can be ruined very easily at this stage. Careless handling can push the hair out of the shape in which it was wound. If this happens some bonds will reform in the wrong position and the perm will drop.

5 Rinse the neutraliser from the hair thoroughly with tepid water. Use a kneading action to squeeze the rinsing water through the hair and do not pull or stretch the hair.

Manufacturers occasionally recommend that, after rinsing with tepid water, the hair should be further rinsed for one minute with cool water. This is good practice as it encourages the cuticle to contract and lie flat. It can be rather uncomfortable for the client so tell her why it is being done. If she objects do not proceed.

6 When the neutraliser has been completely removed, apply a normalising conditioner to insure that the hair is left with the correct pH value. The conditioner will also make the hair more manageable and shiny.

7 Towel dry the hair gently with a clean towel and replace any damp towels or gowns.

8 Comb hair through carefully with a large toothed comb.

9 Assess the results of the perm.

When the perm has been completed

* Style the hair

* Record the result of the perm in the client's record card.

* Recommend appropriate home care treatments, which are for sale in the salon, and advise her not to use hot brushes, tongs or crimpers on newly permed hair.

* Suggest an appointment for the following week to reassess the perm.

9 HAIR COLOURING

Hair colouring goes back to ancient times. The first *metallic dye* was discovered by the Romans who dipped lead metal combs in wine to stain white hair, and the Egyptians liked to colour their hair red using *vegetable dyes* such as henna.

Colouring the hair did not become socially acceptable in Britain until the 1950's although it was introduced before the turn of the century. However it has now become very popular with both men and women, which has led to the introduction of imaginative new techniques for achieving unusual effects. It can also be used to accentuate the lines of a style, to make a full face look slimmer and a thin face wider.

The commercial value of colouring

Hair colouring is perhaps the most important service that the hairdresser can offer his client. It is important to the hairdresser in terms of creativity and commercial value. It is important to the client because colour can alter her appearance and reflect her personality perhaps more than any other hairdressing treatment. Many women now consider hair colouring to be an essential part of their fashion routine, but others need convincing.

To capitalise on hair colouring you must be able to influence the client to try it, and to achieve the result you have claimed. If the client is disappointed with her first experience she is unlikely to repeat it.

To introduce colour effectively you must talk about it. Your specialised knowledge and experience make you the expert, and clients will welcome your advice. Not every client is really sure what colour suits her. Carefully considering each client's preferences, her natural hair colour, skin tone, eye colour, lifestyle, personality and career will guide you in what advice to give. This of course is part of the Consultation and Diagnostic procedure carried out before any salon service.

It is essential that you understand the basic principles of colour, the products available and the effects these have on the hair.

Clynol have produced an excellent publication called 'Viton Colour Facts' which gives most of the information you will need. It is reproduced here in part with their kind permission.

It gives a comprehensive explanation of both basic and more advanced colour theory.

Clynol's Viton S permanent colour is one of the best colouring products on the market. It is ideal for training purposes because the majority of shades are intermixeable, giving a limitless range of colours.

Hair Structure

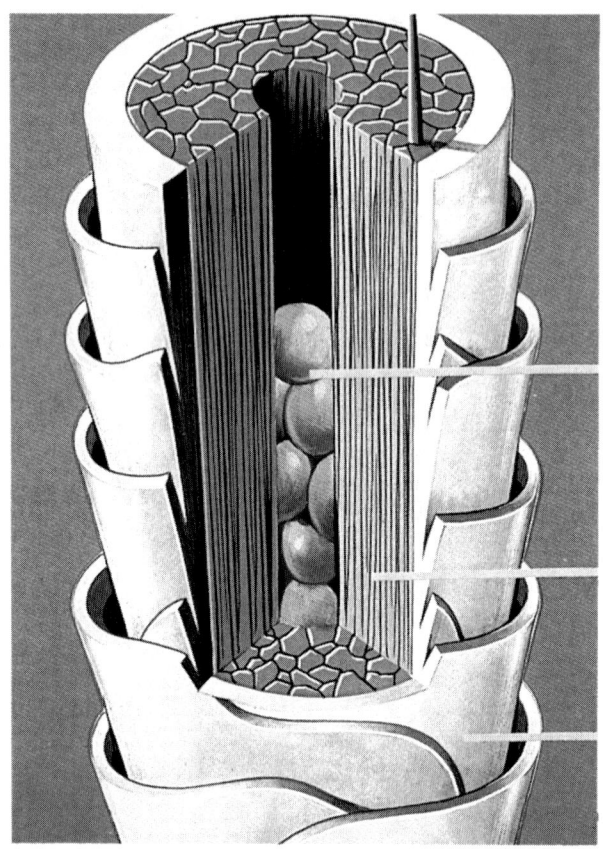

Hair is made up of three separate layers – the cuticle, the cortex and the medulla.

Medulla – plays no part in the colouring process.

Cortex – contains hair's natural pigments.

Cuticle – outer protective layer.

CUTICLE

The Cuticle is the outer layer of the hair and is made up of overlapping scales (like roof tiles!), this gives the hair strength and at the same time, flexibility.

Its purpose is to protect the cortex, which is delicate and can be damaged, weakened, or even destroyed if it is not protected.

CORTEX

The Cortex is the middle, fibrous layer of hair which makes up 75% to 90% of the main body of the hair and it is responsible for its strength, elasticity, pliability, diameter, texture and quality.

The hair's natural colouring is due to the pigment in the cortex. These pigments are known as MELANINS.

The cortex is made up of millions of parallel keratin fibres which are twisted around one another like a rope, these are known as polypetide chains.

Polypeptide chains have cross linkages of sulphur and hydrogen (also known as cysteine or di-sulphide bonds) and vertical linkages (peptide bonds).

MEDULLA

The Medulla is the middle layer of the hair. It can often be broken, and in some instances is not present at all. It does not appear to have any significant purpose in the hair's structure.

What is Colour?

Colour Formation

White light (sunlight) is made up of all colours of the rainbow:

Red   Orange   Yellow   Green   Blue   Indigo   Violet

This can be seen if we shine light through a prism.

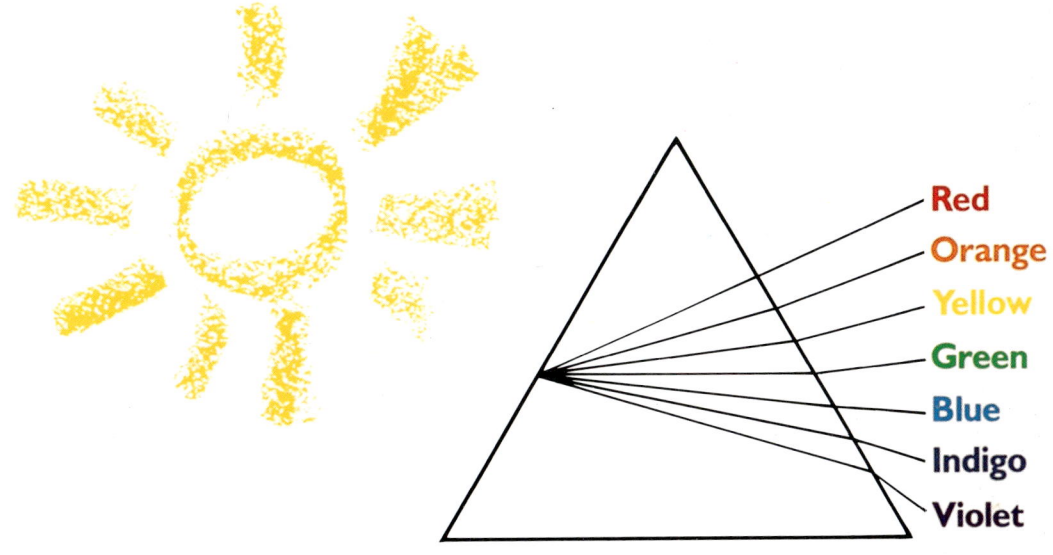

The ability of an object to absorb certain colours shining on them and reflect others gives the eye an appearance of colour.

If an object absorbs all the colours it appears black. If it reflects all colours it appears white.

The colours of the spectrum are split into two groups:

Primary colours

Red   Yellow   Blue

Secondary colours

Orange   Green   Violet

In hair colouring terminology we refer to this as **the colour star**.

The Colour Star

The basic principles of colour

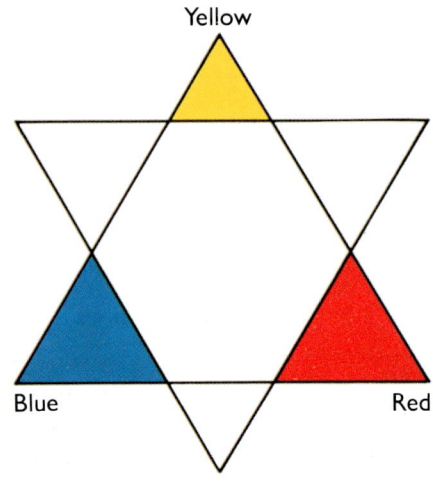

1 There are **3 Primary Colours** from which all colours evolve. They are **Red**, **Blue** and **Yellow**.

2 By mixing these **3 Primary Colours** we can create colour. This is best explained with the help of the colour star.
We can see that
by mixing **Red** and **Yellow** we make **Orange**,
by mixing **Red** and **Blue** we make **Violet**,
by mixing **Blue** and **Yellow** we make **Green**.

Orange, **Green** and **Violet** are secondary colours. By varying the amount of colour we mix together, we can create different shades of **Orange**, **Violet**, or **Green**.

3 To subdue, correct or neutralise colour, we mix colours opposite each colour on our colour star.

e.g. to subdue **Red** we would use **Green**.
to subdue excess **Yellow** we would add **Violet**.

By moving across the colour star we can subdue colour.

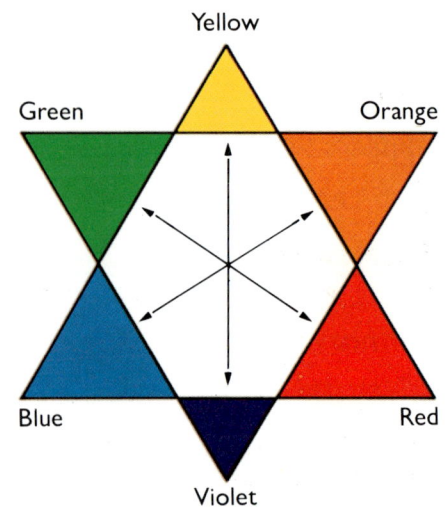

The Colour Star

Viton S Colour star

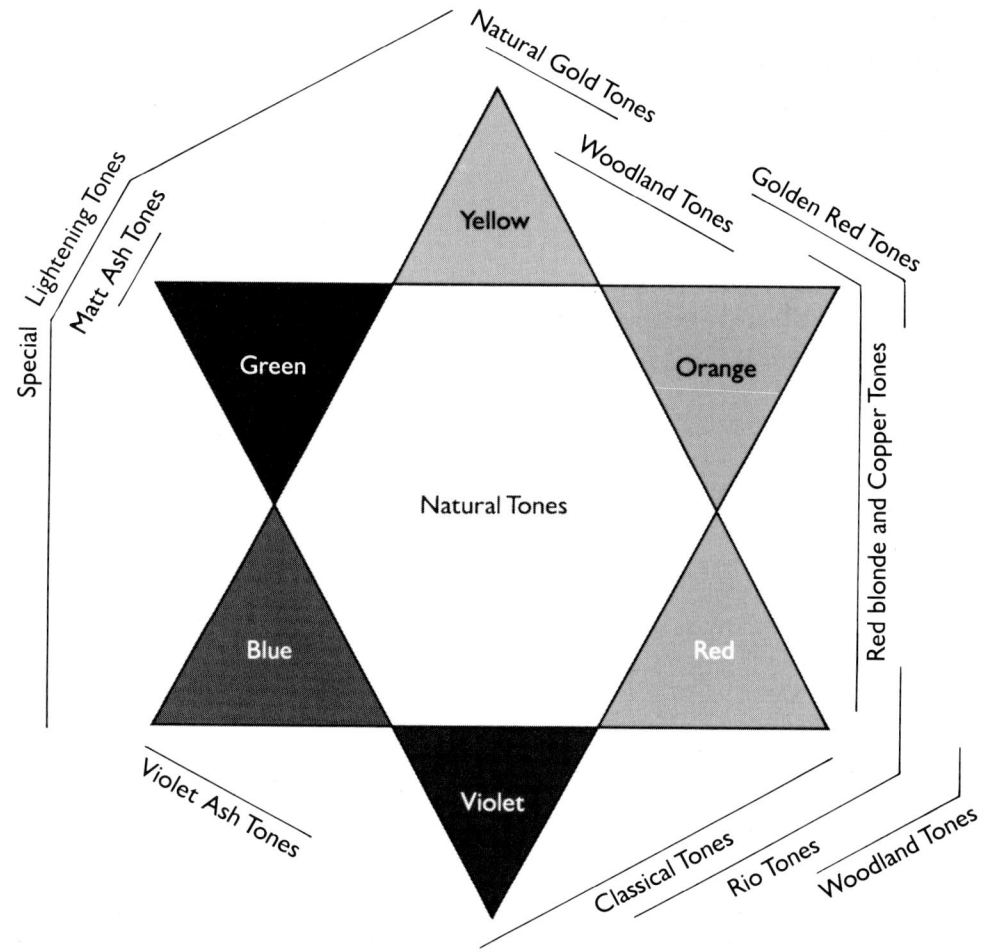

All shades in the Viton S range correspond to the Colour star:

.0 Natural Tones
.1 Matt Ash Tones
.2 Ash Tones
.3 Natural Gold Tones
.4 Woodland Tones
.5 Golden Red Tones
.6 Red Blonde and Copper Tones
.7 Rio Tones
.8 Classical Tones
.9 Classical Tones
.50 Special Lightening Tones
.60 Intensive Tones

Toners – used in small quantities to subtly alter shades:

ICC 12 Ash Concentrate –   **to Gold Ash Tones**
ICC 17 Coral Red –   **to increase or highlight red**
ICC 19 Dark Red Violet –   **to give more purple tones**
ICC 65 Titian –   **mixed-Tone gold**

Different Types of Colour

 **TEMPORARY COLOURS**

These use basic dyes and can be found in coloured setting lotion, eg. Clynol Textra S. These are the least complicated of all dye systems as the way they colour the hair is very simple and easy to understand.

The dye particle comes in an already coloured form and no chemical reaction takes place. The particles of dye lie on the cuticle to brighten and enhance natural hair colour until the hair is next shampooed.

Colour Rinse

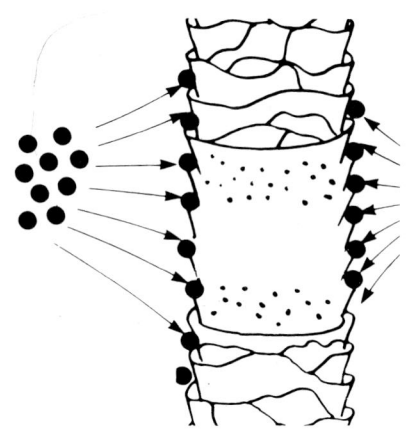

 SEMI-PERMANENT COLOURS

Semi Permanent Rinse

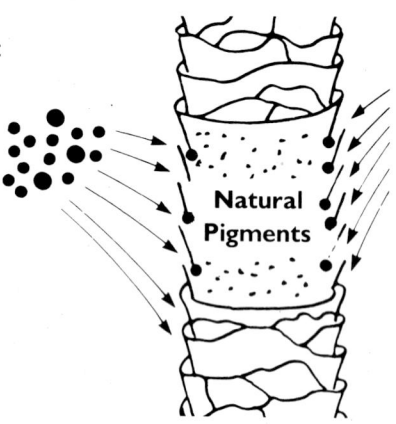

These use direct dyes and are usually incorporated in a shampoo base.

The dye particle comes in a finished form — that is to say it is already coloured in the bottle prior to application to the hair.

These dyes partially penetrate the cortex, so giving a longer lasting colour. They last between 6-8 shampoos, and some wash-out occurs on each subsequent shampoo.

Colour, Condition and Confidence

Different Types of Colour

PERMANENT COLOURS

Permanent Colour is the most important type of colour because of its long lasting effect, its versatility, and its commercial value to the hairdressing market.

Viton S is made up of millions of tiny colour molecules small enough to penetrate the cuticle into the cortex.

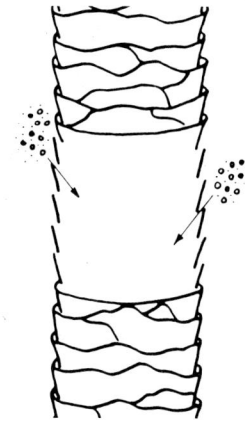

When Viton Cream Peroxide (hydrogen peroxide) is added to the colour creme, a reaction called oxidation takes place; the small colour molecules combine with the free oxygen from the peroxide to form large colour molecules.

These large colour molecules are now unable to get back through the cuticle, they are trapped within the hair structure; this gives permanent colour change.

Clynol's Viton S Creme contains four special conditioning agents to protect and care for the hair during colouring – giving the treated hair superb condition and shine.

Different Types of Colour

BLEACHING

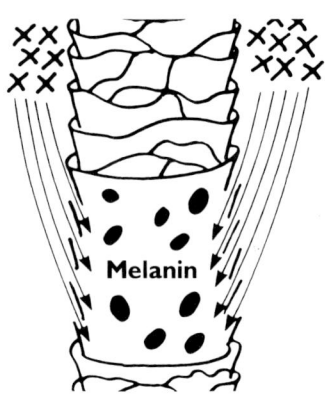

Sometimes it is not possible to lighten the hair sufficiently without using bleach. This works in the reverse way to permanent colour.

Bleach breaks down the hair's natural colour pigments and removes them from the cortex section of the hair.

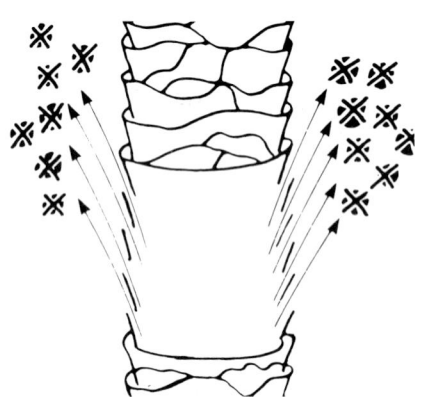

Clynol's Viton Powder Bleach has a controlled lightening action whereby the various lightening agents contained in the product work at varying and controlled speeds, giving a much kinder and gentler processing of the hair and scalp.

Introduction to Viton S

Viton S Permanent Creme Color has undergone massive growth since its introduction in 1980 and is now acknowledged as one of the leading colour systems available to the salon.

Viton S is available in an extensive and comprehensive range of 73 superb colours to meet the demands of the hairdressing market, and there is a colour in the range for everyone – especially as the majority of shades are intermixable, giving a limitless range of colour choices.

The range includes:

NATURAL RANGE

Viton S **Natural ranges** .0, .1, .2, .3, and .4 which provide up to 100% coverage on grey hair. The Natural range consists of:-

Natural Shades
Which relate directly and accurately to the client's natural colour.

Matt Ash Tones
Designed to combat undue warmth in the client's hair.

Blue/Violet Ash Tones
To introduce natural ash tones to the hair.

Natural Gold Tones
To enhance the hair's natural golden lights.

Woodland Tones
To add subtle warmth to bases from dark brown to extra light blonde.

FASHION RANGE

The Fashion Range in Viton S .5, .6, .7, .8, and .9 cover a wide range of vibrant fashion shades from Golden Red tones through Red Blonde and copper tones, rio tones to the classical.

These reproduce the special colouring effects so much in demand by the fashion conscious client.

The 500 series is a range of special lightening shades comprising of 3 beige and 4 crystal tones. These colours will give up to 4 shades lift and can be used on bases from Dark Blonde upwards.

The 600 series is a range of 5 intensive tones for use on natural bases 8, 9 or 10 and pre-lightened hair. Intensive Titian can be used on darker bases without pre-lightening and this will lift approximately 2 shades.

Introduction to Viton S

Toners

Finally, there are 3 concentrated toners within the range:

Ash

A blue/violet ash tone for reducing orange or red tones.

Coral Red

This is both a toner and a shade used in its own right for intensifying red tones, and for pre-pigmenting bleached hair.

Bordeaux

This is both a toner and a shade in its own right. Main purpose is to reduce yellow tones.

All toners should be used sparingly. On light bases 2-3cm may suffice, whilst on dark bases up to 16cm can be used.

In the Viton S formula, maximum emphasis has been placed on hair condition and the creme includes four special conditioning agents to ensure that the hair is left in excellent condition.

The color creme has a built-in shampoo which eliminates any scalp staining, making it easy to remove the colour and minimises the risk of any colour fade.

The Viton Shade Guide

The comprehensive Shade Guide displays the total shade range, and helps provide straight forward and simple shade selection. An important part of this Shade Guide is the numbering system, which is based on the International Colour Code – ICC.

The majority of shades have a double number, eg. ICC 77.

The first number indicates the depth of the colour, and the scale reads from

1 **BLACK** up to

10 **EXTRA LIGHT BLONDE**.

The **second number** indicates the tone as follows:–

.0 Natural
.1 Matt Ash
.2 Ash
.3 Natural Gold
.4 Woodland
.5 Golden Red
.6 Red Blonde and Copper
.7 Rio
.8 Classical – Exotic
.9 Classical – Red Violet/Silver Pearl

N.B. This does not apply to the three toner shades 12, 17 and 19. Although they start with a 1, they do not have a depth of black.

The Viton S Shade Range

The Shade Range comprises:

NATURAL SHADES (.0)

ICC 00	Extra Light Blonde
ICC 90	Super Blonde
ICC 80	Light Blonde
ICC 70	Medium Blonde
ICC 60	Dark Blonde
ICC 50	Light Brown
ICC 40	Medium Brown
ICC 30	Dark Brown
ICC 20	Super Dark Brown
ICC 10	Black

MATT ASH TONES (.1)

ICC 01	Matt Silver
ICC 91	Super Matt Blonde
ICC 81	Light Matt Blonde
ICC 71	Medium Matt Blonde
ICC 61	Dark Matt Blonde
ICC 41	Medium Matt Brown

VIOLET ASH TONES (.2)

ICC 02	Silver Blonde
ICC 92	Super Ash Blonde
ICC 82	Light Ash Blonde
ICC 72	Medium Ash Blonde
ICC 62	Dark Ash Blonde
ICC 22	Blue Black
ICC 12	Ash Concentrate

NATURAL GOLD TONES (.3)

ICC 03	Extra Golden Blonde
ICC 93	Super Golden Blonde
ICC 83	Light Golden Blonde
ICC 73	Medium Golden Blonde
ICC 63	Dark Golden Blonde
ICC 53	Light Golden Brown
ICC 43	Medium Golden Brown

WOODLAND TONES (.4)

ICC 74	Hazelnut
ICC 64	Beech
ICC 54	Chestnut
ICC 44	Mahogany
ICC 34	Dark Mahogany

GOLDEN RED TONES (.5)

ICC 95	Super Light Gold
ICC 85	Light Golden Red
ICC 75	Medium Golden Red
ICC 65	Red Gold
ICC 55	Dark Red Gold

RED BLONDE & COPPER TONES (.6)

ICC 86	Light Copper
ICC 76	Warm Red Blonde
ICC 66	Medium Copper
ICC 56	Copper
ICC 46	Dark Copper

RIO TONES (.7)

ICC 97	Rosewood
ICC 87	Medium Rosewood
ICC 77	Intensive Rosewood
ICC 67	Light Chestnut
ICC 57	Light Mahogany
ICC 37	Aztec Red
ICC 17	Coral Red

CLASSICAL TONES (.8)

ICC 08	Pearl Beige
ICC 88	Beige Blonde
ICC 68	Dark Red Blonde
ICC 48	Medium Red Brown

CLASSICAL TONES (.9)

ICC 09	Silver Pearl
ICC 69	Light Red Violet
ICC 59	Red Violet
ICC 49	Medium Red Violet
ICC 19	Dark Red Violet

PASTEL SHADES (50)

ICC 501	Pastel Beige
ICC 502	Oyster Beige
ICC 503	Light Ash Beige

CRYSTAL SHADES (50)

ICC 505	Crystal Matt
ICC 506	Crystal Ash
ICC 507	Crystal Pearl
ICC 508	Crystal Reflect

INTENSIVE TONES (60)

ICC 601	Intensive Gold
ICC 602	Intensive Titian
ICC 603	Intensive Copper
ICC 604	Intensive Cyclamen
ICC 605	Intensive Violet

Colour, Condition and Confidence

Application Circle

APPLICATION CIRCLE

Within the Viton S Shade Guide, there is a unique application circle, this has been specially designed to make shade selection easy, by illustrating on which base to use the colours, thereby eliminating the need for any guesswork!

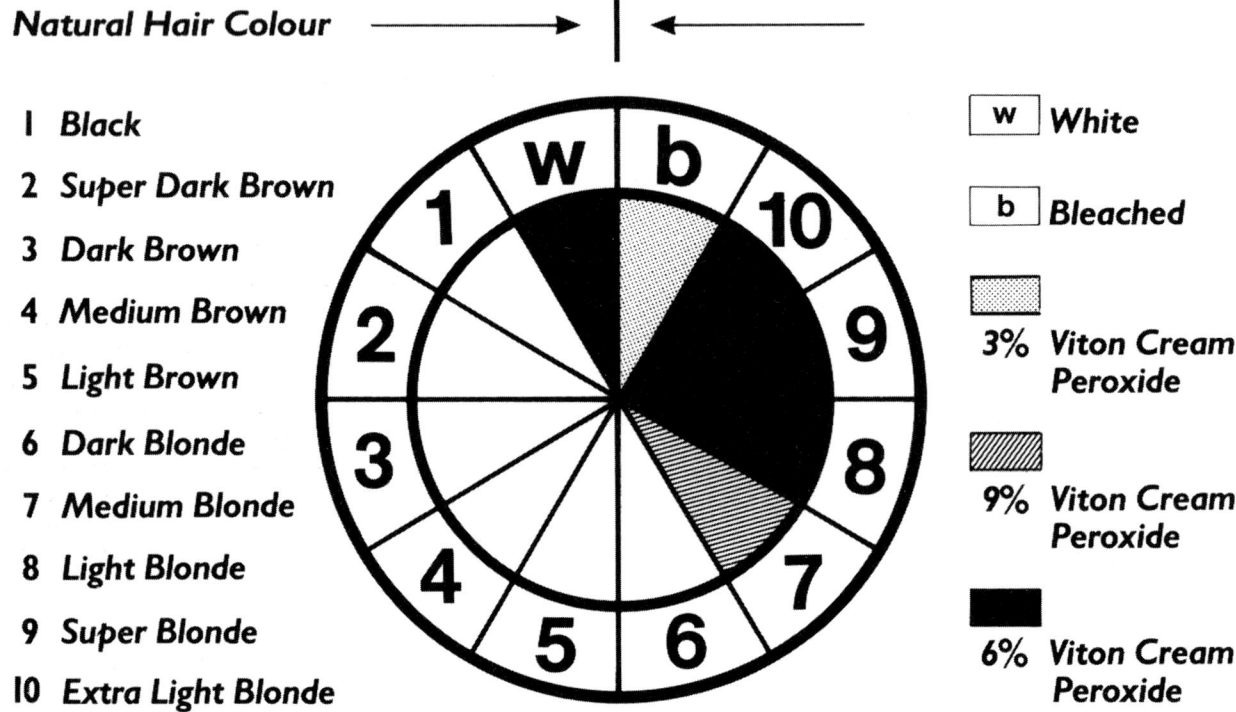

Natural Hair Colour

1 Black
2 Super Dark Brown
3 Dark Brown
4 Medium Brown
5 Light Brown
6 Dark Blonde
7 Medium Blonde
8 Light Blonde
9 Super Blonde
10 Extra Light Blonde

| w | White |
| b | Bleached |

3% Viton Cream Peroxide

9% Viton Cream Peroxide

6% Viton Cream Peroxide

HOW TO READ THE APPLICATION CIRCLE

The circle is marked out in natural hair bases from 1-10, i.e. Black to Extra Light Blonde. The other two bases are "Bleached" and "White".

The parts of the circle marked in black indicate the ideal bases for the shade. In our example these would be "White" or bases 10, 9 and 8.
In all instances, 6% Viton Cream Peroxide would be used in a ratio of 1:1.

The parts of the circle shaded with dots or lines indicate possible Bases. In our example this would be "Bleached or base number 7."
Where the area is shaded with dots (Bleached base) you should mix your tint with 3% Viton Cream Peroxide. You would do this by mixing 6% Viton Cream Peroxide with water on a 1:1 ratio.
Where the area is shaded with lines (Base 7) then you should mix your tint with 9% Viton Cream Peroxide on a 1:1 ratio.

Viton S – Instructions for Use

COLOUR SELECTIONS

- A simple to read colour selection guide, for both Natural and Fashion shades can be found on the back page of the shade guide to assist you with your colour selection.
- The clients natural colour is determined using the Natural series tufts on the first page.
- The Application circles and Viton Cream Peroxide table indicate the best possible base for each shade and the concentration of Viton Cream Peroxide to be used.
- The Viton S Natural Shades **(Series 0, 1, 2, 3 & 4)** give coverage up to **100%** on grey hair.
- All Viton S shades are intermixable. Shades (46, 56, 57, 59, 47) give coverage up to **50%** on grey hair.

MIXING

For normal usage Viton S is mixed with Viton Cream Peroxide 6% in a 1:1 ratio before application.

Complete Treatment: **1 tube Viton S + 60 ml (cc)** Viton Cream Peroxide 6%.
Regrowth Treatment: **½ Viton S + 30 ml (cc)** Viton Cream Peroxide 6%.

Where a natural shade darker than the base colour is used, a mixture with 3% oxidiser will be sufficient. To achieve this, mix Viton Cream Peroxide 6% with equal quantities of water.

Squeeze the Viton S into a non-metallic bowl and gradually add the required amount of Viton Cream Peroxide. Mix to an even cream free of lumps before applying.

APPLICATION

Apply to dry unwashed hair. If the hair is excessively greasy, give one shampoo prior to application. Dry the hair before applying tint.

Complete Treatment: Apply the mixture 2-3cm from the scalp to the middle length and ends of the hair and develop for **10-15 minutes.** Then apply mixture to roots and leave to develop a further **30 minutes**.

Regrowth Treatment: Apply the mixture to the regrowth only working systematically from the back to the front of the head in small partings. After checking the application for coverage leave the tint to develop for **30-40 minutes**. If the colour needs reviving, mix a little water to the mixture remaining in the bowl and apply to the length **5-10 minutes** before development is complete. Massage into length.

DEVELOPMENT TIME

On normal hair develop for at least **30 minutes**. Where hair is very coarse it may be necessary to increase this time up to **45 minutes.**

REMOVAL OF EXCESS TINT

On completion of the full development time, add a small amount of warm water to the hair and massage thoroughly to remove tint from the scalp. Then add more warm water, lather well and rinse clear. Viton S contains its own conditioning shampoo which will normally remove excess tint. If any additional shampoo is used we recommend the after use of a conditioner such as Clynol Salon Formula Conditioner for permed or coloured hair.

EXTRA LIGHTENING SHADES

ICC 00 Extra Light Blonde (Chamois)
ICC 01 Matt Silver
ICC 02 Silver Blonde
ICC 03 Extra Golden Blonde
ICC 08 Pearl Beige (Alaska)
ICC 09 Silver Pearl

Application: **Mix ½ tube of Viton S in a 1:1.5 ratio** with Viton Cream Peroxide 9%. Application the same as for normal treatment. Development time according to the desired result **30-40 minutes**. Remove as for complete treatment.

SPECIAL LIGHTENING SHADES

The shades of series 50.

ICC 501 Pastel Beige
ICC 502 Oyster Beige
ICC 503 Light Ash Beige
ICC 505 Crystal Matt
ICC 506 Crystal Ash
ICC 507 Crystal Pearl
ICC 508 Crystal Reflect

– have been specially developed for the lightening shades dark blonde and lighter. A lightening up to 3-4 shades can be achieved.

Application: The special lightening shades can be mixed with either **9%, 12% or 18% Viton Cream Peroxide (1:1.5)** according to the desired lightening effect. Application as for normal treatment. Development time is **30-45 minutes**, but this can be decreased if additional heat in the form of an accelerator or infra-red unit is used. It is recommended that heat should only be applied after the cream has been active for **10 minutes**.

TONING SHADES

For use on Natural shades above Light Blonde or pre-bleached hair.
For toning all shades in depths 10 and 9 (except Silver Pearl ICC 09) as well as shades 88 and 85 can be used.

Applications: Mix Viton S, Viton Cream Peroxide and water in a **1:1:1 ratio**. The mixed colourant cream is applied from the roots to the tips. Development time **20-30 minutes** according to the desired colouring results.

Note:

Fashion shades (series .5 to .9). Where additional depth is required with the fashion tones on white hair, add to the fashion tone the natural tone with the same shade depth, e.g. to give extra depth to **ICC 65 (Red Gold)** add **ICC 60 (Dark Blonde)**. Shades 46, 56, 57, 59, 77 will give up to 50% coverage on white hair without the addition of the corresponding base shade. Development time for fashin shades is **45 minutes**.
This preparation may cause serious inflammation of the skin in certain persons and should be used only in accordance with expert advice.

Viton Ancillary Product Range

VITON DECOLORANT

An effective colour reducer for use with all oxidation tints. Decolorant can be used to remove or reduce artificial oxidation hair colours. Colours that have been applied to the hair for some time will be the most difficult to remove.
Caution: As Decolorant can cause staining to clothing, the use of a tinting cape at all times is recommended.

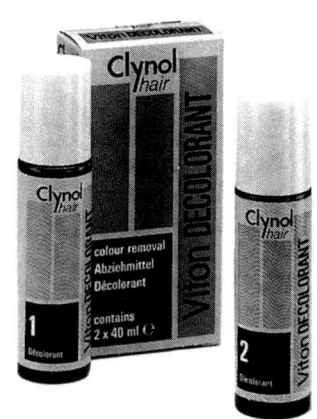

INSTRUCTIONS FOR USE (for full reduction)

Shampoo hair and towel dry. For a whole head reduction mix together Decolorant No.1 and No.2 in a non-metallic bowl.

Application should take place immediately after mixing. Apply with a sponge or a cotton wool pad. If part of the head needs lightening, only apply Decolorant to those areas.

Develop for 15 minutes. This time may be reduced by using a plastic cap and dryer.

Test by drying a strand with a hand towel. If the hair has not lightened sufficiently, rinse well, towel dry and repeat the process.

When the result is satisfactory, rinse and shampoo thoroughly.

Mix 30cc 6% Viton Cream Peroxide with 1 litre of warm water. Rinse the solution through the hair. This rinse will reduce the red tones in the hair. If the hair is still too dark after the rinse, repeat the procedure again.

Finally, apply a conditioner (such as Clynol Intensive Conditioner) to the hair. Leave for 2-3 minutes and rinse clear. When the desired effect is achieved, dry the hair and re-colour.

Remember that the decoloured hair will accept colour very quickly; it is therefore, advisable to use one shade lighter than the colour required, and watch the development carefully (it will normally develop more quickly after Decolorant treatment); this will ensure a correct colour match is made.

For Slight Corrections Decolorant can be used to remove colour that has developed slightly darker than was desired or where the hair is too ash in appearance.

Mix together 7-8cc of Decolorant No.1 and No.2, add 30cc of shampoo.

Lather the mixture over the whole head or areas to be lightened. Leave to develop until the desired colour is achieved.

Rinse thoroughly and finally shampoo.

Hints and Tips

LIGHTING

A point worth remembering is the effect that salon lighting has on hair colouration.

Neon lights tend towards blue, and therefore have a flattening (matting) effect on colours.

Tungsten or spot lighting tend to make the colours look warmer than they actually are.

The best light is natural daylight. Always try and show clients a colour chart in daylight.

If this is not possible in the salon, aim for a mix of neon and tungsten/spots.

COLOUR SELECTION

When a colour is being selected, as well as noting the clients skin tone, eye colour and personality, more importantly reference must be made to the client's natural colour. When both the natural shade and shade required have been chosen, reference should then be made to the Peroxide Chart or application circle to determine which strength of Viton Cream Peroxide is added to the chosen shade. Should the Peroxide Chart or application circle indicate that the colour is unsuitable for that base, then another colour should be selected.

BLEACH TONING

To achieve the best results when toning bleached hair with Viton S, a shade beginning with 8 or 9 should be used, provided the Application Circle indicates they are recommended or possible shades. Shades beginning with 0, Extra Lightening Tones or 500 Special Lightening Tones can be used, but they will give a very delicate result, which will not have the lasting powers of the 8 or 9 depths.

The Intensive 600 Series are also for use on pre-lightened hair.

Hair condition plays a vital role in permanent hair colouring, and Viton S has a specially formulated creme base. The composition of the creme base is such that the alkaline pH and oxidation dye stuffs are counteracted by the moisturising, conditioning and protecting roles of the protein and lipid ingredients, giving the treated hair good condition and shine.

Hints and Tips

Colouring Techniques

a To achieve a really intensive red suitable for bases 4, 5 and 6 mix together ⅔ tube of ICC 602 Intensive Titian and ⅓ tube ICC 603 Intensive Copper.

b When darkening hair with a red shade, add ½ inch to 1 inch of ICC 19 Dark Red Violet or ICC 49 Medium Red Violet to give a rich tone and subdue any Gold.

c When measuring out 1 inch of toners ICC 12 Ash concentrate, ICC 17 Coral Red or ICC 19 Dark Red Violet, or indeed any other shade, use the length of the bristles on the Viton S Tinting brush which are exactly 1 inch long.

d When refreshing colour on porous hair (eg after going on holiday) add 1 to 2 inches of ICC 17 Coral Red to the diluted tint prior to application through the mid lengths and ends. This will avoid a matt colour developing through these areas. The darker the tint used – the more red should be mixed in.

e When presoftening resistant grey hair, apply 6% Viton Cream Peroxide, leave for at least 10 minutes then mix tint as normal and apply over the peroxide.

f If porous ends are too matt, remove the colour with Clynol Decolorant Wash, then apply a slightly warmer Shade.

Always make sure that any colours or treatments used on a client are recorded on a record card. It makes life easier when they come back in for a regrowth touch up!

Pre-pigmenting

When taking a bleached head of hair back to a natural shade, it is necessary to put back the warm tones that were in the hair naturally. If this is not done, the resulting colour will be very flat (matt/green).

Recommended Viton S shades are:

ICC 65	**ICC 601**
ICC 75	**ICC 602**
ICC 17	**ICC 603**
ICC 37	

These can be applied to the hair mixed 1:1 with water.

After 20 minutes development, mix up the required shade of Viton S with 6% Viton Cream Peroxide, blot off surplus pre-pigment tint and apply the required shade immediately on top of the remaining pre-pigment shade. Leave for 20-30 minutes depending on the development of the colour.

Caution

The colour will appear very bright during processing but a high percentage of this will rinse from the hair when the tint is removed.

Hints and Tips

COLOUR CODING

With the current trend towards total colour co-ordination we have taken the unprecedented step of grouping the Viton S shades into **warm** and **cool** seasons. The warm seasons of spring and autumn are predominately **reds**, **golds**, and **coppers**.

The cooler summer and winter shades are based on **ash**, **matt** and **violet**.

WARM COLOURS

ICC 03 Extra Golden Blonde	ICC 34 Dark Mahogany	ICC 97 Rosewood
ICC 93 Super Golden Blonde	ICC 95 Super Light Gold	ICC 87 Medium Rosewood
ICC 83 Light Golden Blonde	ICC 85 Light Golden Red	ICC 77 Intensive Rosewood
ICC 73 Medium Golden Blonde	ICC 75 Medium Golden Red	ICC 67 Light Chestnut
ICC 63 Dark Golden Blonde	ICC 65 Red Gold	ICC 57 Light Mahogany
ICC 53 Light Golden Brown	ICC 55 Dark Red Gold	ICC 501 Pastel Beige
ICC 43 Medium Golden Brown	ICC 86 Light Copper	ICC 601 Intensive Gold
ICC 74 Hazelnut	ICC 76 Warm Red Blonde	ICC 602 Intensive Titian
ICC 64 Beech	ICC 66 Medium Copper	ICC 603 Intensive Copper
ICC 54 Chestnut	ICC 56 Copper	
ICC 44 Mahogany	ICC 46 Dark Copper	

COOL COLOURS

ICC 01 Matt Silver	ICC 22 Blue Black	ICC 49 Medium Red Violet
ICC 91 Super Matt Blonde	ICC 12 Ash Concentrate	ICC 19 Dark Red Violet
ICC 81 Light Matt Blonde	ICC 37 Aztec Red	ICC 502 Oyster Beige
ICC 71 Medium Matt Blonde	ICC 17 Coral Red	ICC 503 Light Ash Beige
ICC 61 Dark Matt Blonde	ICC 08 Pearl Beige	ICC 505 Crystal Matt
ICC 41 Medium Matt Brown	ICC 88 Beige Blonde	ICC 506 Crystal Ash
ICC 02 Silver Blonde	ICC 68 Dark Red Blonde	ICC 507 Crystal Pearl
ICC 92 Super Ash Blonde	ICC 48 Medium Red Brown	ICC 508 Crystal Reflect
ICC 82 Light Ash Blonde	ICC 09 Silver Pearl	ICC 604 Intensive Cyclamen
ICC 72 Medium Ash Blonde	ICC 69 Light Red Violet	ICC 605 Intensive Violet
ICC 62 Dark Ash Blonde	ICC 59 Red Violet	

Colour Problems – Resolved

Question 	Cause	Answer 
Colour too dark	1. Wrong choice of colour. 2. Hydrogen peroxide below strength. 3. Use of too low a % (vol) of peroxide. 4. Hair of fine texture or in a porous condition.	Clynol Decolorant
Colour too light	1. Wrong choice of colour. 2. Too high a % (vol) of hydrogen peroxide used. 3. Coarse hair. 4. Lack of penetration. 5. Resistant hair.	Use one shade darker at next application and take through to ends.
Insufficient coverage on white hair	1. Too light a shade used. 2. Poor application. 3. Too low a % (vol) hydrogen peroxide. 4. Too short a development time. 5. Coarse resistant glassy white hair.	1. Use one shade darker, re-apply. 2. Check development; longer if necessary. 3. Use higher % (vol) hydrogen peroxide.
Lengths too light	1. Ends becoming porous. 2. Colour combed through too often.	Colour needs re-applying to lengths with 3% (10 vol) hydrogen peroxide, or use Color Bath. Apply liberally, leave for 20 minutes, then rinse.
Lengths too dark	1. Colour not left on roots long enough. 2. Ends very porous caused by other treatment. 3. Colour was taken through to ends too quickly. 4. Lengths that had been previously treated with unsuitable preparations.	Wash the ends with a mild solution of Decolorant.
Streaky hair	1. Faulty application of the colourant. 2. Variation in hair porosity and texture. 3. Insufficient colour applied.	Re-check colour chosen, re-apply colour.
Hair not brought up light enough	1. Shade used too dark. 2. Too low a % (vol) peroxide. 3. Hydrogen peroxide below strength. 4. Development time too short. 5. Dark para colour on lengths of hair. 6. Natural hair too dark to achieve colour.	Re-apply lighter colour. De-colour lengths of hair. May be necessary to use bleach.
Colour fades off the lengths too quickly	1. Porous ends. 2. Insufficient colour applied to lengths. 3. Not left on long enough. 4. Effects of the weather.	May need re-pigmenting with colour. Application of colour with 6% (20 vol) peroxide.

NO PROBLEM!

Having studied the Viton Colour Facts you should have a very good idea what hair colouring involves. We will now look at some other factors to do with colouring that you must know.

Condition of the hair

Hair colour, be it natural or synthetic, only looks its best when the hair is healthy. It is the reflection of light on the hair's surface which gives the colour its vibrancy, highlighting the varying shades and making the hair shine. The raised cuticles on damaged hair prevents this reflection taking place so it is important to have the hair in the best condition possible.

Always make sure the hair and scalp are left with their natural pH value after treatment by using an acid balanced shampoo or an acid rinse.

As we discussed in the Consultation and Diagnostics unit, the porosity of the hair indicates what condition it is in. Hair is naturally porous and can absorb up to one third of its own weight of water. This ability allows dye dissolved in liquid to penetrate well into the hair.

Virgin hair, that is hair which has not been treated with any chemicals such as perms, bleaching agents and semi- or permanent colourants, will not absorb as much water as hair which has been treated. This is a very important fact to remember when colouring.

Over-porous hair may need to be treated with a conditioner before colouring.

SAFETY NOTES

All colouring and bleaching agents should be handled carefully. Not only can they cause considerable damage to clothing, but severe irritation if splashed on the skin or in the eyes. If this occurs rinse the affected area thoroughly with water and seek medical advice immediately if irritation persists.

If swallowed give water to drink and again seek medical advice immediately.

Colour classification

Colouring agents are divided into three groups according to the time they remain in the hair.

Permanent colours remain in the hair indefinitely, **semi-permanent** tints last from six to eight weeks and **temporary** colours wash out with the next shampoo.

Permanent colours

Permanent tints are made with 'para' dyes such as *para-phenylenediamine*, *para-toluenediamine* and *para-aminophenol* or 'meta' dyes such as *meta-dihydroxybenzene*.

They are of more commercial value to the commercial salon than temporary or semi-permanent colours because of their versatility, and also their long-lasting effect which ensures the client returns every four to six weeks to have new growth treated.

Some people may be allergic to the dyes they contain so it is essential to carry out a skin test before applying the tint. You will find out how to do this in the practical section of the Consultation and Diagnostics unit.

Concentrated permanent **toners** are colours which are used in conjunction with other tints to increase the depth of a particular tone. Clynol do three concentrated toners, as you will have observed from their information sheets. Do not confuse these with the semi-permanent products used to add subtle tones to bleached hair.

As you have already learned, the tint is mixed with hydrogen peroxide before being applied to the hair.

Hydrogen peroxide is not a stable substance and very easily releases oxygen. The free oxygen reacts with the tiny molecules of tint after they have penetrated the cortex. This process of oxidation causes large coloured molecules to form which cannot get back through the cuticle and so are trapped in the cortex.

Because the scales of the cuticle are translucent the colour shines through and a permanent colour change taes place. However, if the cuticle is damaged even 'permanent' colour will fade because it gets washed out through the raised or broken scales.

In its unstable condition hydrogen peroxide loses oxygen quickly and its strength as an oxidising agent is rapidly reduced. To increase its shelf life manufacturers produce a stabilised form by adding dilute ascetic acid. To de-stabilise it again during processing, tints produce a small quantity of ammonia which returns the peroxide to its alkaline state. This allows it to release its excess oxygen freely. The stronger the peroxide solution, the more oxygen is available for release.

The ammonia has another function, which is to *raise* the cuticle scales temporarily to allow the unprocessed tint molecules to penetrate deeply into the cortex.

The procedure for selecting which tint to use is covered in the practical section at the end of the unit.

If hair has been bleached prior to tinting the natural warm tones must be put back in the hair first or the resulting colour will be flat with a *greenish* tinge. This restoration of natural colour is called *pre-pigmenting* and is covered in the Clynol information sheets.

The 3 types of permanent colour

1 Oil based
2 Cream based
3 Combined oil and cream emulsions

Oil based tints

These mix into a thick gel which is easy to apply and will not run.

Sometimes they do not cover fine white hair which has a tight smooth cuticle. This type of hair is referred to as 'glass hair' because when you look through a hair which has been coloured and then retouched there is a visible line dividing the two applications.

Cream based tints

Cream tints are popular because they give good coverage and do not fade easily. They cover resistent white hair better than oil based tints.

They are thick and more difficult to mix than the other types.

Combined oil and cream tints

Oil and cream emulsions combine the advantages of separate oil and cream based tints. They give excellent coverage and are easy to apply because of their consistency.

Advantages of Permanent Colour

* They can cover grey hair completely and permanently giving the hair a natural looking colour.

* A wide range of shades is available which can be mixed to suit individual requirements.

* They will not rub off on clothing or run when wet.

* They can lighten hair colour as well as add to it.

* They usually contain conditioners which leave the hair shining.

Disadvantages of Permanent Colours

* A skin test must be carried out before each application as serious allergies can occur.

* They take between 20 and 45 minutes to process.

* They require skilled application.

* Permanent colour is not easily altered if the client is not happy with the result.

* They are more expensive than other colourants.

* Accurate record keeping is essential for matching colour when treating regrowth.

Strand test

This is a simple test carried out during the processing of a permanent colour in order to monitor its development. It is used when colouring regrowth to check when it is ready to be combed through.

The procedure for carrying out the test is in the practical section.

Semi-permanent colours

Semi-permanent colours come in cream, liquid and mousse form. They do not penetrate far into the cortex so do not usually require to be processed for as long as permanent tints.

If an application of semi-permanent colour is made to porous hair the dyes can penetrate more deeply into the cortex than intended and be retained after eight shampoos causing a regrowth problem.

Some semi-permanent colours contain a small quantity of the para dyes used in permanent tints to make them last a little longer. These must be mixed with peroxide before applying and necessitate a skin test being carried out first as they can cause an allergic reaction.

Although semi-permanent colourants cannot lighten natural hair colour, they can alter the tone and add depth to both bleached and coloured hair. They are not recommended for grey hair as they will not cover resistent white hair and the final colour is often too vivid.

Temporary and semi-permanent colours are made with direct dyes, that is dyes whose colour is present before application to the hair.

There is no true brown direct dye so various colours have to be mixed together to achieve a brown shade. The colours used include blue, yellow, red, mauve and grey. However, these components fade at different rates and what was initially an acceptable brown shade will tend towards the most enduring of the component colours after a few shampoos. Usually this is blue, green or mauve.

Advantages of Semi - Permanent Colours

* They are easy to use.

* They give clients the opportunity to try out a new colour on a non-permanent basis.

* Most contain conditioners so add shine and tone to natural and permanently coloured hair which has faded.

* They will not rub off on clothing.

Disadvantages of Semi - Pemanent Colours

* If the product contains a para dye a skin test will be required.

* They are not very successful on grey hair with over ten percent white.

* Red tones tend to persist after the base shade has faded.

* Processing takes longer than temporary colours.

* Brown shades may gradually change colour.

Temporary Colours

Temporary colours are water based. They usually contain an **aso** dye. Some products contain several other colouring ingredients such as *methyl blue, nigrosine black* or *fuchsin*.

They come in various forms from gels to 'paints'.

Temporary colours do not have to be processed because they lie along the cuticle and do not penetrate the cortex at all. This means that the colour change is immediate.

SAFETY NOTES

Setting lotion, mousse and foam types of temporary colours contain solvents such as *ethanol isopropanol*. These are flammable and should not be used near a naked flame.

Advantages of Temporary Colours

* The client has an opportunity to try out a new colour before deciding to have it permanently.

* They give clients the opportunity to wear a colour for a special occasion only.

* No skin test is required before application.

* Some are ideal for adding tone or depth to natural or permanently coloured hair which has faded.

* They are quick and easy to apply.

Disadvantages of Temporary Colours

* If polymers are not incorporated in the product they can rub off on clothing, or the colour may run if the client perspires excessively.

* They can give hair a dull appearance.

* They are not suitable for covering grey hair

Lightening the Hair by Bleaching

Bleaching is an *oxidation* process which lightens the hair by changing some or all of the natural pigment to colourless molecules.

To lighten dark hair to blonde the colour is first oxidised from black to brown, then to red, to gold, to yellow and finally to pale blonde. This is because natural colour is made up of two different melanin pigments. The darker granular melanin pigment is oxidised more easily than the pigment responsible for red and yellow tones, known as *pheomelanin*.

Modern bleaches are formulated to oxidise the melanin with as little oxidation of the sulphur bond as possible.

Bleaching is usually a preparatory process for tints or toners, carried out because the client's natural colour is too dark for the shade she requires. The hair must be lightened to the correct base shade for the particular tint or toner you wish to use.

Because bleaches are *strong* alkalies some damage to the hair is inevitable and bleached hair tends to be dull with poor elasticity. Regrowth is more obvious on bleached hair so retouching has to be done frequently at the risk of further damage. Conditioning treatment is therefore a very important addition to a service involving the use of bleach lighteners.

It is vital that bleaches are rinsed out of the hair thoroughly or they will continue to oxidise slowly and weaken the hair when the client has left the salon. This is known as 'creeping oxidation'.

Types of lighteners

Bleaches today are available as emulsions, oils or powders.

The original hair lightener was a solution of hydrogen peroxide mixed with ammonium hydroxide. Because of its watery consistency it was almost impossible to confine to a specific area and it tended to run over the whole head causing the ends to become lighter than the rest of the hair. It was a popular home treatment and the users were referred to as 'peroxide blondes'.

Emulsion bleach

Emulsion bleaches are usually a combination of hydrogen peroxide, oil, other ingredients, and a booster to accelerate the release of oxygen.

Boosters come in powder form in a separate sachet. Usually either *potassium* or *ammonium persulphate* is used.

Emulsion bleaches also contain buffers to maintain the pH value around 9, and cooling agents which keep the scalp comfortable during the lightening process.

<u>It is essential to follow manufacturer's instructions.</u>

This type of bleach is popular because it will not drip, flake or dry out. They are quite strong bleaches and can lift up to seven shades although two separate applications are often required to maintain the lightening action when bleaching black hair to pale yellow.

Oil bleaches

Oil bleaches are a combination of an alkali, usually *ammonium hydroxide,* a wetting agent and a gelling agent such as *lauryl diethanolamide* although some contain *sulphonated castor oil* as an alternative thickener.

The alkali, with a pH value of **9** to **9.5**, speeds up the release of oxygen from the hydrogen peroxide which is mixed into the bleach as well as opening the cuticle.

Oil bleaches may have added boosters to release extra oxygen as with emulsion bleaches. They will only lighten up to four shades resulting in golden blonde shades. They are suitable for either lifting the hair to a base shade before a tint application or for highlighting the hair.

Oil bleaches are the mildest of bleaches and are ideal for clients who do not want a drastic colour change.

Powder bleaches

Powder bleaches are a combination of powdered *magnesium* and *ammonium carbonate*. Ammonium carbonate is the oxygen releasing agent in this type of bleach.

Just before use the powders are mixed to a paste with hydrogen peroxide. The strength of peroxide used depends on the treatment required so always check the manufacturer's recommendations.

These bleaches are more likely to cause damage to the hair than other types because the hydrogen peroxide is not diluted with any other liquid. They are also more inclined to dry and flake.

Powder bleaches do not contain coolants and have a pH value around **10** so will cause irritation if applied directly to the scalp and could damage the hair if used carelessly. They are usually only used for partial bleaching treatments such as frosting, tipping and streaking so that the bleach does not come in direct contact with the skin.

Removing 'permanent' colours

Temporary colours, as we have seen, are generally removed from the hair with the first shampoo, and semi-permanents wash out over a period of normally 5 - 6 shampoos. Permanent dyes, on the other hand, can only be removed by chemical means.

Although many hairdressers continue to use bleaches to do this it is not advisable because of the damaging effect they have on the hair. Special decolourants known as **strippers**, or **reducers**, have been produced for the purpose which are kinder to the hair. They come in both powder and liquid form.

Decolourants reverse the oxidation process by removing oxygen from the large oxidised molecules of colour. This reduction process breaks down the large molecules into smaller particles, and the cuticle is swollen to allow these to escape when the hair is shampooed. Reduction agents used are either *formaldehyde, sulphoxylate* or *sodium dithionite*.

You will find that you are left with streaks of yellow, orange and red. Red will predominate because the red component of the dye has smaller molecules which are difficult to remove. This of course will be covered by the tint you use to re-colour the hair, but it can be quite a shock for the client so warn her first!

When the decolourant has been removed from the hair, an *acid pH* conditioner must be applied prior to any further application of colour. The tint you use should be one shade lighter than the required colour. The colour will probably develop quicker than usual, so it is necessary to watch the development carefully.

SAFETY NOTE

Take care not to inhale bleach or decolouring powder when mixing. If powder is inhaled move into fresh air. Seek medical advice if breathlessness persists longer than ten minutes.

Commercial value

Hair colouring is perhaps the most important service that the hairdresser can offer his client. It is important to the hairdresser in terms of creativity and commercial value. It is important to the client because colour can alter her appearance and reflect her personality perhaps more than any other hairdressing treatment. Many women now consider hair colouring to be an essential part of their fashion routine, but others need convincing.

To capitalise on hair colouring you must be able to influence the client to try it, and to achieve the result you have claimed. If the client is disappointed with her first experience she is unlikely to repeat it. To introduce colour effectively you must talk about it. Your specialised knowledge and experience make you the expert, and clients will welcome your advice. Not every client is really sure what colour suits her. Carefully considering each client's preferences, her natural hair colour, skin tone, eye colour, lifestyle, personality and career will guide you in what advice to give. This of course is part of the Consultation and Diagnostic procedure carried out before any salon service.

PRACTICAL SECTION

Before commencing any colouring treatment go through the Consultation and Diagnostics procedure covered in the practical section in the unit of that name.

Selecting a permanent colour

Procedure

1 Establish the client's natural hair colour by comparing it with the sample tufts in the manufacturer's shade guide.

2 Ask if the client would like to go darker or lighter than her natural shade, and what tone she would prefer.

3 Select a suitable colour from the manufacturer's shade chart used in your salon. If the hair is fine textured and abundant it will look darker when coloured. Explain this to your client and advise a colour one shade lighter than what would otherwise be selected.

Determine whether the selected shade is suitable for the colour base. If it is not suitable you must select an alternative. Guidance on selection will be included in the manufacturer's instructions.

If you are using 'Viton S' use the application circle mentioned in the Clynol information sheets.

Let's look at an imaginary example of colour selection to help you put this into practice.

Suppose our client has a base shade of **6**, which is dark blonde, and she wants her hair to be a copper shade. Looking through the shade guide we select warm red blonde, **ICC 76**. This will give the desired red copper tones.

By looking at the application circle we can see that **76** is suitable on a base of **6**. Our client has coarse textured hair. This means we can use the selected shade knowing that it will not appear darker than required.

The manufacturer's directions indicate that we need to use **6%** hydrogen peroxide with **ICC76** on a base of **6**.

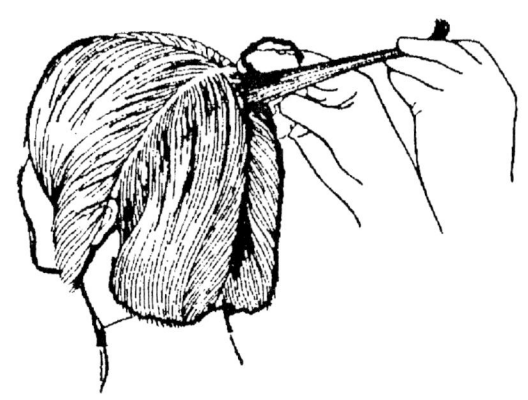

Strand test for colour development

Take a small mesh of hair and remove the colouring agent from the area you wish to test with either damp cotton wool or the back of a comb. If the colour is uneven more development time is needed before rinsing off.

Applying a permanent colour or bleach to virgin hair

The application and processing of a tint is exactly the same as for a bleach so we will describe them together.

The application sequence takes into account the varying degrees of porosity along the hair shaft. Because the ends of the hair are usually the most porous part of the hair having been subjected to the effects of destructive physical factors for a longer time, they allow the bleach or colour to penetrate the hair shaft quickly. The roots, being the youngest area, are less porous but will lift or colour quicker than the mid length because of the heat of the scalp.

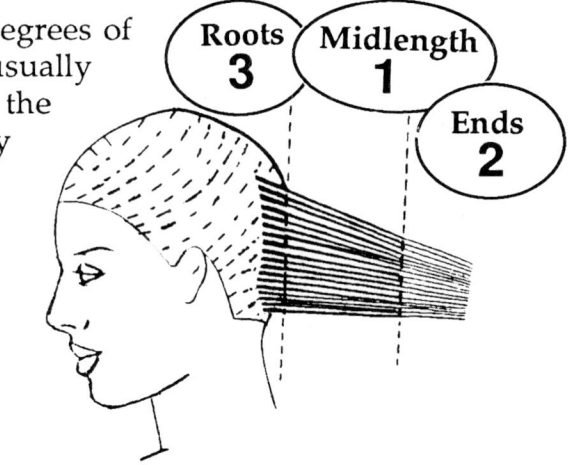

The order of the bleach or colour application then is the mid length first, followed by the ends and finally the root area.

(If the hair is very short this sequence will not be applicable.)

Requirement checklist

* Record card, and release form if required.
* Protective gown
* Towels
* Shampoo supplies
* Gloves
* Cotton wool strip
* Applicator bottle or bowl and brush
* Colour or bleaching product
* Hydrogen peroxide
* Measuring container
* Stain remover for tinting
* Section clips
* Timer

Procedure

1 Prepare the client for service with protective gown, cape and towel.

2 Shampoo the hair only if very greasy.

3 Part the hair into four equal sections.

4 Wearing protective gloves, mix the product with hydrogen peroxide in a plastic bowl or a bottle applicator.

If using an applicator remember to shake the bottle vigorously.

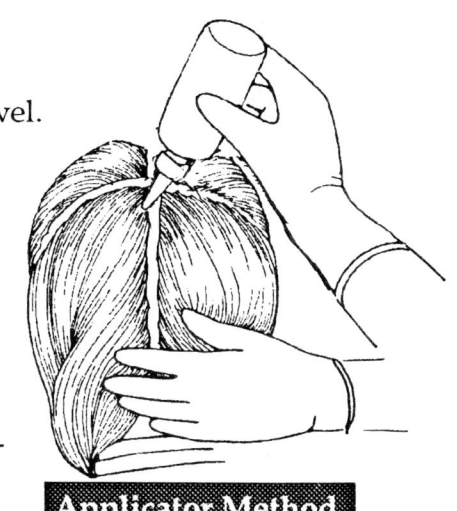
Applicator Method

3 Commencing at the top right back section, make a horizontal parting and apply the product 2 cm away from the scalp and work up the middle of the hair until you reach 2 cm from the ends.

Continue in this way, making the partings a centimetre apart, and work towards the nape area. Repeat on the top left section.

6 Go back to the right front section and follow the same procedure as above, working towards the hairline. Repeat on the left front section.

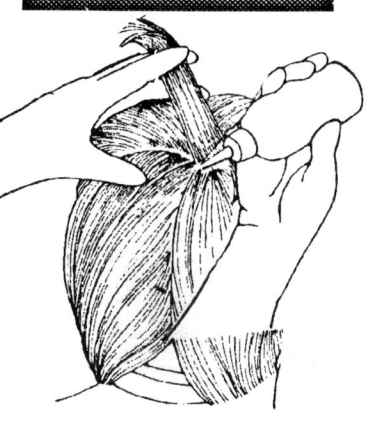

7 Following the same sequence and method apply the product to the ends of the hair.

8 Place a strip of cotton wool round the hairline to absorb any drips.

9 When half the time recommended by the manufacturer is up, mix a fresh amount of product and apply to the root area, following the same sequence and method as before.

<u>Work quickly so that all the roots will be processed for the same length of time.</u>

10 Remove any colour on the skin with stain remover.

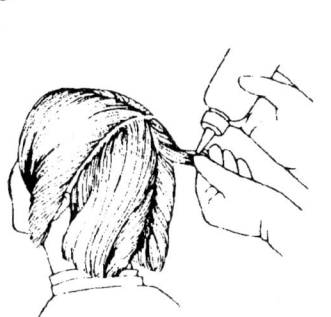

11 After the recommended time is up carry out a strand test for evenness of colour. The colour on the ends of the hair should match that on the middle and roots.

If it is not even, leave a few minutes and repeat the strand test. Continue to do this until colour is even.

1 Rinse the hair with tepid water then shampoo with a non-stripping acid shampoo.

13 Apply a normalising conditioner to neutralise any traces of alkali.

14 Record the products used and the results.

15 Advise the client on follow-up hair care, recommending suitable products for sale in the salon.

Bleaching or Colouring Regrowth

Requirements checklist is the same as for applying bleach or colour to virgin hair.

Procedure

Follow steps **1** to **4** of the procedure for applying bleach or colour to virgin hair.

1 Apply the colourant to the regrowth area fron the nape to where the partings cross at the crown area.

2 Using 2cm horizontal partings apply the colourant or bleach to the root regrowth in the right back section.

Work from the top of the section to the nape hairline.

Brush Method

3 Repeat this sequence on the left back section.

4 Go to the left front section and continue applying the colourant from the top of the section to the face hairline.

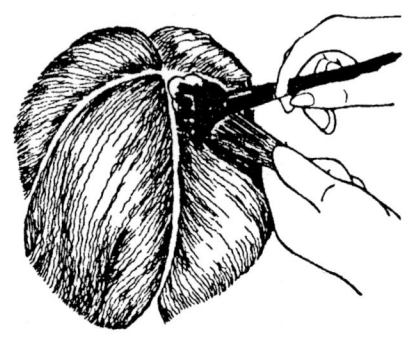

5 Repeat this sequence on the right front section, working from the top of the   section to the face hairline.

6 Check for complete coverage by taking partings in the opposite direction.

7 Allow air to circulate throughout the root area by gently lifting with a tail comb. This helps the product to process evenly.

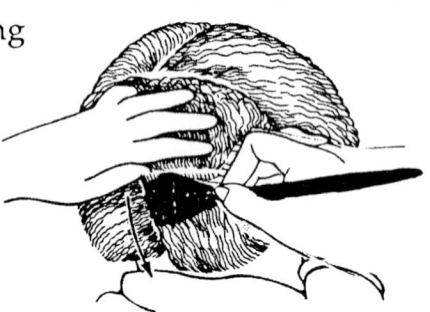

8 When the recommended time is up carry out a strand test to assess development. Leave longer if required, testing every few minutes.

9 <u>For colour application only</u> Dilute the tint mixture with a little shampoo and comb the mixture through the rest of the hair. This will refresh the previously coloured hair.

Process further according to the manufacturer's instructions.

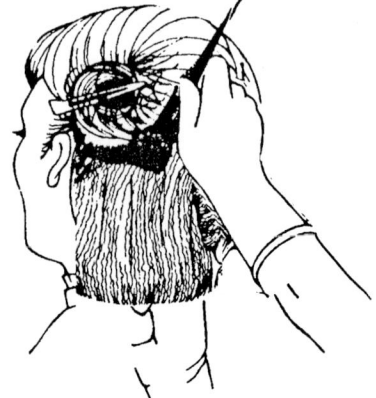

10 Remove the tint or bleach by rinsing the hair with tepid water and shampoo with a non-stripping acid shampoo.

11 Apply a normalising conditioner to neutralise any traces of alkali.

12 Record the result.

Applying a Semi-Permanent Colour or Toners

Requirements checklist

* Record card, and release form if required.
* Protective gown
* Towels
* Shampoo supplies
* Semi- permanent colour product
* Gloves
* Cotton wool strip
* Applicator bottle or bowl and brush
* Timer

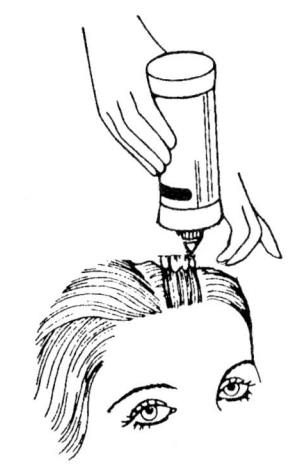

Procedure

1 Prepare the client for service by protecting her with a gown, cape and towel.

2 Shampoo and towel dry hair.

3 (If colour requires to be mixed with hydrogen peroxide, mix and apply according to the manufacturer's instructions. Otherwise, the colour will come in its own applicator.)

Shake the container to mix the contents, making sure nozzle is sealed. Remove the seal cap and apply the colour directly from the applicator bottle working it into a lather.

Commence at the nape area which is normally the most resistant. (If you want to mix two shades together you will need to remove them from their containers, mix them together and apply with a brush or sponge).

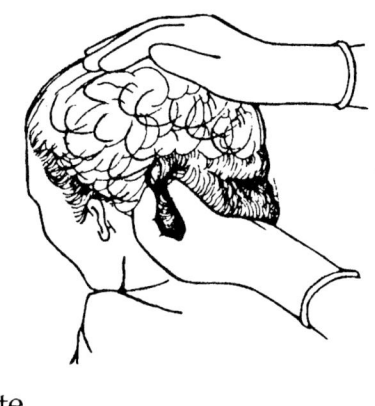

4 Massage gently and comb with a wide tooth comb to distribute the colour evenly and pile the hair loosely on top of the head.

5 Remove any colour on the skin with stain remover.

6 Some manufacturers recommend that a plastic cap is worn so that heat from the scalp speeds up processing. Others recommend additional heat for the same purpose. Follow the instructions for the particular product you are using.

7 At the end of the recommended development time carry out a strand test. Leave to process longer if required, testing every few minutes.

8 Rinse the colour from the hair until the water runs clear. (Modern products contain shampoo which makes removing the colour much easier.)

9 Apply an acid rinse if there is no conditioner incorporated in the colour. Record the results on the client's record card.

Applying Temporary Colourants

Requirement checklist

* Record card and release form if required.
* Protective gown
* Towels
* Shampoo supplies
* Temporary colour product
* Gloves
* Cotton wool

Procedure for using a mousse

1 Shampoo and towel dry the hair.

2 Shake product can well.

3 Hold nozzle downwards and apply an amount about the size of an egg into the palm of your hand and spread evenly over the damp hair. Increase the quantity for longer hair.

Mousse can also be applied to the tufts of a brush and then brushed into the hair.

4 Do not rinse out.

5 Style as required.

Application of paints, crayons and sprays

These are all applied to **dry** hair.

Paints

These are painted on to the hair a with a small brush supplied with the product.

Crayons

These are simply stroked on where the colour is required.

Sprays

Spray colours come in aerosol cans and should be applied sparingly.

11 SELLING

Perhaps you are wondering why a guide to hairdressing should include a unit on selling. The reason is simply that salons, like every other business, have to make a profit. They do this by selling their skills, services and retail hairdressing products.

Even the most junior member of staff can help to increase the productivity of their salon if they learn to apply some of the basic rules of salesmanship.

Successful salons not only attract new customers but have a regular clientele who return time and again because they are happy with the treatment they receive. We will look at some of the factors which attract clients to one salon rather than another and encourage them to come back again.

These include

* the right image
* the right atmosphere
* the right attitude

We have already discussed these points in relation to reception work, and as they are relevant to both selling and hairdressing in general we recommend that you study this unit in conjunction with the related topics in Unit 1.

The Right Image

Image is vitally important. The impression a prospective client gets from the external appearance of your salon is the one on which she will base her decision about whether or not to make a first appointment.

What do people look for before they are prepared to make that initial visit?

Most people would put cleanliness and efficiency at the top of their list. Shabby, untidy premises and staff who do not take a pride in their appearance reflect a careless attitude, sloppy workmanship and unhygienic conditions.
Every salon should be spotlessly clean inside and out, and every member of staff should be smartly dressed.

Most people find bright, airy salons more attractive than small, cluttered looking ones. On the other hand, many people prefer the privacy of older style salons to modern ones which are open to the view of passers-by.

Apart from these more obvious qualities, potential clients are also looking for signs to assure them that the salon is able to cater for their individual needs and tastes.

Teenagers, for instance, will usually try to assess whether the salon and its stylists are sufficiently up-to-date to produce the latest styles. They will look first at the staff themselves. Are their hairstyles 'dated'? Do they wear trendy clothes? What about the salon? Does it have modern fittings and equipment?

Pensioners on the other hand may be more interested in the cost of services and enjoying a social visit. They could be be put off by a very exclusive, sophisticated image which suggests expensive treatments, or by ultra modern seating which sacrifices comfort for elegance.

Few salons have a universal appeal and owners/proprietors are well advised to research the market carefully before deciding on the type of clientele they wish to attract.

Most salons cater for a fairly wide range; others concentrate on one specific group. The image the salon presents to the public should be designed to appeal to the target customers.

Whatever image is portrayed, it is essential that it reflects the type of service the client can expect to receive during her visit. There is no point in presenting an up-to-the-minute image if you are not able to produce the latest fashion styles to go with it.

The right atmosphere

Clients who enjoy their visit to a salon, and are pleased with the results of their treatment, are likely to return on a regular basis. A relaxing, warm and friendly atmosphere is an essential ingredient in providing a pleasurable experience for your clients.

Comfortable seating and room temperature, magazines to read and the availability of refreshments all contribute to a relaxing environment.

Perhaps even more important is the atmosphere created by the staff themselves. Nothing will make clients more ill at ease than an undercurrent of ill-feeling or, worse still, open hostility between members of staff. Not only does this give a very unprofessional image which will undermine the client's confidence in the salon, but is a very unpleasant working environment which can easily lead to a rapid turnover in staff.

On the contrary, when staff work together as a team, showing courtesy and respect for one another as well as their clients, the salon will function efficiently in a pleasant atmosphere.

A team spirit which develops through friendly cooperation with colleagues, provides the ideal working environment because it fosters the acceptance of individual responsibility and commitment to clients, colleagues and work.

Disagreements and grievances will arise on occasion even in the best of salons. These should be discussed calmly and sensibly as soon as possible. If allowed to fester they will rapidly lead to the hostile atmosphere referred to above.

Never discuss staff problems in front of clients. Difficult clients should also be dealt with quickly, tactfully and out of the earshot of other clients.

* Study the references to verbal and non-verbal communication in the Reception Unit in relation to creating the right atmosphere.

The Right Attitude

Selling has more to do with a positive attitude to your clients, your salon and your work than the practice of any high pressure sales techniques.

A stylist who has a genuine concern for her clients and interest in their hair will automatically try to sell the skills, services and commodities available in the salon which she feels would be of benefit to them. Clients who sense the sincerity of her interest, and have confidence in her judgement, are likely to act upon her advice.

Key factors in selling

* the seller's attitude

* the ability to convey a genuine concern

* the knowledge and skill necessary to give the right advice

* the ability to supply the recommended goods and services

A positive attitude

Your attitude to your work, your clients and your salon is the outward expression of how you feel about them in your own mind. It shows in your actions, your facial expression and the way you communicate with others.

As we noted when discussing the right atmosphere, you are more likely to develop a positive attitude in a salon where the staff work agreeably together as a team. It is very difficult to maintain the right attitude in a hostile environment, so it is worth making a real effort from the outset to develop a harmonious relationship with everyone employed in your salon, from the most junior up.

Conveying sincerity

Building up a good relationship with your clients is the first step in convincing them that you have their interests at heart.

Find out about your clients' likes and dislikes, their interests and needs, their lifestyles and their occupations by listening carefully to what they tell you. To encourage clients to talk about themselves ask open questions which require a thoughtful reply rather than just 'yes' or 'no'.

<u>Never gossip or talk about other clients, and do not ask personal questions.</u>

Always be honest with your clients and you will soon gain their trust and respect. If you cannot answer a question admit that you do not know and offer to find the answer for her. Do not promise results you are not certain can be achieved, and do no try to sell a service or product which the client does not need.

If you recommend a treatment which is more expensive than usual explain your reasons clearly and make sure the client understands.

Building a good relationship with a client does not mean chattering incessantly! Many clients like to relax quietly during their visit. They may have demanding jobs and want to 'switch off' for a while; they may just want to read or sit and watch what is going on around them. Don't persist in trying to initiate conversation if the client is not responsive.

Some clients like to confide in their stylist and discuss personal matters with them. It is not advisable to encourage this. Listen, but do not pass judgement or give advice about personal problems, and never repeat what you have been told or discuss it with other people.

Avoid high pressure selling

Once you have made your recommendations do not put pressure on a client to buy. Perhaps she is unable to afford the recommended treatment and you will only succeed in embarrassing her.

If a client shows signs of interest, perhaps by asking questions or watching another client having the recommended treatment, you can suggest that she might like to have the service there and then. If she remains hesitant suggest that she should think about it and wait until her next appointment before deciding.

Let the client volunteer her decision about whether or not to have the treatment when they return for their next appointment. If she does not want the service she may be embarrassed about saying so outright.

The right time to sell

Do not keep offering advice and making recommendations about the client's hair throughout her visit. The ideal time to 'sell' services and treatments is during the consultation and diagnostics stage when both you and the client are concentrating on her hair, discussing her needs and what she wants done.

If, for example, you think a requested style would be more successful if the hair was permed, this is the time to say so; not half way through when it is too late. Again, ask open questions so that the client has to think about your advice instead of rejecting it out of hand. For instance, instead of asking, 'Would you like a perm to give body to this style?' you might say, 'This style really needs more body to be successful. How would you feel about having a perm first?'

Be sure to tell clients the cost of a treatment before they decide to have it.

Occasionally during a treatment you may feel it is particularly appropriate to make a suggestion. If so, do it as casually as possible, so that the client remains relaxed and does not feel she has to start making decisions all over again.

After Care

Good aftercare is essential for most salon treatments. Permed, coloured and bleached hair should only be washed with acid balanced shampoos, and need proper conditioning at home. All salons should provide for this home care by selling quality retail products, and advising clients about their use.

It is a good policy to carry retail goods produced by manufacturers whose products are used in the salon as clients will see that you have confidence in their quality. Display them attractively in an easily accessible part of the salon, making sure they are clearly priced.

Many salons fail to offer this professional service. In doing so they miss a potentially lucrative market, leaving the supermarkets and chemists to profit from their negligence.

The dressing out stage is a good time to sell retail products for home hair care. Usually clients are again concentrating on their hair at this time and therefore open to advice.

It is also a good time to suggest making another appointment, perhaps to asess the results of a perm or colour or to have a conditioning treatment if is necessary.

Know your job

In order to sell successfully you must know what you are talking about. Learn all you can about hair and skin, about the services and treatments available in your salon, about the products used and sold there and their cost.

You should be able to explain the advantages and special features of one service, treatment or product in relation to others. Visual aids are helpful when doing this.

Present the facts clearly and simply. Do not blind the client with science. Clients are more interested in how a treatment or product can benefit them than how it works.

It is not a good idea to offer too many alternatives as this can be confusing. Research shows that a maximum of three choices should be offered.

You should also have the necessary skill to make an accurate diagnosis of the client's needs. Can you assess the condition of her hair? Can you tell from the texture and growth pattern how the hair will adapt to a particular cut? Can you detect any evidence that the client has used a product containing metallic salts on her hair?

Such skills will develop with experience, so it is important to practice consultation and diagnostic procedures as often as you can. Your clients' confidence in your judgement will increase with every successful treatment she receives from you.

Be prepared

Obviously, if you recommend a particular style, cut, treatment or product to a client you should be able to 'deliver the goods'.

Perhaps you are not quite sure how to produce the style or cut the client wants, or you are not very good with long hair. Do not go ahead and risk disaster by attempting the service yourself. Instead, refer your client to a stylist who has the required skills.

This may mean making another appointment for the client, so be ready, if possible, to suggest an alternative service which is immediately available. Be sure to watch when the service is being given and practice it so that you will be able to do it yourself in future.

Make sure you have a particular treatment, colour, perm lotion or other product in stock before recommending it to a client. If the client agrees to accept the recommended product and it is not available, she will feel she is only getting second best if you have to use an alternative.

Selling retail

As we noted already, aftercare is an essential part of hairdressing treatments. Permed, coloured and bleached hair should only be washed with acid balanced shampoos, and need proper conditioning at home.

All salons should provide for this home care by selling quality retail products, and advising clients about their use. It is a good policy to carry retail goods produced by manufacturers whose products are used in the salon as clients will see that you have confidence in their quality.

Display them attractively in an easily accessible part of the salon, making sure they are clearly priced. Many salons fail to offer this professional service. In doing so they miss a potentially lucrative market, leaving the supermarkets and chemist to profit from their negligence

Finally......

Be open to constructive criticism. No-one is perfect, and even the best stylist or consultant can learn from others.

Always be willing to adopt new ideas if they will benefit your salon and clients. It is not always easy to adapt to change, but hairdressing is a fashion industry and to stay in business hairdressers have to keep abreast with the latest trends and techniques.

Sometimes innovations are such that they change the whole face of the industry. Blowdrying, for instance, completely replaced roller setting in some salons when it was first introduced. In this age of high technology we can expect change to be rapid and far-reaching so be ready to adapt when it comes.

Index

accidents 15, 16
acidity 21, 22, 46, 48, 49, 54, 55, 56, 100, 101, 137, 138. 143
acid mantle 10
AIDS (disease) 15, 37
aids (styling) 78, 98
allergy test 35
alopecia 26, 27
akalinity 21, 45, 46, 54, 55, 56, 99,
amino acids 19, 21, 49
ammonium thioglycollate 101
anagen 23
appointments 2, 3, 4, 13
backbrushing, backcombing 93
banking 9, 12, 14
bleach, bleaching 46, 56, 101, 122,
   application 142 - 144
   chemical processes 137
   colour problems 132
   damage 14, 138, 139
blowdrying 74 - 85
   aids 75, 78
   hints 78
   techniques 77
cash 9, 10, 11
catagen 23
client 1 - 5.
   appointments 2, 3, 4, 13
   complaints 5
   consultation 19, 42, 43
   preparation 14
consultation checklist 42, 43
clippers 60
club cutting 61,
colouring 115 - 146
   basic principles 118, 119
   colour coding 131
   colour formation 133 - 134
   colour problems 132
   colour selection 127, 12
combs 67, 76, 79, 89, 91, 93, 98,
communications 2,
conditioning 44 - 52
   hair condition 66
   procedure 51, 52
   types 47 - 49
consultation checklist 42
cortex 20, 22, 48, 49, 100, 116, 121, 122, 137
crimping irons 77
curl 77, 87, 102
curl test 36, 112
cutting 59 - 73
cystine 21
daily takings 11
damaged hair 44, 49
dandruff 27
decolourants 128
dermis 22

disorders, hair, scalp 24
disinfectant 38
disulphide bond 21, 100
elasticity 21, 29, 30, 39, 43, 47
epidermis 22
face shapes 32, 33
finger waving 89, 92
first aid 15
follicle 19, 20, 22
fragilitis crinium (split ends) 26
growth patterns 31, 66
guidelines 63, 72, 73
hair 19, 20, 23, 24, 26, 30, 31, 32
   colour 21, 22, 116
   composition 20
   condition 44 - 52
   damage 21, 44
   density 32
   disorders 24
   growth 31, 66
   structure 19, 20, 21
   tests 35, 36, 39 - 42
   texture 31, 65
   types 23
hairdryers 76
henna 36, 49
hepatitis 15, 37
hot brushes 77
hygiene 1, 37
impetigo 25
incompatibility test 40
international colour code 131
infectious conditions 24, 26
keratin 19, 20
lanugo hair 23
massage 50
medulla 20, 21, 116
monilethrix 26
neucleic accid 49
neutralising 107
non - cash transactions 9 - 11
non - infectious disorders 26 - 28
payment prcedures 8
permanent colours 115 - 146
permanent waving 99 - 106
   chemical action 100
   consultation 109
   lotions 101
   neutralising 107
   post - damping 106
   pre - damping 106
   problems - cause 108
   processing 106
pH 46, 48, 55, 56
pH scale 46, 48, 55
pheomelanin 141
pincurling 87, 88, 91
pityriasis (dandruff) 27
plaiting (braiding) 94 - 97

polypeptide 21, 100
porosity 21, 29, 30, 39, 43, 47
porosity test 39
precautionary tests 39
pre - perm test 41
protective covering 8, 14
psoriasis 28
razors 60, 62
reception 1 - 18
release forms 8
ringworm 25
rollers 86, 88
scabies 25
scalp treatment 50
scissors 59, 61,
sebaceous cyst 28
seborrhoea 28
sectioning, cutting 63, 68, 70
security and safety 12
selling 147 - 153
   right image 147
   right atmosphere 148
   right attitude 149
semi - permanent colours 120 -145
setting 86 - 98
shampooing 53 - 58
   action 54
   chart 56
   purpose 53
   pH 46, 48. 55
skin 22
   acid mantle 22
   amino acids 19. 21, 49
   keratin 19, 20
   dermis 22
skin tests 35, 39, 133, 135, 136
style, choosing of 30
telephone 5
   making calls 5
   services 7
   types of calls 6
telogen 23
temporary colours 120, 136, 137
terminal hair 23
texture 32, 65
texturising 62
thinning scissors 62
tinea capitas 25
tints 134
thioglycollic acid 100
tongs 77, 98
tools, equipment 98
trichorrhexis nodosa 26
ultra-violet cabinets 38
vellus hair 23
warts 26
water, hard and soft 53
wedge cut 70, 71
winding techniques 104